The Dragon and the Crown

Royal Asiatic Society Hong Kong Studies Series

Royal Asiatic Society Hong Kong Studies Series is designed to make widely available important contributions on the local history, culture and society of Hong Kong and the surrounding region. Generous support from the Sir Lindsay and Lady May Ride Memorial Fund makes it possible to publish a series of high-quality works that will be of lasting appeal and value to all, both scholars and informed general readers, who share a deeper interest in and enthusiasm for the area.

Other titles in RAS Hong Kong Studies Series:

Reluctant Heroes: Rickshaw Pullers in Hong Kong and Canton 1874–1954
Fung Chi Ming

For Gods, Ghosts and Ancestors: The Chinese Tradition of Paper Offerings
Janet Lee Scott

Hong Kong Internment 1942–1945: Life in the Japanese Civilian Camp at Stanley
Geoffrey Charles Emerson

The Six-Day War of 1899: Hong Kong in the Age of Imperialism
Patrick H. Hase

Watching Over Hong Kong: Private Policing 1841–1941
Sheilah E. Hamilton

Public Success, Private Sorrow: The Life and Time of Charles Henry Brewitt-Taylor (1857–1938), China Customs Commissioner and Pioneer Translator
Isidore Cyril Cannon

East River Column: Hong Kong Guerrillas in the Second World War and After
Chan Sui-jeung

Resist to the End: Hong Kong, 1941–1945
Charles Barman, edited by Ray Barman

Southern District Officer Reports: Islands and Villages in Rural Hong Kong, 1910–60
Edited by John Strickland

The Dragon and the Crown
Hong Kong Memoirs

Stanley S.K. Kwan
with Nicole Kwan

香港大學出版社
HONG KONG UNIVERSITY PRESS

Hong Kong University Press
14/F Hing Wai Centre
7 Tin Wan Praya Road
Aberdeen
Hong Kong
www.hkupress.org

ISBN 978-988-8083-17-6

British Library Cataloguing-in-Publication Data
A catalogue record for this book is available from the British Library.

Printed and bound by Kings Time Printing Press Ltd., in Hong Kong, China

CONTENTS

FOREWORD

It is very gratifying to see that the Royal Asiatic Society Hong Kong Studies Series has indeed become a Series since our first volume appeared in 2005. The publication of Stanley Kwan's memoirs brings our total to six — and there are significantly more than that in various stages of consideration and production.

Originally writing for his family, friends and relatives, Mr. Kwan was happily persuaded to consider reaching a wider audience. A Chinese version was produced in 1999 in Canada, and I am delighted to present here a re-written and fuller version in English, produced with the collaboration and assistance of his niece Nicole Kwan. Mr. Kwan's background and experience have given him recollections and observations that are unique and fascinating to anybody interested in Hong Kong's social and economic transformation over the past seventy years. The journey he records, from patriotism to socialism and to capitalism, includes his one-time belief in socialism and Mao Zedong thought, and his establishment of the ultimate capitalist measure of Hong Kong — the Hang Seng Index.

The publications in the Studies Series have been made possible initially by the very generous donation of seeding capital by the Trustees of the Clague Trust Fund, representing the estate of the late Sir Douglas Clague. This donation enabled us to establish a trust fund in the name of Sir Lindsay and Lady Ride, in memory of our first Vice President. The Society itself added to this fund, as have a number of further generous donors.

The result is that we now have funding to bring to students of Hong Kong's history, culture and society a number of books that might otherwise not have seen the light of day. Furthermore, we were delighted to be able to establish an agreement with Hong Kong University Press which sets out the basis on which the Press will partner our efforts.

Robert Nield
President
Royal Asiatic Society, Hong Kong Branch
July 2008

FOREWORD

Some of the most influential and important people in our world are the quiet, thoughtful ones who see the need for a change or an innovation and set about bringing it into being. One of these people is Stanley Kwan, the creator of the Hang Seng Index, one of the key tools of financial information in Hong Kong, not just for Hong Kong, but also for the world.

Hong Kong has evolved since the end of World War II from a colonial port on the China coast into a major centre of the global economy. Social and cultural development has gone hand in hand with the economic, but has been much less well documented in the scholarly literature or the popular press.

Many men and women contributed to the making of Hong Kong society. Some were rich and famous, or did great deeds that were recorded in print or on stone. Most just struggled quietly to survive in difficult conditions. The life stories of these men and women give us a deeper, fuller understanding of the evolution of Hong Kong.

Stanley Kwan belongs to both these categories. He has given the world some of the most widely recognized and frequently cited indicators of the Hong Kong economy; yet with the self-effacing modesty characteristic of the scholar-merchant (*rushang*) that he is, he has led a quiet and simple life.

His world, part and parcel of the evolving open and pluralistic Hong Kong, and so beautifully described in this book, is one in which his involvement with banking goes hand in hand with a profound dedication to Chinese culture and history. This book is therefore not only a "people's history" of Hong Kong, but also a probing analysis of Hong Kong identity, and what it means to be living in a Chinese society.

As the return to Chinese sovereignty drew near, Stanley Kwan went through a process of analysis and questioning about the past and the future, a process that eventually led him to emigrate to Canada. His description of his decision-making is deeply moving; he articulates, with care and sincerity, the process that has so enriched Canada, and connected this country so closely to Hong Kong.

Scholars as well as general readers who have an interest in Hong Kong and modern China owe Stanley Kwan a great debt for sharing his touching and thoughtful story, first in the Chinese version which we edited as Volume 2 of the *Hong Kong Life Stories* series published in 1999 by the University of Toronto–York University Joint Centre for Asia Pacific Studies, and now in this enriched and re-written English version. Reading his memoirs is an enlightening and enjoyable treat.

Diana Lary   Bernard Luk
Vancouver   Toronto

As a third-generation Hongkonger, my life and family fortune have been inexorably tied to the fate of the former British colony during the past century. We were wedged between the East and the West — the Dragon and the Crown.

I was born, in 1925, into a banking family steeped in Chinese culture and tradition, but I studied at King's College under the British colonial system. I served as an army interpreter during the war, liaising between the Nationalist Chinese and American forces in southwest China. After the war, I worked for a British firm, then the American Consulate General and finally, back to my roots, a local Chinese bank — Hang Seng Bank — where, as head of the research department, I launched the Hang Seng Index and witnessed the dramatic ups and downs of the Hong Kong economy.

As Chinese in Hong Kong, we benefit from easy access to both China and the West, but we are also the passive subjects, and sometimes victims, of international agreements. Many of my generation felt deep humiliation at the cession of Hong Kong to Britain after the Opium War, but we benefited from the stability and prosperity of the colony. All of us should have celebrated when Britain handed back Hong Kong to Chinese sovereignty in 1997, but many greeted the occasion with feelings of uncertainty and anxiety.

We have all been deeply affected by developments in China and, as a result, our lives have taken very different directions. Our patriotic feelings for China soared during the Anti-Japanese War, but our reactions to the Communist takeover in 1949 were mixed. My two younger brothers and some of my friends and relatives went back to China to join the revolution, but others emigrated and settled overseas. Still others came to Hong Kong in search of a better life and stayed, contributing to the colony's prosperity. I myself stayed in Hong Kong until 1984, when I retired and emigrated to Canada.

I have tried to look back on my life and explore the contradictions and dilemmas that we faced in Hong Kong, as well as the social, economic and political forces which shaped our destinies. It is my hope that this can contribute to the discussion on Hong Kong identity and our understanding of where we came from and where we are going.

This memoir was written primarily from my own memories, observations and reflections, and supplemented by our own research and personal interviews. The authors are solely responsible for any errors.

Stanley Kwan

ACKNOWLEDGEMENTS

As I began to make preparations to write my memoirs in English in the new millennium, my wife, Wing Kin, was diagnosed with Alzheimer's disease, and I was about to give up this project and devote full time to my new unaccustomed role as a caregiver. Fortunately, my niece Nicole offered to help me with the research and writing, and her brother Cheuk gave us his full support and encouragement.

Many people contributed to this book. Man Kwok Lau, my former King's College schoolmate and mentor at Hang Seng Bank, provided valuable insights and information for the sections on Hang Seng and the banking industry in Hong Kong. John Ho, Fan Meng Siang and Liu Wen Lin, my former army interpreter comrades, helped refresh my wartime memories during our many reunion luncheons in Toronto. Barbara Yang, my neighbour, read and commented on our manuscript.

My brothers, Tse Kwong and Yuan Kwong, shared with us their thoughts and experiences, without which my memoirs would be incomplete. Aunt Rose and my cousins Kwan Lin Chee, Kwan Sai Kwong and Tang Wai Han provided us with details of the history of the Kwan and Tang families which greatly enriched this book. Chan Hang Chuen, my sister-in-law, provided me with information on her siblings on the Mainland; her daughter, Man Si Wai, first gave me the idea to write down my life experiences.

I am also grateful to: Elizabeth Sinn, who took an interest in my memoirs and introduced us to the Royal Asiatic Society; Robert Nield of the Royal Asiatic Society and Colin Day at Hong Kong University Press, who supported this project; and Diana Lary and Bernard Luk, the editors of the original Chinese version of my memoirs in 1999, who encouraged us and wrote the Foreword.

Last but not least, to my wife, Wing Kin, and my daughters, Yvonne and Elaine, who sustained and supported me in my endeavour, I owe them my deepest gratitude.

Stanley Kwan

We are immensely grateful to Peter Geldart and Judy Maxwell who gave their valuable time to help us edit the manuscript. Without their assistance, we would not have a finished book.

I would also like to thank my family and all my friends and relatives who supported and encouraged me in this project, in particular: Eileen Cheng who inspired me with her keen interest in Hong Kong history and was the first to read our draft; my uncle Wong Man Fai who recounted stories of the Wong family over our many dim sum breakfasts in Hong Kong; my aunt Wong Wai Sum who took me to visit Ching Lin Terrace, the site of our old family mansions; and all my teachers and classmates at the Journalism and Media Studies Centre at the University of Hong Kong, from whom I learned the joy of reporting and writing.

Nicole Kwan

Editorial Conventions

For all places, institutions, publications and well-known persons in Hong Kong with Chinese names, we have retained their prevailing (or most commonly known) Romanized forms (for example: Wing Lok Street, Tung Wah Hospital, Ta Kung Pao, Chung Sze-yuen).

For all friends and relatives, we have used their Romanized names whenever we know them; otherwise, we have taken the liberty to Romanize their Chinese names using Cantonese pronunciation. In both cases, we have put their last names first under Chinese convention.

Chinese names and terms unique to Hong Kong are Romanized using Cantonese pronunciation; otherwise, they are Romanized using the pinyin method.

For all persons, places, publications and institutions on mainland China, we have used the pinyin Romanization method, with two exceptions: for persons already well-known before 1949, we have retained their most commonly used Romanized names (for example: Sun Yat-sen, Chiang Kai-shek); for certain places in the Pearl River Delta, we have Romanized their names using local dialects when talking about the pre-1949 period (for example: Kaukong, Hoiping).

The Chinese characters for less well-known terms, places, personal names, literary and artistic works, publications and institutions are listed in the Glossary. The Chinese names of relatives are listed under the respective family trees in Figures 1–4 of the Genealogical Tables. (Only those mentioned in the text are included.)

The Chinese characters for the teachings of Chairman Ho quoted in the text are provided in Appendix III. The Chinese characters for selected sayings, slogans, and literary quotations used in the text are provided in Appendix IV.

The text follows the house style of Hong Kong University Press.

Genealogical Tables

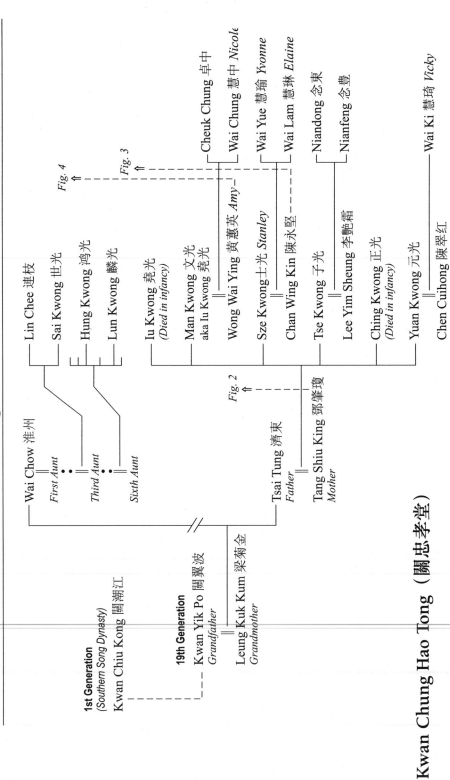

Figure 1 The Kwan Family

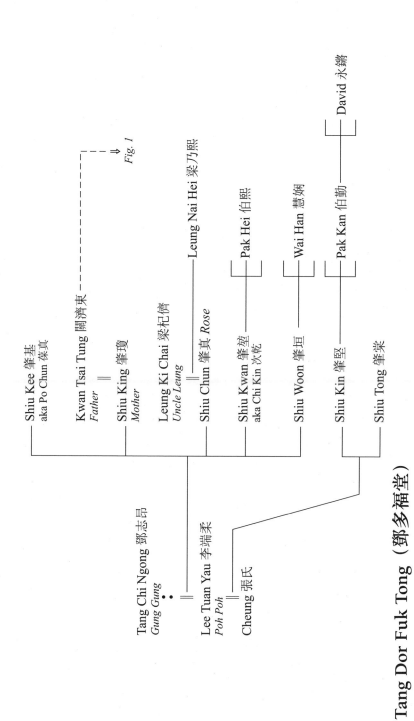

Tang Dor Fuk Tong（鄧多福堂）

Figure 2 The Tang Family (my maternal relatives)

Chan Yee Yeung Tong （陳義讓堂）

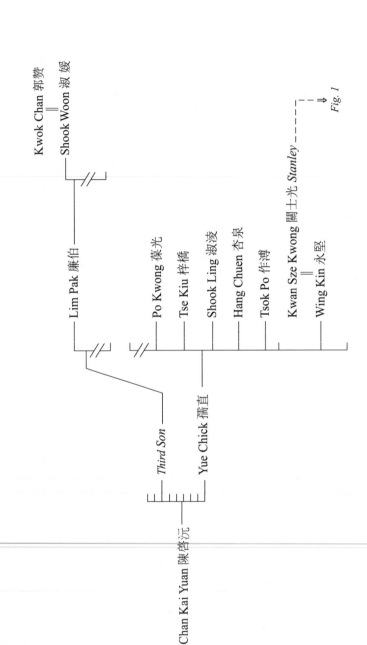

Figure 3 The Chan Family (my in-laws)

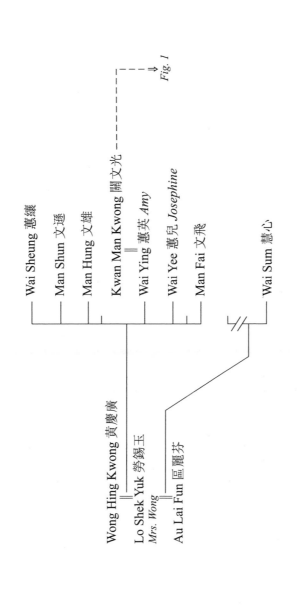

Wong Kwong Sin Tong（黃廣善堂）

Figure 4 The Wong Family (our Ching Lin Terrace neighbours)

1
Roots

Ancestors

My earliest memories of the family house were the four large characters of our household name — Kwan Chung Hao Tong — in sweeping brush strokes. Written in gold on a five-foot-long black wood panel, the characters hung high in the middle of our family hall. Household names traditionally highlighted each family's values and aspirations, and ours were *chung* and *hao* — loyalty to the emperor and filial piety. Our household was thus the "Kwan Family Hall of Loyalty and Filial Piety," and these words haunted me as I was growing up.

Mindful of our family values, I was properly deferential towards my parents and family elders and never got into any trouble — but loyalty to the emperor was another matter. By the time I was born in the British colony of Hong Kong in 1925, China had become a republic and no longer had an emperor; instead, we were to pledge loyalty to the King of England. The symbols of the British monarchy were everywhere: the Royal Crown on the red cylindrical pillar post-boxes and the caps of the policemen patrolling the streets; the Royal Coat of Arms on government documents and posters; the portrait of King George V in school halls and government offices; and "On His Majesty's Service" stamped on all government envelopes.

In reality, however, the British monarchy was far removed from our daily lives. Except for the few who attended English-speaking schools, the vast majority of the local Chinese could hardly understand or speak any English. We interacted with each other daily in areas where the Europeans rarely ventured, so it never occurred to me, my family or any of my friends that we owed loyalty to the King of England. Instead, even though the emperor was gone, we found ourselves remaining loyal to five thousand years of Chinese tradition and history.

In police stations, aside from the photo of the King, we could just as easily find the statue of Guan Yu — a Chinese general from the Three Kingdoms period of the third century who was later deified and given the title of *Guandi* (Emperor Guan). With a dark red face and a long black beard, *Guandi* was often depicted carrying a large sword with a long handle in his right hand and a book in his left — a symbol of bravery, righteousness and loyalty. He was also worshipped in many temples, restaurants and shops throughout the colony.

Many Chinese families could trace their lineages back hundreds of years. The earliest record of my ancestors was in 1273, the ninth year of the reign of the Southern Song (Sung) Emperor Du Zong, when Kwan Chiu Kong took refuge in Kaukong (Jiujiang) or Nine Rivers, a village in the southern province of Guangdong. The event was described in surprising detail in our family genealogy record — the *Shixilu* (a record of relations over the generations).

During the reign of Emperor Du Zong (1264–74), the Southern Song dynasty was on its dying breath, and the country was ravaged by wars and famine. By 1271, Kublai Khan, the grandson of Genghis Khan, had overrun northern China and crowned himself emperor, thus establishing the Yuan dynasty. When the Mongolian army swept down the country to destroy what was left of the Southern Song dynasty, inhabitants of Anhui, Zhejiang and Jiangxi migrated southward to escape its onslaught. It was reported in the *Shixilu* that our ancestor Kwan Chiu Kong joined this refugee tide. Leaving his home province of Jiangxi, he wandered south with the refugees, begging for food and shelter along the way.

The long trek took him past the border post of Nanxiong to what is now the province of Guangdong. He then travelled down the North River (Bei Jiang) on a wooden raft, uncertain of where he was headed, until the raft was finally damaged on the river's lower reaches and he had to wade ashore to look for shelter. Our ancestor Chiu Kong eventually settled in Kaukong, a village in the middle of the Pearl River Delta where the North River merges with the West River (Xi Jiang) and the East River (Dong Jiang) to flow onwards to the South China Sea as the Pearl River (Zhu Jiang). Here, where the soil was rich, the climate wet and mild, and the crisscrossing waterways teemed with fish, our ancestor finally found a place which could support him and the many generations of his descendents.

Within a few years of our ancestor Chiu Kong's journey, Kublai Khan's armies swept into the Southern Song capital of Hangzhou in Zhejiang province in 1276 and captured Emperor Du Zong's successor Gong Di. This would have dealt a final blow to the long-decaying dynasty, except that Gong Di's two younger brothers escaped and fled south with their entourage. The older brother was crowned Emperor Duan Zong, but did not live long and was succeeded by his younger brother Ping Di in 1278. By then the Mongolian armies were closing in so, refusing to surrender, Ping Di's loyal official carried him on his back and jumped off a cliff into the South China Sea.

The tragic fates of the young emperors would have been just another footnote in the tomes of Chinese history, except for one unexpected legacy. While in exile, Duan Zong built a temporary palace on top of a small hill near the west bank of what is now Kowloon Bay in Hong Kong. Over the centuries, the palace collapsed but a boulder remained on the spot, on which later generations engraved and painted three large characters in bold red: Sung Wong Toi — the terrace of the Song Emperor. Although the Japanese occupied Hong Kong during World War II and levelled the hill to make way for the extension of the former Kai Tak Airport, a block of the boulder bearing the three characters remained intact. In 1945, the colonial government built a small garden around this remaining block, which now rests on a low granite platform framed and shaded by trees at the far end of the garden. The three characters are faded but remain clear-cut and visible. Near the entrance to the garden stands a pair of six-foot-high steles depicting the story of the young emperors in Chinese and English. Apartments, grocery stores and garages now thrive across the street and double-decker buses, taxis and minivans careen around the corner, but within the stillness of the garden the solid block is imperturbable — a silent witness to Hong Kong's distant past and its early ties to imperial China.

My family would not move to Hong Kong until the turn of the twentieth century, by which time China had witnessed the passing of four imperial dynasties: Southern Song, Yuan, Ming and Qing (Ch'ing).

My grandfather Kwan Yik Po, who gave us our household name, belonged to the nineteenth generation of our ancestor Chiu Kong's descendants in Kaukong. Born in the ninth year of the reign of Emperor Xian Feng of the Qing dynasty (1859), Grandfather aspired to join the imperial government, like others of means and learning at the time.

Serving in the imperial government had been the most prestigious and sought-after career path in China over the centuries. To qualify, all candidates needed to pass numerous stringent examinations. Testing the candidates on a vast range of Chinese classical thoughts and writings, these examinations were administered at various levels: twice every three years in the county, once every three years at the provincial capital, and finally once every three years at the imperial capital. Only those who advanced to the highest level successfully were admitted to the imperial government service. Tall and robust, with a red face like *Guandi* and famously outgoing, Grandfather was fond of learning from an early age and showed talents for writing and literature. Kaukong village elders had high hopes of him securing a post in the imperial government and he diligently studied the classics for many years, but success in the examinations eluded him.

Then, in 1898, Emperor Guang Xu introduced the Hundred Days' Reform in an effort to resuscitate a rapidly decaying dynasty. As part of his attempts to institute a modern education system and introduce mathematics and science into the curriculum, he abolished the traditional examination system. The reforms eventually failed, but Grandfather did not sit for any more examinations and, instead, devoted himself to teaching in his own village where he acquired quite a reputation as a teacher. By the time he passed away at forty-six, in the thirtieth year of the reign of Emperor Guang Xu (1905), thousands of years of imperial rule over China were slowly but irrevocably grinding to an end.

My father Kwan Tsai Tung was deeply influenced by Grandfather's teachings. He would later update the family *Shixilu* and describe Grandfather's achievements in great detail. The youngest of seven children, of whom only four survived to adulthood, Father was slight in build, quiet and scholarly, with large, sensitive eyes and a thin, kindly face. True to tradition, he remained totally submissive to his elder brother Wai Chow, who took over as patriarch of Kwan Chung Hao Tong after Grandfather passed away. Uncle Wai Chow was the opposite of Father in physique and personality: tall and well built, with a high forehead and stern eyes. He decided to try his hand at business and set the family on a totally different path.

The *Yinhao* and Our Family Fortunes

By the turn of the twentieth century, foreign powers had forced China to "open up", exacting trade and territorial concessions, and the Qing dynasty was on its last breath. The economy, which had long teetered under heavy taxes and corruption, came close to ruin with a flood of foreign goods, including opium, and the rapid drain of silver from the country. Kaukong, even with its abundant fish ponds and rich farm lands, was no exception and many started to leave the village to look for better livelihoods elsewhere. While villagers from other coastal areas headed primarily for Southeast Asia and North America, many Kaukong natives ventured even further and settled in Central and South America (including Cuba, where the Havana Chinese cemetery holds the remains of many Kwan's from Kaukong).

Those who preferred not to go too far headed for Hong Kong, within a day's journey from Kaukong. Ceded to the British in 1842 after the first Opium War, the colony was transformed rapidly from a sleepy fishing village into a busy trading port and financial centre, and was thriving by the end of the Qing dynasty. Uncle Wai Chow arrived in Hong Kong at the age of thirteen and was apprenticed with his maternal uncle's small, traditional bank — Hung Tak Yinhao — at 165 Queen's Road Central.

Kaukong villagers who moved to Hong Kong during this period typically made their living operating traditional banks called *yinhao* (silver shops). They were also known as *qianzhuang* (money dealers) in other parts of

China, and foreign businessmen generally called them "native banks". *Yinhao* played a major role in the local economy during the colony's first hundred years, handling most of the deposits and loans within the Chinese business community as well as remittances from overseas Chinese who originated from the Pearl River Delta. Many *yinhao* also actively traded currencies and bullion, which led to the founding of the Chinese Gold and Silver Exchange Society in 1910.

Uncle Wai Chow proved himself a fast understudy at Hung Tak and within a few years he was representing the *yinhao* at the Gold and Silver Exchange. He was a talented if somewhat aggressive trader, and rapidly made a name for himself. By his early twenties, he had accumulated enough capital and business contacts to start his own business. He set up Wing Tak Yinhao and Wing Tai Yinhao with capital and support from his Kaukong business network which stretched as far as San Francisco, Mexico and Havana. Wing Tak and Wing Tai imported silver from Mexico for minting into silver dollars for mainland China, and also traded heavily on the Gold and Silver Exchange.

In 1916, the West River broke its banks and flooded vast areas of the Pearl River Delta. Many lives, houses and livestock were destroyed in Kaukong. Uncle Wai Chow hired a boat to rescue his mother, his young wife from an arranged marriage and his younger siblings, and brought them to Hong Kong. That was when Father started his banking career, at the age of eighteen, assisting Uncle Wai Chow in his *yinhao*.

Most of the *yinhao* congregated in the narrower streets of the Chinese business area of Sheung Wan, between Queen's Road and Des Voeux Road, just west of the Central District. In contrast to Central, where foreign banks and corporations occupied imposing Victorian buildings with tall pillars and high ceilings, Chinese businesses in Sheung Wan were housed in three- or four-storey traditional southern Chinese tenement houses with narrow staircases and balconies. The balconies extended out to provide a covered passageway along the shop front — a convenience during the hot summer months and the long rainy seasons. The names of the shops were written in bold characters across the front of the tenements, and their businesses or products were itemized vertically on the pillars supporting the balconies.

Guarded by tall iron bars at their entrances, the *yinhao* were surrounded by gold retailers, jewellery shops, Chinese herbal stores, Western pharmacies, and shops trading in dried seafood and textiles. Tea houses serving *dim sum* steamed in little bamboo baskets would open at six in the morning, so that businessmen and shopkeepers could take their breakfast before starting work. Many shops would hang out large wooden panels or pennants from the upper floors to advertise their names and products, forming a busy and colourful parade of signs over the pedestrians and rickshaws passing along the streets below.

Further to the west of Sheung Wan was Sai Ying Poon which was filled with shops selling and distributing dried sea products such as sharks' fins, scallops and abalones. To the west of Sai Ying Poon was Shek Tong Tsui where the most famous Chinese restaurants and legalized brothels congregated, and where much of the real business was conducted in the evenings. Uncle Wai Chow would go home for a short rest after closing shop in the evening, put on his best dark-blue silk gown, and depart for his nightly visits to Shek Tong Tsui with his clients and fellow bankers. The biggest restaurants there occupied three or four storeys over an entire block and would all be brightly lit and filled with the sweet smell of braised abalone and the aroma of flowing rice wine. Loud voices rising from the crowded tables would overpower the high-pitched singing and the gentle whining of the *erhu*, a two-stringed instrument, in the background. These festivities would spill over to the brothels in the surrounding buildings, many of the better known of which would occupy several storeys. On the upper floors, rolls of wooden shuttered doors would open out onto narrow verandas lined with intricate cast iron rails and decorated with pots of ferns and tropical house plants. Light, music and voices would continue to flow from the rooms all night long.

To consolidate his business network beyond his nightly contacts, Uncle Wai Chow needed to form more permanent alliances within the banking circle. The same year that my uncle rescued his family from the floods of the West River, another Kaukong banker, Tang Chi Ngong, gave generous sums of money to the village to help its reconstruction, in recognition of which the village leaders named a newly rebuilt bridge after him.

Tang Chi Ngong was lightly built with taut features and clear sharp eyes. A thick moustache drooping over his broad, lightly clinched lips gave him an air of shrewdness and confidence. Much older than Uncle Wai Chow, Tang Chi Ngong had come to Hong Kong in the early 1870s at the age of twelve. At first he helped his uncle in his currency exchange stall on Queen's Road and then, after his uncle passed away, he worked as an apprentice at Hung Yu Yinhao where he quickly rose through the ranks. When Hung Yu closed for business and distributed its capital, Tang Chi Ngong was given a handsome sum of silver dollars which he used to set up Tang Tin Fuk Yinhao, where he was sole proprietor. Tin Fuk was located at 171 Queen's Road Central at the end of a string of *yinhao*: Shui Kut, Tai Yau, Hung Tak, and later Wing Tak and Wing Tai. Hung Tak was where Uncle Wai Chow was initially apprenticed, and the two became acquainted with each other first as neighbours and later as business associates.

Unlike Uncle Wai Chow's *yinhao*, Wing Tak and Wing Tai, which mainly traded currencies, gold and silver, Tin Fuk specialized in making loans against property mortgages. Its business was less risky and grew briskly as more people settled in Hong Kong and property became increasingly in demand. Whenever borrowers were unable to service their debts, Tin Fuk would take over the property and rent it out. With a steady flow of rental income, its basement vault was always full of silver dollars. As Uncle Wai Chow needed funding from Tin Fuk to take on increasingly large stakes in trading currency and bullion, it was to his advantage to consolidate the relationship between the three *yinhao*. Since there could be no more effective way to seal the bond than through marriage, my father was introduced to the quiet, serious-looking and diminutive seventeen-year-old girl with large dark brown eyes who would become my mother.

Mother, Shiu King, was the thirteenth child of Tang Chi Ngong, by his second and favourite concubine. For unknown reasons which haunted the family, all her older brothers except for the twelfth had died before they turned eighteen, and all her older sisters who lived long enough to be married died within a hundred days of their marriages. Mother's marriage to Father was therefore an occasion for both celebration and apprehension.

My maternal grandmother Lee Tuan Yau, whom we called *Poh Poh*, was a sharp-looking woman with handsome features and quick movements despite the inconvenience of her tiny bound feet. *Poh Poh* was the fifth daughter of a Qing dynasty official and the only one of Tang Chi Ngong's wife and four concubines who was educated. Grandfather Chi Ngong, whom we called *Gung Gung*, took *Poh Poh* with the intention that she would manage his household and attend any social function if needed. *Poh Poh* therefore wielded great authority within the Tang household. Since Mother was her first daughter to be married, and aware of the sad history of previous marriages in the family, *Poh Poh* was determined to spare no expense in making the marriage a success.

Mother married into the Kwan household on the tenth day of the tenth lunar month of 1917. Carried to her new home in a sedan covered by bright red silk with delicate multicoloured embroideries, she brought as her dowry thick round gold bracelets carved with phoenixes and dragons symbolizing marriage, jade earrings and pendants of the deepest shades of translucent green, two young housemaids from the Tang family, and a full set of elaborately carved blackwood furniture. One of the most prized of Mother's dowries, however, was a Western-style desk clock. Finely inscribed in black along the lower rim of the clock face were the words: "Manufactured by Ansonia Clock Company, New York, United States of America". Its intricate mechanism was housed in a foot-high rectangular glass case with a gilded metal frame, the four legs were shaped like animal faces, and on top was a gold beacon standing erect in a sea of glistening waves and floral patterns. I used to be mesmerized by the clock: the delicate metal hands ticking along the black roman numerals on the face, the gold and glass pendant swinging with the clockwork, the melodic chimes on the hour, and the sunlight sparkling through the glass and glittering off the golden frame. The clock was all that remained of Mother's dowry after the war and has stayed in the possession of our family to this day.

Perhaps because of *Poh Poh's* unswerving determination to make the marriage a success, the hundred-day curse was finally lifted; Mother lived to be eighty-four and bore six sons, of whom four lived to adulthood. Her life in the Kwan household, however, did not turn out to be an easy one. My parents' first child, a son named Iu Kwong, died in infancy and, despite the rich dowry that Mother brought, Father was a man of moderate means. Dependent on Uncle Wai Chow for his livelihood and forced to work under his shadow, Father worked obediently and diligently but received only a modest salary.

My second brother Man Kwong and I, the third child, were born in an old tenement house on Wing Kut Street, close to the area where the *yinhao* congregated. The street was a narrow lane running between Queen's Road and Des Voeux Road and not accessible to motor vehicles. Hardware stores, grocery shops, barber shops and small restaurants occupied the ground floors of the tenement houses, with middle- and lower-income families living on the upper floors. A year after I was born, however, we were able to move up in our housing status.

Reaping the profits of his hugely successful business, Uncle Wai Chow bought two houses on Ching Lin Terrace, an affluent neighbourhood on the mid-levels of Kennedy Town in Western District. Although adjacent to Shek Tong Tsui, Western District was then a quiet area with few commercial activities other than some grocery stores and rows of warehouses (called "godowns") along the harbour front. Uncle Wai Chow liked this largely residential neighbourhood and completely renovated two houses, combining them into a big mansion equipped with flushing toilets and gas for cooking and heating, all of which were rare luxuries at the time. He moved into the mansion with Grandmother and his rapidly expanding household, which now consisted of his wife, two concubines and eight children. He felt magnanimous enough to accommodate our family in one of the suites and my fourth brother, Tse Kwong, fifth brother, Ching Kwong (who died in infancy), and sixth brother, Yuan Kwong, were born there.

Ching Lin Terrace was the centre of my childhood. Midway up the hill on the western end of the island, the terrace commanded a panoramic view of Victoria Harbour and its ships of all descriptions: squat Chinese junks with large brown sails, white steam ships puffing smoke from their long funnels, and small tug boats and sampans that darted back and forth to service the ships and ferry the passengers. Ching Lin Terrace was the third highest among the five parallel residential terraces that were cut into the side of the hill and reinforced with blocks of granite. Mount Davis towered over us at the western end, and on the summit a British army fortress housed the big guns intended for Hong Kong's coastal defence.

Uncle Wai Chow's mansion occupied numbers 10 and 11 in a row of fourteen three-storey houses, one of a number of stately houses renovated or re-built with solid masonry on a granite base with large glass windows and wide balconies. The outer walls of the mansion were constructed with "green bricks" — high quality greyish bricks with a deep green hue. The long yard in front of the houses was wide and shaded by a row of leafy candlenut trees, and on summer evenings the elderly would sit outside on wooden stools to chat and fan away the warm humid air.

On the ground floor of our mansion was a large family hall which opened onto a wide backyard. The black wood panel bearing our household name Kwan Chung Hao Tong hung on top of a dark brown, intricately carved wooden arch which soared from wall to wall and divided the hall in two. In the front was a Western-style living room with a teakwood floor and wall panels, and a set of heavy sofas upholstered in bright floral patterns. In the rear was a Chinese-style living room with a set of elaborately carved blackwood furniture with round black and white marble panels in the backs of the chairs. At one end of the room, a large mirror hung against the wall over a long, narrow blackwood altar table. On the table were two-foot-high porcelain statues of three legendary elders in traditional Chinese robes, representing fortune, wealth and longevity — *Fu, Lu, Shou*. In the backyard of the mansion was a goldfish pond surrounded by neatly trimmed shrubs and flowers in ceramic pots.

There were five residential suites: one on the ground floor beside the family hall and two on each of the upper floors. Grandmother occupied one of the suites on the second floor, and Uncle Wai Chow and his wife (whom we call First Aunt) the other. Our family lived in one of the third floor suites, and two of Uncle Wai Chow's five concubines (whom we called Third Aunt and Sixth Aunt in accordance with the sequence in which they were brought into the family) lived in the other suites with their respective children. (Uncle's other concubines had either died or left the family by the time we moved to Ching Lin Terrace.)

Grandmother Leung Kuk Kum was small-framed and plain but kindly. Like *Poh Poh*, she had bound feet no more than four inches long, as was the custom among women of well-to-do families during the Qing dynasty. She used to wear miniature shoes made of black silk cloth delicately embroidered with brightly coloured floral patterns. Because she swayed while she walked and could manage only relatively short distances, whenever she went out Uncle Wai Chow would order a sedan chair carried on the shoulders of two footmen to take her from the terrace down the slope and back up again. Born in Hong Kong under British rule, Mother was not as constricted by tradition as many of the girls in similarly well-to-do families in mainland China. By the time she turned eleven, the 1911 National Revolution led by Dr. Sun Yat-sen had toppled the Qing dynasty. To usher in a new era of freedom and progress, the new republican government ordered all men to cut their queues and the end of the practice of binding girls' feet.

Although she escaped the fate of having her feet bound, Mother continued to be fettered by the traditional obligations of a wife and daughter-in-law which, since she came from a well-respected family, she was expected to follow diligently. The foremost among her duties was to obey Father's wishes. Father, for his part, took to heart our family value of filial piety which, after Grandfather Yik Po passed away, he lavished on Grandmother. Mother therefore had to work extra hard in her role as daughter-in-law. She would prepare tea and serve it to Grandmother on the first and fifteenth days of the lunar month while wishing her good health and long life, a ritual that was particularly important on Grandmother's birthday. One of my earliest memories was of Mother kneeling and serving tea to Grandmother.

Another of Mother's duties was to keep the family shrine in immaculate condition. Uncle Wai Chow had given Grandmother a three-bedroom suite and one of the rooms was used for ancestor worship. Against the main wall of the room was a large, deep blackwood altar table supporting a two-foot-high red tablet housed in a blackwood frame. Written in gold on the tablet were the words: "The Shrine of the Successive Generations of Ancestors of the Kwan Family". This room was Grandmother's domain, where she would say her morning and evening prayers to *Guanyin* (the Goddess of Mercy) and the Kwan ancestors and seek their blessings. She would also supervise ancestor worship rituals for key days of the lunar calendar: New Year, the Qing Ming and Chong Yang festivals (which both commemorated the deceased), Grandfather's birthday, and the anniversary of his death.

On such occasions, the rituals would be highly elaborate and the offerings on the altar table would be three rows deep. Directly in front of the ancestral shrine stood a large rectangular bronze incense burner, flanked on both sides by pairs of bronze joss stick stands and candle stands. Along the second row large porcelain plates held the main dishes — a whole cooked chicken and a chunk of roasted pork or a whole suckling pig — surrounded by side dishes such as fried fish, steamed buns, vegetables and fresh fruits. The outer row contained three pairs of red lacquered chopsticks, three red porcelain bowls piled with rice, and three small red porcelain cups filled to the brim with rice wine.

Before the ceremony began, Mother and other female members of the household would light up pieces of camphor wood piled up on a heap of incense dust inside the burner, as well as the joss sticks and red candles in their stands. Then, led by Uncle Wai Chow, each family member in order of seniority would perform the act of *kowtow* in front of the ancestral shrine by kneeling down and touching his or her forehead to the ground three times. The entire act would be performed three times consecutively — in total kneeling three times and touching the head to the ground nine times (*san gui jiu kou*). When the ceremony was over, the food offerings would be served on the dinner table; for us children, this was the best part of the entire ceremony.

After Grandmother died, Mother kept the rituals alive for our own family, with simpler food offerings, but instead of performing *kowtow* we reduced the ritual to just standing and bowing three times, much to my relief. Having gone to school and learned about Western ideas and practices, I was no longer willing to submit to the ritual of *kowtow* as I felt offended or humiliated whenever I heard that the Chinese were a "kneeling" nation.

As well as the solemn rituals and often strict rules of behaviour within Uncle Wai Chow's household, there were also lighter moments. After Uncle Wai Chow and Father left for work in the mornings, Mother would keep Grandmother entertained by playing mahjong with her and would often invite First, Third and Sixth Aunts to make up four players. Although First Aunt would usually oblige, Third and Sixth Aunts would often find excuses not to participate, which was perhaps understandable since the games were usually slow and boring given Grandmother's poor eyesight and faltering memory. Mother would then enlist the help of our neighbours, especially her good friend Mrs. Wong Hing Kwong who lived in unit number 8 and would often come to join the game. From a wealthy Cantonese family which made its fortune in Shanghai, Mrs. Wong was graceful and considerate, and would often strategically slip a few tiles on the table to let Grandmother win the game. Sometimes Lin Chee, Uncle Wai Chow's eldest daughter, and Wai Sheung, Mrs. Wong's eldest daughter, would also join to help make up a foursome at the mahjong table. The children of both families quickly became friends, and Mrs. Wong later became an in-law when her daughter Amy married my second brother, Man Kwong.

Although Grandmother got on relatively peacefully with her many daughters-in-law all under one roof, all was not well among Uncle Wai Chow's wife and concubines. First Aunt was his wife through an arranged marriage in Kaukong, but after he moved to Hong Kong and made his fortune, Uncle acquired five concubines in rapid succession. The first was a housemaid and the others he met in Shek Tong Tsui. However, three of the concubines had left him before we moved to Ching Lin Terrace and only Third and Sixth Aunts stayed with us. Uncle Wai Chow had fourteen children in all, although only eight survived to adulthood. First Aunt did not have any children, and this gave Uncle Wai Chow all the excuses he needed to have concubines. Plain and uneducated but strong willed and unyielding, First Aunt put up a good fight and resisted to accept Uncle's concubines into the household for some time, but when they started bearing his children her defences broke down. Gradually, her influence in the household waned and she eventually retreated to a nunnery in Sha Tin where she stayed until she passed away, surviving Uncle Wai Chow by a few years. Third Aunt, who was soft-spoken, delicate and fair, played the *yangqin*, a stringed percussion instrument, and sang to the accompaniment of her father on the *erhu* in Shek Tong Tsui, where she met Uncle Wai Chow. She respected First Aunt but held her place in the household since she had a daughter and a son. Sixth Aunt, who was tall, sharp and assertive, bore four sons and two daughters and fiercely expanded her sphere of influence within the household and even into Uncle Wai Chow's business.

As children, we were only vaguely aware of the intrigues of our extended family and mixed easily with our cousins as well as with other children living on the terrace. For us, the long yard in front of our house was our playground, a battlefield and the centre of our after-school activities.

We especially loved to play soccer in the wide open space at the end of the terrace in front of the Temple of Lu Ban — the god of carpenters and masons. On top of the temple's grey tiled roofs were two turquoise dragons twirling in the clouds and chasing a large green pearl. Beneath the dragons, a row of figurines depicted the life and work of the Master. Inside the temple, Lu Ban's bearded figure wearing a golden belt and a green robe sat solemnly on a high wooden pedestal at the far end, contemplating the offerings of incense, fruits and flowers before him. I used to linger in the cool shade inside the temple, watching the tall pillars rise to meet the dark wood ceiling, reading the black and gold characters on the large wooden panels on the walls, and feeling drowsy as I watched the thin ribbons of smoke from the incense dance and swirl gently and effortlessly to the ceiling.

Uncle Wai Chow's *yinhao*, Wing Tak and Wing Tai, thrived during the early 1920s, reaping significant profits from his active trading in gold, silver and foreign currencies. However, the markets suffered a major setback in 1925, the year I was born. Spearheaded by communist labour leaders and supported by the Guangzhou (Canton) government, the Canton–Hong Kong General Strike began that year and brought business activities in Hong Kong to a standstill. The strike was initially launched in response to a nationwide movement to protest against the killing of demonstrators in Shanghai on 30 May. However, on 23 June, five days after the strike began in Hong Kong, British soldiers in Guangzhou shot at demonstrating workers, killing 52 and wounding 117 in what was known as the Shakee Massacre. This brought nationalistic and anti-British sentiments to a new height. In protest, some 250,000 workers left Hong Kong for Guangzhou with their families. The strike lasted sixteen months as unions boycotted all British goods and any ship using Hong Kong, and demanded better working conditions and greater rights. Alarmed by this explosive situation and questioning Hong Kong's future viability, many wealthy businessmen fled the colony with their capital. Those who stayed took out their savings in cash in case they had to flee, and this led to widespread bank runs and a sharp drop in the prices of property and stocks. Many smaller and under-capitalized *yinhao* became illiquid and eventually closed down.

Fortunately, Wing Tak and Wing Tai survived and expanded as weaker players went bankrupt and left the market. Uncle Wai Chow became even more active and consolidated his reputation as one of the most aggressive traders of his time. But his penchant for speculation eventually led to his downfall when, during the Great Depression of 1929, the American economy took a nose dive and brought down financial markets worldwide. With large exposures to the markets, Wing Tak and Wing Tai had to close their doors; Uncle Wai Chow went bankrupt and Father became unemployed.

For a time, life went on as usual. I was too young to realize the full extent of our misfortunes, although I did notice that the adults were looking more sober and seemed to have a lot on their minds. It was not until I started going to school that I began to feel the degradation of my family's material life, and the shame and agony of my parents. Uncle Wai Chow, however, was undaunted by this setback and continued to search for opportunities to make a comeback. Then Mother's family extended us a helping hand, and the strategic alliance Uncle had made earlier proved its real worth.

The Tang Family to the Rescue

Unlike Uncle Wai Chow who traded heavily in gold and foreign exchange, *Gung Gung* Tang Chi Ngong had remained cautious and seldom strayed from real estate lending. When his clients failed to pay their debts he would take over their properties and hold them as long-term investments, and as there were many bankruptcies during the General Strike and the Great Depression he steadily accumulated his wealth. At one point, Tin Fuk owned over forty shops for rent in the Sheung Wan area, and dozens of residential and commercial properties in Shek Tong Tsui and Happy Valley. While the traditional values of the Kwan family were loyalty and filial piety, those of the Tang family were *Dor Fuk* or "many fortunes", from the auspicious saying: "Many fortunes, long life and many male descendants." *Gung Gung's* household name was thus Tang Dor Fuk Tong — the "Tang Family Hall of Many Fortunes".

By the time he passed away in 1932, *Gung Gung* had indeed amassed an enormous fortune. But he had always been keen about sharing some of his wealth with those in need and enjoyed the public recognition this brought. In 1905, capping a series of substantial donations, he served as chairman of the board of Tung Wah Hospital, which was then the most influential charitable and community organization among the local Chinese. In 1916, after the flooding of the West River, he donated money for rebuilding Kaukong (with a bridge named after him), and later funded the building of Nanhai Secondary School and Kaukong Secondary School in his native town. He reached the apex of his public career on 28 September 1931, when Hong Kong governor William Peel officially opened the Tang Chi Ngong School of Chinese at the University of Hong Kong. *Gung Gung* had donated sixty thousand dollars for the building of the school in response to requests by the previous governor, Cecil Clementi, and leaders of the Chinese community. Much to *Gung Gung's* delight, Governor Peel commended him highly on his contributions to the development of Chinese culture in the colony and, in recognition, gave him special permission to hold a huge celebration for his seventieth birthday.

Gung Gung lived with his large family in a majestic mansion at 35–39 Gough Street, slightly up the hill from the financial district of Sheung Wan. He had nineteen children from his wife and four concubines, but by the time I was born, only six — four sons and two daughters — survived. His wife had passed away early, but three of his concubines and all of his surviving children, except for Mother after she married, lived in the mansion with their families. After *Gung Gung's* death, his surviving concubines and some of his children and their families continued to live there until it was sold in 1955.

Gung Gung's mansion, constructed with fine "green bricks", was three storeys high and divided into three sections: the main, east and west wings. Large rectangular windows with eaves covered by lush green tiles were interspersed with smaller octagonal multicoloured stained glass windows. The entrance of the main wing was on the northern side of the street, facing south in good Chinese architectural tradition, with a thick granite door frame twelve feet high and ten feet wide. Guarding the entrance was a wooden gate made of heavy logs about five inches in diameter attached horizontally to a large wooden frame that could slide back and forth across the doorway. The logs were about six inches apart, narrow enough to prevent people from getting through. At the top of the granite frame were the characters of the household name — Tang Dor Fuk Tong — and immediately behind the main gate were two large wooden doors. The entrances to the east and west wings had wooden doors instead of a sliding gate and could be reached through two private lanes on either side of the building. Unusually long and deep, the mansion had three levels of basement and was reportedly a government building before *Gung Gung* purchased it for his own residence.

The main foyer was separated from the main hall by a large rosewood screen elaborately carved with flowers, trees and birds, and inlaid with ivory and semi-precious stones. Visitors would enter or exit the main hall from either side of the screen. In the main hall, where *Gung Gung* received and entertained guests and held many of his banquets, four large mirrors hung on the walls, two on each side. The floor was covered by large smooth grey tiles. Adjacent to the hall was a courtyard with granite slabs which opened up to an atrium in the centre of the mansion, covered by a large glass skylight window. Across the courtyard was the rear portion of the main wing which housed *Gung Gung's* first concubine, a large kitchen serving the family and guests and, most important, the ancestral hall which held the shrines of Tang family ancestors.

Mother would always bring us to the ancestral hall to bow and pay our respects whenever she went home for visits, which became more frequent as Father's financial condition deteriorated. In the main wall of the ancestral hall was a large rectangular wooden niche the size of a big wardrobe which housed many red wooden tablets with gold characters. Names of recent ancestors were individually inscribed on foot-high tablets, and for more distant ancestors there was one large tablet bearing the inscription: "The Shrine of Successive Generations of Tang Family Ancestors".

On the other two sides of the courtyard were the foyers of the east and west wings, with stairs leading to the upper floors. *Gung Gung's* suite was located on the second floor of the main wing and consisted of a bedroom, a study and a big living/dining room. His fourth concubine lived in a suite directly above his, and his second concubine — our *Poh Poh* — lived on the ground floor of the east wing with my Seventeenth Aunt Rose (Shiu Chun), occupying three bedrooms and a living/dining room. On the upper floors were the suites of Eighteenth Uncle Chi Kin (Shiu Kwan) and his family and Nineteenth Uncle Shiu Woon and his family. Twelfth Uncle Po Chun (Shiu Kee) and his family lived on the ground floor of the west wing. On the upper floors were Fourteenth Uncle Shiu Kin and his family, and his birth mother — *Gung Gung's* third concubine. Each family suite had its own kitchen and bathroom and was equipped with gas for cooking and heating.

The Tang family had over twenty housemaids, some of whom came to the family as young girls and ended up spending the rest of their lives there. There were also a chef, a watchman, and a rickshaw driver who took *Gung Gung* to and from his office at Tang Tin Fuk Yinhao. *Gung Gung* hired a chauffeur in the late 1920s when he purchased his first automobile — a black four-door sedan — and soon the rickshaw was discarded. The rickshaw driver lost his job, but *Gung Gung* gave him a handsome sum for his retirement.

Despite his sharp business acumen, *Gung Gung* was warm and loving towards his grandchildren. My earliest memories of him were on the second day of Chinese New Year when by tradition we would go with Mother to pay our respects to him in the main hall of the mansion. Seated on an embroidered silk cushion in a spacious blackwood armchair, *Gung Gung* would beam and open his arms to greet us. As soon as we stepped across the threshold to the hall, my brothers and I would rush towards him and bow, wishing him prosperity and good health. He would gather us in his arms and give each of us a hug and a kiss on the cheek, his prickly moustache rubbing against our faces. And he was always generous with his *lai see* — a small red packet containing money for good luck. *Gung Gung's lai see* was always soft and would usually yield a ten dollar banknote, which was equivalent to three months' pay for a housemaid at that time.

Gung Gung doted on his four sons, who each had an entourage of servants when they were growing up and were given a free reign to spend as much money as they wanted and in whatever manner they pleased. They ended up pursuing widely different careers. Twelfth Uncle Po Chun, the scholar of the family, graduated from Queen's College, an elite English secondary school in Hong Kong, and Lingnan University in Guangzhou. He completed his graduate studies at Columbia University in New York, a rare achievement for well-to-do gentlemen of his time. Unfortunately Twelfth Uncle chose not to join the family banking business after he returned to Hong Kong, causing *Gung Gung* much disappointment. He suffered from diabetes and died at the relatively young age of fifty. Eighteenth Uncle Chi Kin and Nineteenth Uncle Shiu Woon also stayed away from the family business and both led high-flying lifestyles. In their youth they were among the few Chinese in Hong Kong to own automobiles — flashy two-door coupe convertibles — but neither was able to build up his own fortune. Eighteenth Uncle tried his hand at a variety of businesses, including trading and restaurants, but none of them turned out to be successful. Nineteenth Uncle indulged in horse racing, became quite a well-known jockey in Hong Kong and even went to Inner Mongolia to buy horses. He lived in Shanghai for a period before the Japanese occupation raising horses and dogs, and mingling with the rich and famous.

Gung Gung eventually looked to Fourteenth Uncle Shiu Kin to continue the family business. Uncle Shiu Kin attended St. Stephen's College in Hong Kong, a private English secondary school primarily for children of well-to-do families. Although his grades were mediocre he was diligent and obedient and, at *Gung Gung's* request, he left school to join Tang Tin Fuk Yinhao where he worked his way up from the ranks until he was able to manage the business upon *Gung Gung's* retirement. Uncle Shiu Kin thus became the guardian of *Gung Gung's* fortunes and even surpassed him in philanthropic achievements. In 1928, at the age of twenty-seven he became the youngest chairman on record on the board of Tung Wah Hospital, where he oversaw the expansion of the hospital group, and five years later he became chairman of Po Leung Kuk, which was then well-known for harbouring abducted girls and orphans. In the same year, he set up the Kowloon Motorbus Co. (1933) Ltd. with several partners and later became its chairman and managing director. Always wearing his trademark Chinese long gown, Uncle Shiu Kin mingled easily among the rich and famous within both Western and local Chinese communities. In recognition of his contributions, he was appointed Justice of the Peace in 1929, awarded the MBE (Member of the British Empire) in 1934, and received various awards and decorations from the British and colonial governments during successive years. In 1964, he was knighted by Queen Elizabeth II. To this day, hospitals and schools bearing his own or *Gung Gung*'s name testify to his extensive contributions to charity. Both the Tang Shiu Kin Hospital and Tang Chi Ngong Specialist Clinic in Wanchai continued to be well known and used by the Hong Kong public. His grandson, David Tang, who founded the China Club and Shanghai Tang, later became a successful businessman and celebrity in Hong Kong in his own right.

When *Gung Gung* passed away, his estate was primarily divided among his four sons, but a portion went to *Poh Poh*, his favourite concubine and the mother of five of his surviving children. It was *Poh Poh* who saved our family from an early ruin, even though her own health was failing from a serious injury she suffered at the race course.

On 26 February 1918, *Poh Poh* led a party of thirteen to the horse races in Happy Valley. They included her own children Aunt Rose, Eighteenth Uncle Chi Kin and Nineteenth Uncle Shiu Woon, and Sixteenth Uncle Shiu Tong, son of *Gung Gung*'s third concubine. A fire broke out from the cooking on the ground and quickly spread to the bamboo-built spectators' stand above. The crowd panicked and broke into a huge stampede. Fortunately, Eighteenth Uncle and Nineteenth Uncle were watching the race at the front and did not get caught as the stand collapsed. Sixteenth Uncle, however, was trapped in the confusion and died in the fire. *Poh Poh* was pinned down by a fallen beam but managed to survive; her maid later found her and stayed at her side until the ambulance arrived. Aunt Rose, who was then only thirteen, miraculously escaped unhurt and walked all the way home crying for help. Some six hundred people lost their lives in the fire — the highest number of fire casualties in the history of Hong Kong.

Suffering from poor health since the tragedy, *Poh Poh* became a devout Buddhist and would retreat each summer to her villa in Tai Po in the New Territories where she often invited nuns from a nearby abbey to chant with her and share her vegetarian dishes. When Father's health failed after the bankruptcy of Wing Tak and Wing Tai, she asked him to stay in the villa until he recovered. Worried about Father's misfortunes and Mother's difficulties in making ends meet, *Poh Poh* eventually gave Father fifty thousand dollars to start his own business.

Uncle Wai Chow was elated by this turn in fortune and was soon back in business. He quickly obtained additional capital, again from Kaukong natives overseas, and arranged for Father to set up another bank — Shiu Yuan Yinhao — in 1931. Father was nominally the bank's manager and licence holder but Uncle (who claimed greater savvy and experience) ran the show. Later, they also set up an affiliate — Seng Yuan Company — and registered it with the Chinese Gold and Silver Exchange Society to trade gold bullion.

To regain his losses, Uncle took increasingly larger positions on the market, but his luck did not improve and later he became entangled in lawsuits. To finance his legal costs, Uncle Wai Chow appropriated money from the bank and was subsequently charged and briefly jailed. After only three years, Shiu Yuan went the way of Wing Tak and Wing Tai and closed down. Father was too ashamed to go back to *Poh Poh* for any more help, so he declared bankruptcy and looked for jobs to support the family. He first worked as a broker in Fook Chai Insurance, an insurance company subsequently started by Uncle Wai Chow, but business was unstable and Father's meagre commissions were often not enough to cover our living expenses. Mother, who had enjoyed the luxury of a multitude of servants and unlimited amenities before she was married, was despondent and became even quieter than before. Her lips were always tightly clinched, and I seldom saw her smile anymore.

I suspected that aside from our deteriorating financial situation, Mother was also upset that Father had to live under the shadow of Uncle Wai Chow. Even though our family helped him re-start his business, he continued to assert authority over all of us as the Kwan family patriarch. One Sunday afternoon, when I was playing soccer in front of the Lu Ban Temple with my brothers and friends, he passed by on his way home and shouted at us to stop playing and go home. "If you keep on playing you'll neglect your school work and fail in your examinations," he ranted, "and you'll become a janitor or factory worker. You're not going to have any future!"

I was angry and humiliated and secretly vowed that I would work hard to prove him wrong. But by this time, our conditions had further deteriorated. Uncle Wai Chow had long mortgaged his mansion on Ching Lin Terrace, and his bank finally sold the property when he could not pay his debts. We had to move out and rent the ground floor of house No. 12 as our residence, which further increased our living costs.

During this trying period, it was Aunt Rose, Mother's younger sister, who provided much-needed relief from the cloud of impending ruin hanging over us by taking us out for treats. "Where shall we go today?" she would call out to us even before she stepped inside our living room. "How about some ice cream?"

Thoroughly modern and in tune with the latest trends, Aunt Rose would treat us to the small Western luxuries which were gradually becoming popular in Hong Kong, such as movies, ice cream and steaks. With a square well-set face, sparkling dark eyes, spectacles and a booming voice, Aunt Rose was the opposite of Mother in style and temperament, though as the only two surviving girls in the family they were very close. Unlike Mother, who received only primary school education in a local Chinese school, Aunt Rose studied at the Italian Convent, an English secondary school run by the Canossian Sisters. Jovial, energetic and quick on her feet, Aunt Rose was determined to experience life to its fullest rather than just get married after graduation. She taught in a school, joined a swimming club and a martial arts team and, to her family's consternation, worked for a circus and toured Southeast Asia with them, visiting Thailand, Malaysia, and Singapore. All this was totally unheard of among young women of her time but *Gung Gung* indulged her, and she unerringly took her life into her own hands.

Following Aunt Rose, we frequented Boston Café and Canada Café which were popular among local Chinese for the novelty of eating Western food, using knives and forks. A typical dinner in these restaurants would comprise a bowl of borscht, served hot in Hong Kong style, a pork chop with fried onions, and a small scoop of ice cream or jelly as dessert. We did not know at the time of course that this was Western food with a Chinese flavour, so-called "soya sauce Western dishes". Sometimes, Aunt Rose treated us to a Western breakfast and my favourite order would be pancakes with butter and syrup. We also went regularly to the Queen's Theatre and the King's Theatre in Central to watch Mickey Mouse and Donald Duck cartoons and, later, films with Shirley Temple who became the dream princess of many Hong Kong children. We also watched Charlie Chaplin, and Laurel and Hardy whom local fans called the "Slim Guy" and the "Fat Guy".

In summer Aunt Rose would take us to Repulse Bay, where she would teach us how to swim, and when the weather turned cool in autumn we would spend our weekends picnicking in the New Territories. Both pastimes were considered very "Westernized" by the older generation. Once or twice a year, Aunt Rose would treat us to afternoon tea in the lobby of the Peninsula Hotel, known as just "The Pen", a large Victorian-style hotel by the harbour then considered the pinnacle of Western luxury. We would take the Star Ferry from Central and walk to the hotel from the Tsim Sha Tsui ferry terminal. In the cool, spacious lobby we would sit contentedly in roomy arm chairs with white covers, eating scones with jam and whipped cream and sipping black Ceylon tea with milk and sugar. Our eyes would rove in wonder at everything around us: the tall white ceiling with gilded rectangular panels; soaring white pillars capped with golden floral patterns; the dark brown wooden chandeliers hanging above; the meticulously polished silver tea pot reflecting our faces; knives and spoons stamped with a crown and lion emblem; and the fair complexions, brown hair and blue eyes of the Europeans around us sipping tea and speaking in English. Amid the soothing flow of stringed music, sunlight would gently filter into the lobby through large arched windows, glide over the white tables and chairs, and illuminate the potted palms in the hall. Sometimes I would wonder whether all this was real or just a dream.

While Aunt Rose spoiled us, *Poh Poh* was also always looking for ways to help us. Even though our family budget was tight, both Father and Mother insisted that my brothers and I receive a good education. My elder brother Man Kwong, *Poh Poh's* first grandson and one of her favourites, wanted to attend Pui Ching Middle School, so she offered to pay for his tuition and boarding fees and thus took the burden off my parents. Pui Ching, one of the most prestigious Chinese secondary schools in Guangzhou and Hong Kong at the time, was founded by a Christian mission and maintained high academic standards; its graduates had little difficulty entering well-known universities in China and even in the US. With *Poh Poh's* help, Man Kwong attended Pui Ching in Hong Kong, Guangzhou and Macao until graduation.

School Days and the Seeds of Patriotism

By the time I started school in 1931, China was under the rule of the Nationalist government. Following the National Revolution of 1911, Dr. Sun Yat-sen helped found the Nationalist Party (Kuomintang) and made a series of attempts to unify the country. After his death in 1925, Chiang Kai-shek assumed leadership of the Nationalist forces and officially unified the country under a republican Nationalist government three years later. The elementary school that all my brothers and I attended — Western District School — was a neighbourhood Chinese school under Hong Kong's Education Department but also registered as an "overseas Chinese" school with the Nationalist government's Ministry of Education.

Inheriting Grandfather Yik Po's love of Chinese culture and literature, Father insisted that all his sons become learned in Chinese even though we were living in a British colony. He was so intent on continuing the family literary tradition that when Man Kwong, Tse Kwong and I started school, he personally took each of us through a traditional Confucian school-entrance ritual on our first day, which I still remember vividly.

Father and I arrived at the school at about seven in the morning. The school was a small grey Western-style brick building on a side street flanked by traditional Chinese shops selling groceries and dry sea food. The headmaster, a thin, stern elderly man in a grey Chinese gown, directed me to a classroom and pointed out my seat. The room was small and dimly lit, with about twenty small wooden desks and chairs and a portrait of Confucius, looking serene, on one of the walls. On my desk were a bamboo writing brush, a stone inkpad, and a writing pad with calligraphy paper. Father stayed outside the classroom out of deference to the headmaster, but from the corner of my eyes I could see him standing by the door and watching me attentively. I felt nervous and wished that he would come in and stay with me. Before I took my seat, the headmaster told me to pay my respects to Confucius, the "Saint among Teachers", and remembering

Father's instructions, I obediently knelt and performed the ritual of *kowtow* in front of his portrait. Then I sat behind my desk, and the headmaster and I proceeded to symbolically carry out the acts of teaching and learning. First, he read aloud a few verses from a book of Chinese classics, and asked me to repeat them after him, which I did three times. Next, he taught me how to hold a writing brush and, with his hand guiding mine, I wrote a few simple characters on the writing pad. After I finished, Father came into the classroom, thanked the headmaster and gave him a red paper packet containing some money. This signalled the conclusion of my school-entrance ritual.

Since Western District School was classified as an "overseas Chinese" school by the Nationalist government, its curricula generally followed those of mainland Chinese schools and we studied Chinese literature and history. More important, it taught us that China was our motherland and tried to instill in us a feeling of patriotism. Every Monday morning, all the teachers and students would assemble in the school hall and sing *San Min Zhu Yi* (The Three Principles of the People) — the anthem of Nationalist China. Then we would observe three minutes' silence in honour of the martyrs of the National Revolution, led by Dr. Sun Yat-sen, which overthrew the Qing Dynasty. At the end of the assembly, we would recite Dr. Sun's *Last Will and Testament*:

> For forty years I have devoted myself to the cause of the National Revolution, to raise China to a position of independence and equality among nations ... to achieve this, the people must be aroused ... The Revolution has not yet been successfully concluded. Let all our comrades continue to make every effort to carry it out.

These words found a deep resonance in my heart, and I can remember every word to this day. So, in the end, it was not loyalty to the emperor that would guide me, but rather my new-found love for my country.

My feelings of patriotism surged to new heights in the ensuing years. On 18 September 1931, the Japanese invaded the northeast provinces of China, an area known as Manchuria. On 28 January the following year, they launched an attack on Shanghai, but met with staunch resistance from the 19th Route Army which held out for over a month despite orders to retreat. News of the Japanese invasion and the army's heroic resistance stirred up unprecedented patriotic feelings among Hong Kong Chinese and, to this day, the numbers "918" and "128" continue to arouse emotions of sadness, anger and patriotism among those of my generation.

In the British colony of Hong Kong, however, we were safe for the time being. Aside from following the latest news from mainland China, life seemed to go on as usual. Little did I realize then that this was the beginning of a series of events in our lives that would irreversibly split and splinter my entire family.

My brothers and I went to school everyday and played soccer with our neighbours in front of the Lu Ban Temple when we came home. Father changed jobs a number of times to try to make a better living, and even worked for a time as a clerk in a dance hall operated by Uncle Wai Chow and his friends. The China Dance Hall occupied the top floor of the large, modern China Emporium Building on Queen's Road Central. China Emporium was at that time one of the leading department stores in Hong Kong, selling many imported goods. After the dance hall closed, again because of mismanagement, Father found work briefly escorting cargo back and forth between Hong Kong and cities on the Mainland. Mother became even more worried since Father had already turned forty and his health was failing. Later, when Japanese troops started to attack southern China, the transport company also folded. Luckily, Eighteenth Uncle Chi Kin was able to offer Father a position as a cashier in his Windsor Café. Uncle Chi Kin had asked *Poh Poh* for fifty thousand dollars — the same amount that she had previously given Father to start his own business — and she consented on the condition that he offered Father a job in whatever business he set up. Occupying an upper floor of Entertainment Building above the King's Theatre, also on Queen's Road Central, Windsor served up-market Western dishes and catered mainly to upper-middle-class Chinese.

All of my brothers and I completed our elementary school education at Western District School, but it was not easy considering Father's financial plight. Since the school was not subsidized by the Hong Kong government, Father had to pay twenty dollars a term for each of us which was a large expense for him. However, a good private Chinese secondary school like Pui Ching cost even more. After Man Kwong enrolled in Pui Ching with *Poh Poh*'s help, Father was too embarrassed to ask her for any more financial support so, against his principle of providing us with a Chinese education, he had to enrol my younger brothers and I in government-run secondary schools which taught in English and charged minimal tuition fees. Father enrolled me in Class Seven (Grade Six) at Ellie Kadoorie School in 1936 and King's College the following year, and I, of course, owed my knowledge of English and my future careers to his change of heart. I would have graduated from King's College in 1942, but my secondary school education was cut short by the Japanese invasion of Hong Kong in December 1941.

King's College (founded in 1926) and Queen's College (founded in 1889 as Central College) were, and still are, Hong Kong's top government schools. Many of their graduates went on to attend the University of Hong Kong. Dr. Sun Yat-sen attended Central College and graduated from the Hong Kong College of Medicine for Chinese (later the medical faculty of the University of Hong Kong) in July 1892. When he visited the University in February 1923, Dr. Sun reminisced about his days in Hong Kong, where he said he first developed revolutionary ideas:

I feel as though I have returned home, because Hong Kong and its
university are my intellectual birthplace … I began to wonder how it was
that foreigners could do such things as they had done with the barren
rock of Hong Kong within seventy or eighty years, while China, with a
civilization of over four thousand years, had no place like Hong Kong.
(Wiltshire, *Old Hong Kong*, Volume Two 1901–1945, p. 7)

King's College stood on Bonham Road on the mid-levels of Sai Ying Poon,
opposite the University of Hong Kong and directly across from the stairs leading
to the Tang Chi Ngong School of Chinese. A three-storey Victorian-style red-brick
building overlooking an enclosed courtyard, with rows of white Doric columns
and covered verandas on the outside, the school stood out prominently among
the traditional Chinese tenement houses in the neighbourhood. Providing cover
to the arched main entrance at the corner of Bonham Road and West Street was
a semicircular white concrete canopy supported by six Ionic columns. The floor
above the entrance bore the Royal Coat of Arms and supported a tall hexagonal
tower with a flag post from which the Union Jack flew. The tower was destroyed
during World War II but the Coat of Arms and the white canopy remain.

King's was at that time the most modern and well-equipped school in Hong
Kong. We had a swimming pool (the first among Hong Kong secondary schools),
a modern gymnasium, chemistry and physics laboratories with the most up-to-
date equipment, and a library stocked with books of all kinds. Our principals,
successively Mr. Alfred Morris, Mr. William Kay and Mr. H.G. Wallington, were
all British, but they were open-minded and did not demonstrate any sense of
superiority over the primarily Chinese students. We used to address them as
"headmaster" or *tai sin sang*. Our teachers were of different nationalities and
were generally highly qualified. Among the most memorable were my Class
Six mistress Miss Thom, a Chinese American with an M.A. degree from
Columbia University, and my Class Two mistress Miss Gray, who held an
M.A. from Oxford. Among the better known Chinese teachers then were our
physics teacher, Cheung Wing Min (M.Sc., Oxford), and geography teacher,
Leung Fung Ki (B.A., Hong Kong), who both later pursued highly successful
careers in education. Overall, King's offered a vigorous curriculum of language,
mathematics and science equal in quality to those of British schools. Many of
the graduates became doctors, accountants or engineers, or worked as clerks
in commercial firms, or went on to join the civil service (which was one of the
original purposes of setting up government schools in the colony).

The school's rather liberal policy towards its students extended to our dress
code. Officially, our uniform comprised a Western-style dark blue blazer with
pockets and notched lapels, and a pair of Western-style grey flannel trousers.
However, not too many students could afford the school uniform and, aware of
this, the school authorities decided that school uniform was not compulsory and

throughout my King's College years I never wore the regular school uniform. Most of us wore an "East meets West" combination consisting of a loose-fitting traditional Chinese-style hip-length coat with buttons on the right side of the chest, known as *tai kum sam*, and a pair of Western-style trousers nicknamed *lap cheung fu* (sausage trousers). After war broke out with Japan, to demonstrate their patriotism many students put on "Sun Yat-sen suits", a hip-length tunic with Western-style cutting, a stiff high collar and two or four pockets, designed by Dr. Sun Yat-sen. After the overthrow of the Qing dynasty, Sun Yat-sen suits became the standard uniform for civil servants and military personnel under the Nationalist government. Later, Communist Chinese government officials also wore this style of jacket, now commonly known in Western countries as "Mao suits".

My studies at King's College were highly comprehensive and fulfilling, my only complaint being that we had to study European instead of Chinese history and that we learned about China through the filter of British lenses. To understand China better I had to study by myself or seek out other sources, such as my brother Man Kwong who, because he attended Pui Ching, was a steady and reliable source of information on China. Even though he later attended school in Guangzhou we stayed in close touch, and through him I learned about the exploits of the Europeans, Japanese and Americans in China, the pillage of the imperial palace, the Opium Wars, the unequal treaties, and the National Revolution. I started feeling resentful towards the British, but I also found it difficult to reconcile my feelings with the fact that I was in a British school and the beneficiary of a colonial education. Although the contradiction troubled me deeply for a long time, I never felt any loyalty towards the British.

Instead, events soon after I entered King's College heightened my patriotic feelings towards China. Following the occupation of the three northeast provinces of Liaoning, Heilongjiang and Jilin in 1931 and their formation into the puppet state of Manchukuo, Japanese forces gradually infiltrated north China as Chinese forces withdrew. On 7 July 1937, the two forces clashed in what was later known as the "Marco Polo Bridge Incident" which led to the outbreak of the full-scale "War of Resistance against Japan" (the Anti-Japanese War). After occupying Beijing (then known as Peiping), the Japanese Imperial Army marched southward to take the key cities of Shanghai and Nanjing (Nanking) and committed what was known as the Nanking Massacre in December 1937. By the second half of 1938, Chinese armies evacuated the strategic industrial city of Wuhan in Central China, and the Nationalist government took refuge in Chongqing (Chungking) in the western inland province of Sichuan. In October, Guangzhou fell into Japanese hands and my brother Man Kwong and many of his schoolmates had to leave and return to Hong Kong.

The speed and ferocity of the Japanese invasion shook Hong Kong to the core and aroused in many local Chinese deep feelings of patriotism that had remained dormant under British colonial rule. Students, especially, responded frantically to the call to support China's war efforts. They formed the "All-Hong Kong Students' National Salvation and War Relief Association" on 20 September 1937, after the Marco Polo Bridge Incident, and King's College students lost no time in joining this organization. We also saved up every coin from our lunch and pocket money to buy National Salvation Bonds and raised funds for the purchase of medical supplies to be shipped to the Mainland. Some senior students even left to join service corps in the war zones. Others who stayed boycotted Japanese goods and smashed the show windows of department stores selling Japanese merchandise. A group of my classmates formed the Xingwu (Self-awakening) Society to improve themselves and support each other in what they saw was a fight against foreign imperialist powers. Wearing Sun Yat-sen suits, its members held weekly group discussions and closely followed developments in China's Anti-Japanese War. They also ran a free evening school for children of underprivileged families.

The highlight of the students' patriotic activities at King's College was the holding of a charity bazaar to raise funds for disaster relief in China on 26 February 1938. The bazaar was held in conjunction with the performance of the Wuhan Ensemble which was then touring Hong Kong to publicize and raise funds for China's war efforts. Members of the ensemble were among the best singers and artists in China, and their performances created a great sensation. Their repertoire included songs depicting the sufferings of the people and extolling China's war efforts: "Defend our Country China", "March of the Volunteers", "On the Songhua River", "Fight Our Way Back to the Northeast" and "Ode to the Eight Hundred Heroes". The concert was a rousing success, and as the voices of the singers soared to the tall white ceilings of our school hall so did our spirits. Thunderous applause resounded through the hall after each song. The headmaster, William Kay, was deeply moved and became so sympathetic to the students' cause that, aside from urging the audience to donate as much as they could, he himself presented the manager of the ensemble with a big cheque. It was one of the most emotional moments of my life. Eleven years later, in 1949, "March of the Volunteers" became the national anthem of the People's Republic of China.

Despite their heroism, however, Chinese forces were often overwhelmed by the superior firepower of the Japanese. I felt powerless at China's weakness and longed for the day when China could manufacture its own weapons to defend its territory. I began to look for books and magazines in libraries and bookstores that would give me information about warships, airplanes, tanks and various types of modern weapons; *Jane's Fighting Ships* was one of my favourite books. I tried to imagine what modern weapons China could have and started to draw the most powerful warships, airplanes and tanks I could find: the British battleships HMS *King George V* and HMS *Prince of Wales*, the German battleship *Bismarck*, the British Spitfire fighter, the Japanese Zero fighter, the US B-17 Air Fortress, and the British Centurion tank. I would share my drawings with Chu Hark Keung who sat next to me in class. Chu was strong and athletic, jolly and talkative, but when it came to matters of national pride he would become totally serious and fired up by patriotic feelings. Chu would later become the Chief Telecommunications Officer at Kai Tak Airport, a high position in the colonial government, but he remained full of enthusiasm and support for China.

I too wished for a strong and independent China and, at that time of our youth, our hopes and aspirations were boundless. I would finish my homework in the evenings, open my school atlas on the wooden desk in the comfort of my bare but snug room, and gaze at the map of China under a bare light bulb. I would try to imagine what China would be like if Dr. Sun Yat-sen's "Plan for National Reconstruction" and "The Three Principles of the People" were realized. Would it be a country which could stand up to foreign powers? Would everyone be able to make a decent living and have a voice? I would close my eyes and imagine such a day, allowing feelings of patriotism to swell inside me.

During the early years of the Anti-Japanese War, the British colonial government was sympathetic toward China and turned a blind eye to anti-Japanese activities in Hong Kong. However, Britain changed its attitude following the Japanese occupation of many parts of southern China and its own losses at the outset of the war in Europe. In order to keep Japan on its side, the government declared that Hong Kong was a neutral city, forbade anti-Japanese activities and closed the border with China so that strategic materials could no longer reach the Mainland through the colony. Hong Kong Chinese who were supporting China's war efforts were outraged, and feelings began to turn against the British.

During the war years, the British Information Service produced documentary films depicting the bravery of the British in their struggle against Nazi Germany. These films were distributed throughout the British Empire, and were shown in cinemas and government institutions in Hong Kong. At King's College we saw films on many well-known episodes such as the evacuation of Dunkirk, German air raids on London, dogfights in the Battle of Britain and the sinking of the *Bismarck*. Since we saw the parallels between Nazi Germany and Japan we became excited and used to cheer the British on, but when the colonial government's attitude toward Japan shifted, our responses also changed. One day, a few students started to boo when King George VI appeared on the screen and clap when they saw Adolf Hitler; our headmaster was mortified.

We carried our protests to other areas. At the end of a film show, when the cinemas played the British national anthem, "God Save the King", and the audience would stand at attention, my schoolmates and I would rush out before the music started to avoid having to stand. Childish as this might be, it was our gesture of protest against the policy of appeasement of the Japanese by the British. The ultimate refutation of this appeasement came not long afterwards when the Japanese invaded Hong Kong on 8 December 1941 and the British soon surrendered.

During the years immediately before the Japanese occupation of Hong Kong, I felt torn by the many conflicting forces tugging at me: China was my country, but I had to live under British rule; I loved China, but I was distressed by its weakness; and all I wanted was to study hard and find a good job, but the spectre of war and revolution loomed over me.

The plight of my family added to my distress. Father's job as a cashier at the Windsor Cafe could barely support our family, but he never asked Mother's family for financial support again despite his deep regret in not succeeding as a banker. Perhaps hoping that one of his sons could succeed where he had failed, after I turned fifteen in the summer of 1940, Father took me to see Fourteenth Uncle Shiu Kin, who was then managing Tang Tin Fuk Yinhao, to ask whether I could be an apprentice at his bank.

Tin Fuk was located at the western end of Queen's Road Central close to a number of other banks. When we arrived we saw an armoured van unloading gold ingots and silver coins in front of the bank's entrance. Guarded by policemen and supervised by Tin Fuk's senior officers, coolies carried these precious commodities on their backs, bag by bag, to the bank's vault in the basement. The bank hall was filled with noise: the clattering of the abacuses behind the counter, the chatter among bank clerks and customers, and the shouting of the coolies. This was my first introduction to banking.

Uncle Shiu Kin's office was on the second floor, and Father and I walked quietly up the dark, narrow stairs with heavy hearts. Father and Uncle Shiu Kin used to dine together at business banquets and often joked with each other after a few drinks, but those happy days were gone. After Father went bankrupt, he lost contact with Uncle Shiu Kin, and he looked sheepish and uneasy as we climbed the stairs. He must have been embarrassed at having to ask Uncle Shiu Kin for a favour which he knew he could not return and, sensing his predicament, I grew apprehensive and felt an urge to turn and run.

Seated behind his reddish-brown rosewood desk, Uncle Shiu Kin rested his tall frame on the back of his chair and measured me up and down with cool sharp eyes. I recalled that when I was younger, he used to be all smiles when he handed me my Christmas presents. Now his face was expressionless.

"Tsai Tung, look at you," he said to Father. "Why do you want your son to be a banker? It's very hard to do well in this business, as you know. Besides, I am not sure we have an opening."

Father gawped as if Uncle Shiu Kin had poured a bucket of cold water over his head. His face turned a deep red and my heart sank to the floor. Luckily, Uncle Shiu Kin's elderly assistant manager came into the room in time to overhear what he had just said. Having been with the bank a long time, he knew my father and wanted to help.

"I may be able to find something," he said soothingly. "But don't expect too much. Without a school certificate or any work experience, Sze Kwong can only work as an apprentice. He will not receive any salary or bonus, but we will give him two free meals a day, one at noon and one in the evening."

Uncle Shiu Kin took a long look at me and consented to the proposal. Sweating, Father thanked him for "giving me a chance." I was dumbstruck throughout the meeting, and barely summoned enough will-power at the end to open my mouth and thank Uncle Shiu Kin. Over and over again I repeated to myself an old Chinese adage: "Only by bearing the hardest hardship can one rise to the top."

So I had my first taste of banking. And hardship it was. My duties included sweeping the floors, dusting the furniture and counters, and cleaning the spittoons in the offices of Uncle Shiu Kin and his senior officers, which had to be the most gruesome part of my routine. I also served tea to visiting customers and ran errands, which ranged from delivering important letters and documents to buying cigarettes and newspapers for the bank officers. I never had the chance to count gold ingots, silver coins or banknotes, or learn to use the abacus — all basic skills that Father had hoped I would acquire. What I did learn, however, was a thing or two about the inconstancy of human relationships.

Thankfully, the apprenticeship lasted only one month and I went back to school after the summer. That was the last summer of my childhood. The following year, the Japanese swept over southern China and overran Hong Kong, and banking was farthest from my mind. Little did I know that more than twenty years later I would indeed succeed Father and take up banking as my career.

1. Studio portraits of Grandmother Leung Kuk Kum and Father Kwan Tsai Tung after they arrived in Hong Kong in 1916. Note Grandmother's bound feet.

2. My maternal grandfather Tang Chi Ngong (*Gung Gung*) (left) touring Summer Palace, Beijing in mid-autumn 1922.

3. Portrait of the extended Wong family (our neighbours) taken at Ching Lin Terrace in 1937. Wong Hing Kwong is seated right with his arm around my future sister-in-law, Amy.

5. A twenty-five-year-old Aunt Rose, 1931. My thoroughly modern aunt treated us to afternoon teas at the Peninsula Hotel and other Western pastimes.

4. Man Kwong with Tse Kwong (left) and me (right), circa 1929.

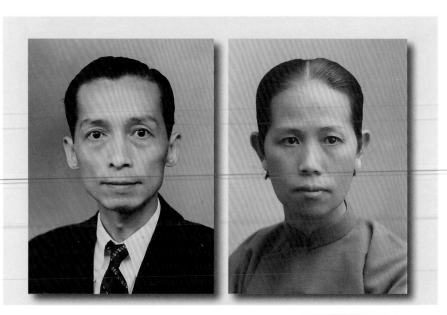

6. Father and Mother circa 1940.

7. Wartime in Liuzhou, Guangxi, 1942. Aunt Rose is flanked by cousins Nai Hei and Lin Chee. Tse Kwong is standing behind me.

8. In my Chinese army uniform with captain insignia on my collars, 1943.

9. Interpreter Training School parade, Kunming, Yunnan, 1942.

10. With colleagues at Motor School, Qujing, Yunnan, 1943. I am third from right in the middle row. Note the couplet on the pillars.

Man Kwong

Sze Kwong

Tse Kwong

Yuan Kwong

11. The Kwan brothers in Hong Kong, 1949. Tse Kwong and Yuan Kwong left to join the revolution soon after these photos were taken.

12. With Mother, Man Kwong, Amy and their son Cheuk before they moved to Singapore, 1951.

13. Mother visiting Yuan Kwong (right), and Tse Kwong, Yim Sheung and their son Niandong in Guangzhou, 1963.

14. A studio portrait with Wing Kin for our wedding, 1956. This picture has always hung in our bedroom.

15. Wedding day, February 4, 1956. The car, a Wolsely, belonged to Aunt Rose who bought it from Dodwell Motors.

16. Uncle Wai Chow with his wife and concubines on my wedding day. First Aunt is seated next to him, with Third Aunt to her right. Sixth Aunt is standing behind him, and Aunt Rose is on the far right.

17. The Tang family at my wedding party. Nineteenth Uncle Shiu Woon is seated far right.

18. In Civil Aid Services uniform, 1957, with Victoria Harbour in the background.

19. The Chan family on the gold wedding anniversary of my parents-in-law in 1958. Hang Chuen and Wing Kin are standing third and fourth from left in the second to last row. I am behind Hang Chuen. The four Chan siblings who left Hong Kong to join the revolution are not in the photo.

20. King's College classmates reunion at a wedding party in the early 1960s. I am at the far left, Wing Kin is seated fourth from right, Tam Ting Kwong and Chu Hark Keung are standing second and third from right.

21. Wing Kin in Sung Wong Toi Garden, 1959. The three Chinese characters on the stone are "Sung Wong Toi" — the terrace of the Song emperor.

22. Wing Kin on board US aircraft carrier in Victoria Harbour, 1959. The former Kowloon railway station with its clock tower is in the background.

2

Baptism by Fire

Before the Storm

During the early stages of the Anti-Japanese War, the British believed that Hong Kong, like Singapore, was "an impregnable fortress" and that as long as Britain remained neutral, Japan would not attack Hong Kong. It took the defeat of the Allied forces on the European continent and the formation of the Germany-Italy-Japan Axis in 1940 to prompt the British into bolstering the defences of these Far East bastions of their empire.

The year 1941 started optimistically with the centennial commemorations of the founding of Hong Kong on 26 January 1841, when a British naval landing party hoisted the Union Jack on the island (at the later-named Possession Point) and claimed the territory for Britain. The landing followed the Convention of Chuanbi (named after the village near Guangzhou where it was signed on 20 January 1841) and marked Britain's *de facto* occupation of Hong Kong. The Convention was never ratified, however, and the better known (or more notorious) Treaty of Nanking, signed on 29 August 1842 and ratified on 20 June 1843, marked Britain's *de jure* occupation. To commemorate the landing, the colonial government erected a bronze statue of King George VI in the Botanical Garden, a popular spot at the mid-levels of Victoria Peak overlooking Government House — the office and residence of the governor of Hong Kong.

In contrast to mainland China, Hong Kong had experienced relative political stability and economic prosperity during its one hundred years of colonial rule. However, all this started to change in the latter half of 1941, by when the war had escalated, the Japanese had occupied Guangzhou and many parts of southern China, and Japan had joined the Axis Powers.

To prepare for a possible Japanese invasion, the colonial government mandated all male British subjects above the age of sixteen to join an auxiliary group, which included: the Air Raid Precaution Service, the Auxiliary Medical Service, the Auxiliary Fire Service, the Auxiliary Transport Service, the Food

Control Service, and the St. John's Ambulance Brigade. These groups would often join in exercises held individually or jointly with such uniformed services as the Hong Kong Garrison, the Volunteers, the Hong Kong Police, the Hong Kong Auxiliary Police, and the Hong Kong Fire Brigade.

Students, government civil servants, and employees of major banks and large corporations were all encouraged to join the auxiliary services. Many responded to the call, even though some were not even British subjects by either birth or naturalization. Some joined out of genuine concern for Hong Kong, some joined out of curiosity, and some simply joined for economic reasons since they would then be entitled to a wartime stipend from the government.

As I was a British subject by birth and had reached the age of sixteen by 1941, I had to join one of the auxiliary services. Since I was still quite young, my parents' preference was for a service with less risk in the event of war and, after evaluating the options, Father decided that I should join the Air Raid Precaution (ARP) Service. "As an ARP warden, you will get the latest news," he said. "You can alert us about when to stock up food and where to escape if the Japanese come. Besides, you will receive a stipend as well as food rations. This is good for the whole family."

In line with Father's advice, elder brother Man Kwong joined the Food Control Service (FCS). He had moved back to Hong Kong after the Japanese occupied Guangzhou, and later enrolled in Lingnan University. While attending Lingnan he also worked in the evenings as a cashier at the Windsor Café and, as a member of the FCS, Man Kwong's job was to manage the stocking of food supplies at the restaurant. It was a coveted post in a time of frequent shortages, and he did his best to keep our family supplied with food whenever we were short.

Both Tse Kwong and Yuan Kwong were still too young to join the auxiliary services, but since he was physically strong and bigger than me, Tse Kwong would often follow me when I was on duty, cheering me on and keeping me company.

As an ARP warden, my work was to alert civilians during air raids and I did not have to carry a gun or go into combat. My duties included ushering people to the nearest air-raid shelter when an air-raid siren was sounded, making sure that every household observed the blackout regulations after sunset, giving first-aid treatment to the wounded, and clearing debris from damaged buildings if necessary. In addition, we were trained to use gas masks and to teach the civilians precautions against poisonous gas attack but, fortunately, the Japanese did not use gas when they attacked Hong Kong.

The Battle of Hong Kong

The ARP had posts all over the colony with ten wardens to each post. Since I was stationed in the Western District at Ching Lin Terrace, where I lived, I was often on duty with our neighbours. We shared a common interest in serving our own neighbourhood and enjoyed the excitement of participating in ARP exercises, which we treated as war games. At times, we even complained that the exercises were not "real" enough.

On 8 December 1941, only hours after they attacked the US and bombed Pearl Harbour, the Japanese started their air assault on Hong Kong. On my way to school that clear, sunny morning, I heard the loud wailing of an air-raid siren and wondered why my commanding officer had not notified me in advance that there would be an air-raid exercise. Then I heard the droning of engines overhead and the distant thunder of explosions and, looking up, I spotted Japanese bombers in the bright blue sky. This was not a game — Hong Kong was at war with Japan! Our air-raid exercises were being put to the ultimate test.

Mark Young, who was governor and commander-in-chief of Hong Kong when the attack started, had taken up his posts only in September that year. Shortly afterwards, the British arranged for two Canadian battalions — the Winnipeg Grenadiers and the Royal Rifles of Canada — to come to Hong Kong to reinforce the colony's defences. I had learned about Canada in school, but my first actual contact with the country was the sight of these battalions as they marched on the Murray Parade Ground on Garden Road. As I squeezed my way through the crowd to watch the parade, I caught sight of the young Canadian soldiers marching side by side with other contingents of the Hong Kong Garrison. To my surprise, they looked only a few years older than me, and I remember their fresh young faces and brisk steps to this day. I learned after the war that many of them were killed when the Japanese attacked, and were buried in Hong Kong.

At the time of the Japanese attack, Major General Christopher Maltby, the colony's military commander, had six battalions of regular soldiers under his command: the Royal Scots and the Middlesex Regiment from Britain; the Rajput and Punjabi regiments from India; and the two Canadian battalions. In addition, he also commanded the Hong Kong Volunteer Defence Corps. Even though he had quite a large defence force, however, the readiness, morale and capabilities of these forces were highly uneven. The British soldiers, known as the "Diehards", had good equipment and combat experience, but there were doubts about their commitment to defend a colony so far away from home. The Rajputs and Punjabis had reputations as fine fighting men, but some suspected that their loyalty was to India rather than Hong Kong. The Canadian soldiers were young, lacked proper training and equipment, and had little combat experience; they were in fact "not recommended for operational consideration" by their commander, Colonel John Lawson. As for the Volunteers, many came from the privileged classes: taipans, government department heads and business executives who had been leading rather comfortable lives. Aged nineteen to sixty-five and representing some seventeen different nationalities, they had little training and no experience. Some journalists even quipped that these men "had never held anything heavier than a glass of whiskey and soda".

The Japanese invasion, on the other hand, was well planned. Long before the outbreak of hostilities, Japanese spies (disguised as restaurant proprietors, department store owners, tourists, bankers or traders) began collecting military, political and economic intelligence in Hong Kong, and the Japanese Consulate was a major centre for gathering intelligence. There were quite a few Japanese shopkeepers in Wanchai, and I remember their smiling faces and courteous service. Even though most local Chinese disliked Japan out of patriotism, many still chose to buy Japanese goods, which were often cheaper than other imports. However, after the start of full-scale war, nationalistic and anti-Japanese sentiments drove many young men and women to take to the streets in protest, yelling slogans like "Down with Japanese militarism" and "Boycott Japanese goods". Some smashed the shop windows of stores selling Japanese merchandise, but Chinese policemen patrolling the streets generally turned a blind eye. A decade after the war, however, Japanese cameras, television sets, electric rice cookers and other goods would once again flood the Hong Kong market, and few consumers seemed to remember the pre-war protests.

Intelligence gathering must have served the Japanese well: their assault on 8 December was swift and effective, and their air force obliterated in one blow the military planes stationed at Kai Tak Airport. The Japanese then bombed the dock facilities in the harbour extensively, putting Hong Kong's navy totally out of action. Immediately following the air assaults, some fifty thousand Japanese troops which had amassed along the border — a battle-hardened force of infantry, cavalry, tanks and artillery — crossed the Shenzhen River to attack Hong Kong. The colony's forces were simply overwhelmed. The line of defence established in the New Territories crumbled within forty-eight hours and, four days after the land offensive started, both the New Territories and Kowloon fell into Japanese hands. The defence forces, along with hundreds of thousands of local Chinese, tried desperately to flee to Hong Kong Island. With Victoria Harbour filled with watercraft of all descriptions — navy landing ships, launches, ferries, junks and sampans — the scene was like the evacuation of Dunkirk (but on a smaller scale).

Following the hurried retreat of the Hong Kong defence forces, Lieutenant General Takashi Sakai, commander of the Japanese invading forces, set up his headquarters at the Peninsula Hotel (where we used to have afternoon teas with Aunt Rose). The Imperial Army was now poised to attack Hong Kong Island.

The emphasis the British placed on coastal defence had put Hong Kong at a disadvantage. The British military authorities had built fortresses at all strategic points along the coast of the island, confident that any attack would come from the sea. Guns mounted on these fortresses were powerful, with a range sufficient to ensure that the colony could put up a good fight if it were to be subjected to a naval assault. Unfortunately, the Japanese offensive came from the air and by land from mainland China, and most of the fortresses never saw action since their guns were pointing in the wrong direction.

As General Maltby concentrated all his remaining forces on Hong Kong Island, the colony braced itself for the siege. On 12 December, the Japanese air force began a week-long series of bombing raids over the island to soften it up for the coming amphibious assault. Japanese planes flew over Hong Kong dropping bombs to destroy the island's fortifications and leaflets calling for surrender. Gun emplacements, pillboxes, power plants, oil storage tanks and warehouses all became targets for the bombers and artillery, and Hong Kong was consumed by fire, smoke, and the deafening roar of exploding bombs and long-range guns. After dark, the illuminating lights of the City of Victoria (a symbol of Hong Kong's prosperity) were gone and, apart from men and women in uniform, nobody would dare to come out of their homes. On the streets military vehicles, fire engines and ambulances rushed back and forth, and we could see flames gushing from the roofs of bombed buildings. Wounded people and dead bodies lay on the pavement, waiting to be picked up by the Medical Services and the Sanitary Department; it was a gruesome sight.

After a week-long bombardment of Hong Kong Island, Japanese forces succeeded in taking control of the bluff on the island's northeast coast on 18 December, and another detachment landed on Repulse Bay Beach to the south (where we used to go swimming in the summer). To advance to the urban areas, the Japanese troops had to go through Wong Nai Chung Gap, a strategic pass with steep hills on both sides, where the Canadian Grenadiers defending the gap put up a good fight. There were only about one hundred Canadians, outnumbered twenty to one, but they succeeded in exacting four times the casualties on the enemy until they ran out of ammunition and were overrun by the Japanese. Colonel Lawson and most of his men died in battle. The sacrifices of the young soldiers were well remembered in Hong Kong but remained a source of deep regret among the Canadians.

Our house (on the west side of Hong Kong Island) was not in the landing path of the Japanese, but could not escape the air assault. Both Ching Lin Terrace and the adjacent Tse Lan Terrace suffered human casualties and extensive property damage from the seemingly endless bombing. The terraces were built on the slope of Mount Davis which, because of the fortress with long-range coastal defence guns on its summit, quickly became a target of Japanese bomber and artillery attacks. Being within close range of the bomb explosions and gunfire was a nightmare for the ARP wardens and the residents of the terraces. A few days before Hong Kong's surrender, a Japanese bomb missed its target and fell on Tse Lan Terrace. We heard a loud bang and saw flames and smoke shooting through broken roofs and windows. Shocked, we rushed to the scene (which was about two hundred metres from our ARP post) to find the ruins of the two houses hit by the bomb and the dead bodies of two young boys. Those who were wounded in the explosion were crying for help, and we quickly pitched in to give them first aid. This was my initiation to the horrors of war.

The Japanese bombarded the island ceaselessly from Kowloon Peninsula and, as countless shells flew over Ching Lin Terrace, we crossed our fingers each time we heard the whizzing above our heads. Then one big shell (about eight inches in diameter) fell on the terrace, landing unexploded on the ground in front of the Lu Ban Temple. Had it exploded, the neighbouring houses would have been wrecked and the casualties horrible, since the schools and shops had closed and most people were at home. The shell lay unattended for a long while after Hong Kong surrendered and the bombardment ended, since the Japanese army engineers were too busy attending to more urgent matters. The residents grew increasingly concerned and impatient and, finally, several young men from the Terrace suggested that we dispose of this dangerous object ourselves. Tse Kwong and I joined the hurriedly-formed amateur shell disposal team; we were young and daring, and did not think about the dangers involved. Equipped with a long rope, two bamboo poles, a pick and a shovel, the team carefully lifted the shell from the ground and carried it to the backyard of the Lu Ban Temple, where we dug a big hole for the shell and covered it with sand and mud. Heaving a big sigh of relief, the residents rejoiced and applauded the bravery of the young men, and many went into Lu Ban Temple to offer incense.

During the war, abandoned weapons and unexploded shells were left scattered all over Hong Kong. With the passage of time, these war-time relics were buried underground and were often discovered much later when construction workers dug into the sites. These were then either dismantled and dumped, or detonated. However, I have not heard of any shell being found at the back of Lu Ban Temple, and wonder whether it is still there.

During the course of battle, we had somehow hoped that Chinese forces deployed in southern China would eventually come to our rescue. There was a widespread rumour that thirty thousand Chinese troops were approaching Shenzhen to attack the Japanese army from the rear. Alas, our hope was in vain and the Chinese troops never appeared. The Japanese landing on 18 December was followed by a week of bloody fighting on the hills and streets of Hong Kong

Island. With mounting casualties and the wanton rape and murder of civilians by Japanese soldiers, the colony capitulated; on Christmas Day, a white flag went up on Government House. Governor Young and General Maltby crossed the harbour — which by this time was a graveyard of crippled vessels — to surrender formally to Lieutenant General Sakai. The surrender ceremony was held in the Peninsula Hotel, and Young himself was held in the hotel before being transferred to the internment camp. This marked the end of the Battle of Hong Kong, which lasted only eighteen days.

Those who survived the battle would remember 25 December 1941 as "Black Christmas Day". Since the government imposed a curfew during the battle and people were not allowed to go out of their homes after dark, on Christmas Eve there was neither midnight mass nor Christmas carols. On Christmas Day, the churches were deserted and Christians could only pray in their houses; all the shops and food stores were closed and everyone braced themselves for the Japanese occupation. The rich buried their jewellery and valuables in the ground, expecting a period of lawlessness as the police force was disbanded. Young women, afraid of Japanese soldiers entering their houses looking for "flower girls", put on old clothes and even rubbed charcoal on their faces, trying to make themselves look old and ugly.

The Japanese Occupation

The triumphant Japanese Imperial Army formally entered the City of Victoria on 28 December. As mounted officers followed by columns of soldiers marched through the streets of Hong Kong, Japanese war planes flew above them in formation. All expatriate soldiers and civilians, especially the British, Canadians, Americans and Dutch, were placed in internment camps. To everyone's surprise, the Volunteers and Canadian soldiers had fought bravely, even though they were the least experienced, and suffered great casualties. Those like me in the auxiliary services who had participated in the battle discarded our uniforms and put on civilian clothes in order to conceal our identities. Every survivor who was not in prison or an internment camp was obliged to come out to greet the Imperial Army. We were now at the mercy of a new master.

During the past century we had enjoyed long periods of stability and prosperity under British rule, but what would our new masters offer us? The Japanese answered our questions through messages on their wall posters and the leaflets dropped from their planes, such as: "Holding high the sacred banner of war, the Imperial Army has come to overthrow the rule of the white men"; and "Through the solidarity of the coloured people, we will build a new order in East Asia".

Then in February 1942, Lieutenant General Rensuke Isogai, the governor of the Japanese Occupied Territory of Hong Kong, made the following announcement:

> There is no question that Hong Kong belongs to Japan, but consideration will be given to the Chinese in the way of administration, which will be based on the new order of Greater East Asia, and that means prosperity for all ... (Wiltshire, *Old Hong Kong*, Volume Two 1901–1945, p. 46)

To be truthful, there was a certain appeal in Japan's call for a new order — the so-called "Greater East Asian Co-Prosperity Sphere" — that would throw out the Western powers. For some of us who had grown up under the humiliation of Western imperialist exploits in China and other parts of Asia, the opportunity to overthrow the white men's domination and take back control over one's country held some attraction. I had to admit that, like other gullible youths, I was initially lured by the idea. But it did not take long before the Japanese occupying forces showed their true colours.

The Japanese set up their Civil Administration headquarters in the massive granite Hongkong and Shanghai Bank Building in Central. They also set up a four-member Chinese Representative Council and a twenty-two-member Chinese Cooperative Council to serve as a bridge between the Japanese occupiers and the local people. But in reality, the councils' main function was to ensure that government orders were carried out smoothly. Representatives in the councils were mostly the rich, famous and influential within the Chinese community, and one of the most supportive members of the Chinese Representative Council was Chan Lim Pak, to whom I later became related through marriage. Chan was a well-known comprador of the Hongkong and Shanghai Banking Corporation (later known as Hongkong Bank and now HSBC). I was also related to two members of the Chinese Cooperative Council: Fourteenth Uncle Shiu Kin, who was the manager of Tang Tin Fuk Yinhao and vice-chairman of Kowloon Motorbus, and Kwok Chan, the son-in-law of Chan Lim Pak, who was the chief comprador of Banque de l'Indochine and vice-chairman of the Hong Kong Chinese Chamber of Commerce. The Japanese also set up another quasi-government agency called the Xingya (Promote Asia) Office to recruit professionals to serve in the civil administration as well as head up important commercial and industrial positions. Quite a number of engineers, technicians, journalists and translators, mostly graduates of Japanese universities, registered with the office.

Flowing with the tide, Hong Kong businessmen stopped dealing with the British *hongs* (trading conglomerates started in the days of the Opium War) such as Jardine Matheson and Swire, and instead transacted business with Japanese trading houses such as Mitsui and Mitsubishi. They also switched their banking relations from Hongkong and Shanghai Bank to Bank of Tokyo or Bank of Taiwan. Many started to study Japanese, hoping to find a job or advance their careers. I was reminded of old Chinese sayings: "We will pay taxes to whoever is the emperor"; and "Those who understand the trend of the times are heroes". Having witnessed the rise and fall of successive emperors and dynasties, and the more recent coming and going of foreign powers, most Hong Kong people had learnt to adapt to change and to work with whoever was in charge.

Nevertheless, the promise of a "Greater East Asian Co-Prosperity Sphere" did not stand the test of time, and life in Hong Kong under the Japanese soon became a nightmare. Residents lived in terror of the murder, rape and looting committed by undisciplined soldiers of the Imperial Army. Wanchai quickly became a special zone for brothels catering to the soldiers. On strategic posts along the main streets, fierce-looking soldiers with bayoneted rifles would demand to inspect pedestrians and cars, and those passing by had to bow to the soldiers and subject themselves to searches. Inevitably, some were slapped down or thrown into custody.

Food was in dire shortage. Immediately after entering the city, the Japanese forces took over all public and private warehouses and shipped whatever goods they deemed to be of strategic value back to Japan. Rice, Hong Kong's most important staple food, was rationed, and individuals were allowed to purchase only 6.4 taels (about half a pound) of rice per day at official rates. Any quantity in excess of this amount had to be purchased in the black market, at exorbitant prices, and non-staple foods such as meat, fish, poultry, fruits and vegetables almost completely disappeared from our family dinner table since they were in short supply and extremely expensive. As a result, the poor often suffered from malnutrition and some of the poorest died of starvation.

We were also forced to accept Japanese Military Notes as a medium of exchange. In the beginning, the exchange rate between Military Notes and Hong Kong bank notes was one Yen to two Hong Kong Dollars, but in October 1942, the rate changed to one Yen to four Hong Kong Dollars. In June 1943, the Japanese authorities disallowed the circulation of Hong Kong bank notes, and local people were instructed to surrender any remaining notes to the Bank of Taiwan in exchange for Military Notes. The Military Notes were not backed by Japan's gold or foreign exchange reserves and became totally worthless after Japan's surrender, so many households lost all their savings. Not everyone obeyed the order, however, and those who secretly hoarded Hong Kong bank notes made big fortunes when Hong Kong reverted to British rule after the war.

The Japanese authorities in Hong Kong rewarded some of their collaborators with special concessions; Chan Lim Pak was a well-known example. During the occupation, edible oil was placed on the list of controlled food items, since it had become important in the local diet as meat and fish became scarce. As a reward for his cooperation, the Japanese awarded Chan the sole distributorship of imported and locally refined edible oil in Hong Kong, and thanks to this monopoly his Fook Hing Oil Refinery Company made huge profits. Uncle Wai Chow knew Chan Lim Pak when they were both in the banking business and, with his help, secured a dealership of Fook Hing's products and opened an edible-oil retail shop, Ming On. Since Father, who was then suffering from tuberculosis, could no longer work for Uncle Wai Chow, he sent his eldest son, Man Kwong, instead. The burden of family support thus fell squarely on Man Kwong's shoulders as he took up his post in Ming On.

Chan Lim Pak was one of the biggest beneficiaries of the Japanese occupation, but he was notorious among the local Chinese. In 1924, Chan had organized the Canton Merchants' Volunteer Corps in Guangzhou to try to block Dr. Sun Yat-sen's attempts to launch the Northern Expedition, a campaign to defeat the warlords in north China and unify the country. His close collaboration with the Japanese destroyed what was left of his reputation and he died a hated man. As the war drew to an end, Chan realized that Japan was about to be defeated and took his favorite concubine and his valuables on board a ferry to seek refuge in Macao. He perished when Allied bombers attacked and sank the ferry.

Free China

As food and other materials in Hong Kong continued to be in short supply, the Japanese authorities tried to reduce the local population. Under the pretext of developing Hainan Island to the southwest of Guangdong Province, they rounded up large numbers of young men and shipped them there to work as slaves. Many people also left Hong Kong on their own accord, especially those who had to flee Japanese persecution: colonial government officials, members of the Allied forces who had escaped from internment camps, and people closely connected with the Nationalist government or the Chinese Communist Party. Others left because they refused to live under Japanese tyranny and wanted to look for new opportunities. These included merchants who had business connections on the Mainland, students who wished to continue their studies at Chinese universities, and people who could not make a living in Hong Kong and wanted to stay with relatives and friends on the Mainland.

Those who could leave legitimately were issued a "Return to Native Village Certificate" by the Japanese authorities. However, in the beginning of 1942, scheduled transportation leaving Hong Kong was confined to only two regular ferry services: daily services to Macao, and less frequent services to Guangzhouwan, a seaport on the western coast of Guangdong. Like the New Territories in Hong Kong, which was leased to the British, Guangzhouwan was leased to the French in 1898 for ninety-nine years. When Germany occupied France in 1940, however, control over Guangzhouwan effectively came under the Japanese. Nevertheless, it still served as a buffer zone between the Chinese and Japanese forces in western Guangdong and acted as a gateway through which people could move in and out of mainland China unharmed. Those leaving Hong Kong through Guangzhouwan would usually head for cities in southwest China, such as Chongqing, Guilin, Liuzhou and Nanning, which were still free from Japanese occupation. Others leaving via Macao would head north to Qujiang, the wartime capital of Guangdong in the northern part of the province and an important city along the Guangzhou-Hankou (Hankow) railway line.

We remained in Hong Kong during the first few months of the Japanese occupation. While Man Kwong worked for Uncle Wai Chow, I went to study Japanese hoping that this would help me to find work, but job opportunities were scarce since the economy had almost completely collapsed and I lacked any work experience. As Man Kwong's meagre salary could hardly support a family of six, Father decided that instead of all of us staying in Hong Kong to face hunger, Japanese oppression and possible Allied bombing, the family should disperse. Our opportunity came when we learned that Aunt Rose and her husband Leung Ki Chai had decided to leave Hong Kong to set up business on the Mainland.

After returning from her Southeast Asian tour, Aunt Rose settled back in Hong Kong and started teaching in Yeung Chung, a secondary school for girls which *Poh Poh* had helped to fund. Then, responding to an advertisement, she took up a tutoring job at the household of Leung Ki Chai, a merchant from Shunde, Guangdong who was doing business in Wuzhou in Guangxi Province. Even though Leung already had a wife and six children and was much older, Aunt Rose was charmed by his business acumen and his six-foot frame and handsome looks. Leung, in turn, found himself attracted to Aunt Rose's accomplishments and outgoing personality. Unwilling to become Leung's concubine, she eventually agreed instead to be his *ping tsai* — an "equal" wife — which was then an accepted Chinese custom. Aunt Rose later suffered a miscarriage and was not able to conceive again so, with his wife's consent, Uncle Leung let her adopt his youngest son Nai Hei.

Since Aunt Rose was still single when *Gung Gung* passed away, she inherited some property and a sum of money from his estate. After becoming Leung Ki Chai's *ping tsai*, she became partner with him in a business selling motor vehicle parts and accessories. Their firm, Kung Lee, was originally based in Guangzhou but moved to Hong Kong in 1938 when the Japanese advanced into Guangdong Province. In early 1942, Aunt Rose and Uncle Leung decided to move again with their son Nai Hei to escape the Japanese, this time to Liuzhou, an industrial city in central Guangxi. Sympathizing with my parents' plight, Aunt Rose offered to take Tse Kwong, the strongest among us, with them. Father readily agreed, since he already wanted the family to disperse, and several months later, after Aunt Rose and Uncle Leung had established their business in Liuzhou, Aunt Rose wrote to ask me to join them as well.

Father was happy that I could also go, since Man Kwong's financial burden would then become even lighter; but first he needed to find a way to pay for my ferry ticket to Guangzhouwan, from where I would travel to Liuzhou. Reluctantly, Father went to Uncle Wai Chow to borrow money for my fare, promising him that I would pay him back as soon as I could.

"I'm not sure I want to go," I said to Father. "I'll never be able to pay Uncle back."

"Don't worry," Father said. "This is how you'll do it. Bring extra clothes with you and sell them on the way. Everything is scarce during war time. You'll find people who are willing to pay good money for Western clothes."

"Your cousin Sai Kwong did that on his way to Guilin," Father continued, trying to reassure me. "Besides, you can travel with cousin Lin Chee who will be able to help you."

Sai Kwong, Uncle Wai Chow's son, had already left Hong Kong for Guilin in Guangxi, and Lin Chee, his older sister, planned to join him. I was happy to have Lin Chee's company. She was a graduate of Belilios Public School (a top English girls' school), six years older than me, and very sharp and resourceful. As expected, with Lin Chee's help I sold all my extra clothes successfully and once we reached Liuzhou I quickly remitted the proceeds to Uncle Wai Chow in Hong Kong. Thank goodness I kept my promise as we would never have heard the end of it from Uncle had I failed.

Liuzhou and Guilin were in what was then known as Free China, the southwestern part of the country which, until that time, had remained free from Japanese occupation. Within a few months of the attack on Pearl Harbour scores of Asia-Pacific and Southeast Asian territories including Guam, Hong Kong, the Philippines, Malaya, Singapore, Indonesia and Burma fell rapidly into Japanese hands. However, the occupation of China did not go as smoothly. When Japan started its full-scale invasion of China in 1937 it thought that China would surrender in three months, but nearly five years later it had succeeded in occupying only the northeastern and coastal areas. The Japanese had underestimated the will of the Chinese to resist, and the Southwest remained largely free.

On 1 January 1942 the United States, Britain, the Soviet Union and China signed a joint declaration calling for an all-out effort to defeat the Axis Powers. China's perseverance in fighting alone against a strong enemy had gained the admiration of the Allies and was recognized as "one of the four world powers."

Soon, whenever people mentioned China, they would refer to it as Free China. I found it ironic that China was finally able to achieve an unprecedented international standing just as it was suffering from unprecedented oppression.

After the fall of Hong Kong, local Chinese looked upon Free China as a haven from Japanese occupation, and many headed for cities in the Southwest: Liuzhou and Guilin in Guangxi Province, Qujiang (also known as Shaoguan) in northern Guangdong, Chongqing and Chengdu in Sichuan, Guiyang in Guizhou, and Kunming in Yunnan. Together, these areas were called "The Great Southwest Bastion of China's Anti-Japanese War."

Although Father wanted Tse Kwong and I to join Aunt Rose in Liuzhou, he was quite worried about our leaving since, apart from Man Kwong (who had been at boarding school in Guangzhou), none of us had ever left home before. To hide his anxiety and sadness, when Tse Kwong and then I were preparing to leave, Father reminded us of the Chinese saying: "A young man should have the ambition to go to the four corners of the world." On both occasions, Mother broke into tears as we hugged her farewell. We ourselves were on the verge of crying since we had no idea when or, indeed, whether we would see our parents again.

In the summer of 1942, holding our "Return to Native Village Certificates", Lin Chee and I boarded a steamer for Guangzhouwan. The voyage was highly unpleasant. Passengers on the ship were packed in like sardines, the sea was choppy and, like many around me, I became horribly seasick. After a few days' rest in Guangzhouwan, on a warm sunny morning Lin Chee and I crossed the border separating Guangzhouwan from Free China. We walked across a bridge leading to the Free Chinese side and presented our "Return to Native Village Certificates" to the young Chinese army officer stationed at the check-post. In response, he issued a "Returned Overseas Chinese Certificate" to each of us, which would be our certificate of identity in Free China. After the formalities were over, I looked up and saw the Nationalist Chinese flag swaying gently in the morning breeze in all its splendour of blue, white and red — "The blue sky, the white sun and the red earth underneath". We were on Free Chinese soil at last!

My certificate of identity in Free China classified me as an overseas Chinese, but I found that it had its advantages since I was exempt from compulsory military service; as I later learned, being a conscript in the Chinese army could be a horrible experience. I began to find out more about the real China as we slowly made our way to Liuzhou.

The first leg of our journey was along the highway from Guangzhouwan to Yulin, a town on the Guangdong-Guangxi border about midway to Liuzhou. In an effort to obstruct or delay the advance of Japanese troops, the Chinese army had demolished this section of the highway so that motor transportation was no longer possible. With the very bad road conditions, those who could afford it would travel in sedan chairs carried on the shoulders of sure-footed coolies. We could not pay the fare and had to make the entire week-long journey to Yulin on foot, which was exhausting but gave us a good view of the Chinese countryside. We passed many villages, and in almost all of them the living conditions were primitive. The small wooden houses were all dilapidated, with little or no electricity, no running water and no sewers. The villagers' clothes were usually tattered and dirty, some children ran around without shirts or pants, and it was all a distressing sight.

As Father expected, Lin Chee took charge, planned our route, and made all the decisions regarding meals and lodgings. At Yulin, where we decided to sell some of the clothes we had brought, Lin Chee took charge of all the bargaining, which I was happy to let her do. In return, I volunteered to do the heavy-duty work on our journey and carried our suitcases as we walked.

From Yulin onwards the highway took shape again and it was possible to travel by bus, but our onwards journey was still memorable. Unlike the paved highways in Hong Kong, the so-called highway to Liuzhou was only a dirt road, muddy on rainy days and dusty when it was dry. To my amazement, instead of burning petrol most buses and trucks used charcoal gas as fuel. The buses had a cumbersome iron stove with pipes connected to the carburettor, and the explosion of ignited charcoal gas would propel the vehicle. A large basket holding lumps of black charcoal sat behind the driver's cab. Since charcoal-burning vehicles did not have much power, they would often stall and slide back when going uphill. To prevent the vehicle from sliding back and causing an accident, the bus driver would ask his assistant to get off, run behind the bus, and place two big wooden wedges behind the rear wheels whenever the bus began to slide. The driver would then hope that at full throttle the bus would continue to move forward. This process was repeated at every point on the highway that had a slope, and all the passengers would hold their breaths until the bus succeeded in climbing uphill again.

I learned after arriving in Liuzhou that gasoline, all of which had to be imported, was a vital strategic commodity and in very short supply. Hence we saw posters on city walls saying: "One drop of gasoline, one drop of blood!" Without gasoline, air force fighters and bombers would be grounded and army motor transportation would stand still. However, I found out that even though imported gasoline was allocated only to government and military departments, rich merchants and shrewd drivers could procure this precious fuel easily on the black market.

I started life in Free China full of expectations, and when I arrived in Liuzhou I looked forward to seeing a strong and prosperous country. I was proud of the saying that China was "one of the four world powers." Yet the picture I saw was one of poverty, corruption and incompetence.

The signs that China's economy had been wrecked by war were everywhere. Imported goods were virtually unavailable because of enemy blockades, and commodity prices skyrocketed due to scarcity. The government was forced to print more paper money to procure supplies, which in turn led to even greater inflation. Hoarding, which became commonplace among merchants and manufacturers, further aggravated the situation. This practice was not confined to civilians; government organizations such as the Central Bank, the Bank of China, the Bank of Communications, the Farmers' Bank of China, the Central Trust and many others did the same. These organizations set up their own companies to join in the profiteering, along with many government officials in high positions (especially those in charge of financial and economic affairs). Meanwhile, lower-level civil servants, teachers, clerical staff, factory workers and other salary earners had a difficult time making ends meet. As could be expected, the rich became richer, the poor became poorer, and resentment against the Nationalist government mounted steadily.

To sustain the fight against Japan, the government urged people to join the army. Two popular slogans were painted on walls or hung on banners in cities and villages: "The entire nation in arms" and "Every citizen a soldier." The conscription of soldiers, which continued unabated throughout the Anti-Japanese War, was based on the traditional *baojia* system organized on the basis of households: ten households made up a *jia*, and ten *jia* made up a *bao*. Every year, village, county and municipal governments would report the number of young men eligible for conscription to the provincial government. If there were more than one eligible young man in a household, one of them would be conscripted that year, so that only one son in each family would be exempt. Also exempt were "Returned Overseas Chinese Certificate" holders like myself. Peasants, who accounted for some 80 percent of China's population at that time, made up most of the recruits and suffered the bulk of the casualties.

The peasant soldiers were largely uneducated, had little modern military training and were poorly equipped. Each soldier was armed with only a bayoneted rifle, a small amount of ammunition and two hand-grenades, all of which were usually either crudely manufactured or obsolete. There was no standardization in the weaponry, which the army imported from many places: Germany, the Soviet Union, Japan, Britain, France, and the United States. The soldiers wore uniforms made of coarse cloth, which kept them neither warm in winter nor cool in summer, and none of them had helmets or boots. Many were shod only with cloth shoes or straw sandals although, with little transportation, they had to move primarily on foot. The battlefield rations for the troops consisted of dried fried rice contained in a sausage-shaped sack which the soldiers swung around their shoulders.

Corruption was rampant within the military. Pay and provisions for soldiers in an army unit were allocated in a lump sum to the unit commander for distribution to the troops. As a result of heavy combat casualties, desertion and deaths caused by malnutrition and disease, most army units were under strength and the number of soldiers in actual service was always less than that on the regular payroll. This meant that a unit commander often did not have to distribute all of the pay and provisions allocated to his unit, and quite a few kept the undistributed portions for themselves. To counteract this, the Central Military Commission would send inspectors periodically to the various army units, but a delinquent commander would respond by borrowing soldiers from other divisions or by herding poor peasants into his barracks. When the inspection was over, the peasants would either be driven away or kept in the army to work as coolies.

As salaries could not catch up with inflation, many lower- and middle-level officers would look for ways to augment their income, often through unlawful means. Officers in the quartermaster corps, for example, would purchase military supplies and equipment in the name of the armed forces and then sell them secretly on the black market. High-ranking officers were often bribed to turn a blind eye to such profiteering. While both senior and junior officers benefited from almost unchecked corruption, the ordinary soldiers suffered from poor food and clothing, hard labour and insufficient medical care, not to mention having to risk their lives in combat and sometimes incurring unjust punishment. It was little wonder that both the morale and the fighting capabilities of the Chinese troops were low compared to the more disciplined and much better equipped Japanese soldiers.

China did have some crack troops but many, like those who had fought in Shanghai in 1937 to international acclaim, had been decimated by the superior land, sea and air power of the enemy. More regrettably still, the cream of the Chinese army (some four hundred thousand strong) was reportedly often deployed to contain the troops of the Chinese Communist Party (CCP) rather than to stop the Japanese advance. Founded in 1921, the CCP had built up its own armed forces and was seen as a serious threat by Chiang Kai-shek, who headed the ruling Nationalist government. During 1930–34, Chiang launched five campaigns to try to exterminate the CCP, but some of its troops managed to escape. The survivors undertook the legendary Long March and retreated to Yan'an in the remote inland province of Shaanxi, where they managed to become self-sufficient and successfully held out against Nationalist forces. During the war, the Communists and Nationalists agreed to form a "United Front" against the Japanese, but they remained highly suspicious of each other and continued to deploy troops to counterbalance each other's forces. I was unaware of the complicated political situation then, and believed that all

Chinese armed forces should join together to fight the Japanese instead of each other.

During my stay in Liuzhou in 1942, the land war between China and Japan had slowed down while the armies on both sides regrouped. However, the Japanese air force intensified its activities and bombed undefended Chinese cities in an attempt to demoralize the people and further destroy the Chinese economy. The degree of destruction was unimaginable, with tens of thousands of civilians killed or wounded and the infrastructure of the cities, military installations and civilian property turned to rubble. Running for shelter during air raids became a part of daily life for people living in Liuzhou, Guilin, Chongqing, Kunming and other major cities in the Southwest. The bombing did not break China's will to resist, however, and the fighting wore on.

During the Battle of Hong Kong, the air-raid sirens were sounded only when enemy bombers were already flying overhead, and we often did not have enough time to get into air-raid shelters. The situation in China was better and people had plenty of time to take cover, thanks to the unique air-raid warning system on the Mainland. Underground Chinese agents in Japanese-occupied territories would monitor enemy activities and file intelligence reports to the Chinese government by wireless or long-distance telephone. As soon as they spotted Japanese aircraft taking off from the airfields, they would notify the Chinese air defence command of the direction of their flight, which gave us ample warning of oncoming attacks. Also, as the cities of Liuzhou, Guilin and Chongqing were built on hilly ground and surrounded by mountains, there were many caves which could serve as natural air-raid shelters.

The air-raid warning system was divided into three stages: Stage One denoted that enemy planes had taken off from their base; Stage Two denoted that enemy planes were approaching the city from a distance; and Stage Three that enemy planes had reached the city's air space. To ensure that warning signs were visible to all citizens, large black balls were hoisted on tall poles erected on hill tops. Either one or two black balls would be hoisted to correspond with the initial two stages of warning, and a series of short blares from the air-raid sirens marked the third stage. When enemy planes left the city's air space, the two black balls on the pole would be lowered and the air defence command would sound the "air-raid over" siren, which was a long blare. During night attacks, lanterns were used instead of black balls.

Liuzhou and Guilin were at that time the most popular safe havens for people from Hong Kong. Liuzhou, a city of merchants, industrialists and traders, is the centre of Guangxi's railway and motor road network. Guilin, on the other hand, is a city well known for its culture and spectacular scenery. Many Hong Kong students, including some of my classmates from King's College, continued their higher education in Guilin's Guangxi University. After staying for a short period in Liuzhou, Lin Chee went on to join her younger brother Sai Kwong in Guilin where they were both able to find work. Sai Kwong worked as a clerk in a drugstore run by his Pui Ching schoolmate from Hong Kong, and Lin Chee found work as a receptionist in a photo studio. At that time, the American Volunteer Group (American pilot volunteers led by Claire Chennault) had set up air bases in various parts of the Southwest to help China with its air defence. When off duty, airmen from these bases would come to Guilin for sightseeing, and Lin Chee's fluent English attracted many of them to the studio to develop their films. Lin Chee later married the studio's owner, Kwong Shiu Wah, a merchant from Foshan, Guangdong, while Sai Kwong married a Guangxi native towards the end of the war.

I spent over a year in Liuzhou working in Uncle Leung's auto accessories firm Fook Lee. Aunt Rose had sent Tse Kwong to study bookkeeping and accounting, and her adopted son Nai Hei to attend middle school with the aim of eventually entering university. Although Tse Kwong was contented with learning to be a bookkeeper and later an accountant, I had no intention of giving up hope of going to university and had always thought that I would not be an apprentice for long. However, our dreams were shattered when we heard that Father had died.

The news reached us in a hot quiet afternoon in late July, when most people had stayed indoors to keep away from the heat, the kind of humid, all-consuming heat that enveloped most of southwest China during the summer. I was working in the auto accessories shop, sweating from the heat, when Mother's letter arrived from Hong Kong. I tore it open eagerly, but immediately my mind went blank. In her small, neat handwriting, Mother told us that Father had died of tuberculosis. I was in shock and ran to Tse Kwong's school to tell him the news. We held each other's hands, our eyes swelled with tears and we were at a loss for words. That night, trying to recover from our sadness, we decided to write to Mother to console her, promising her that her four sons would take good care of her.

Surprisingly, Mother seemed to be quite stoic about our loss. Perhaps she knew that she had to keep our spirits up in order that we could survive the war. "I know you must feel very sad," Mother wrote. "But you have to be strong. You are grown ups now. People will look down on us if we become too emotional."

Father passed away on 13 July 1943, at the young age of forty-five. After that, I never had the chance to enter university, and Tse Kwong never realized his goal of becoming an accountant. We both felt strongly that we had to try to earn more money in order to support ourselves. Tse Kwong stopped going to classes and started to work as a clerk in Uncle Leung's shop; later, he became Uncle Leung's assistant and even tried to start his own business. In the meantime, while hanging on to my job, I kept a lookout for other work that could be more lucrative and meaningful. My opportunity came when the United States decided to send its military personnel to China to help fight the war.

Wartime Interpreter

By the late 1930s, all of China's coastal ports had fallen into Japanese hands, and China could depend only on two land supply lines to sustain its war efforts: the Yunnan-Burma highway, known as the Burma Road, and the Yunnan-Indochina railway. After the defeat of France and the British Expeditionary Force by Germany in 1939, the Allies conceded Japan's demand to close both routes. The railway was kept closed until the Japanese surrendered in 1945, but the Burma Road was re-opened after three months because of pressure from the United States. In March 1941, the US Congress passed the Lend-Lease Act to aid democratic countries in their fight against the Axis Powers, and China was one of the recipients. The first shipments of Lend-Lease supplies from the US came through the Burma Road just after the British re-opened it, and to close this last remaining supply line Japanese planes started to attack convoys on the highway. China was helpless since by this time its air force had disintegrated, having lost practically all of its warplanes and most of its pilots.

After repeated negotiations, the Nationalist government succeeded in persuading US president Franklin D. Roosevelt to send aircraft and pilots to China to intercept Japanese warplanes over the Southwest and to keep the Burma Road open. As the US was not yet at war with Japan at that time, Roosevelt had to issue an executive order quietly on 15 April 1941, permitting pilots to resign their existing positions in the armed forces temporarily and go to China to fight the Japanese as mercenaries. They were enticed by salaries of up to US$750 per month, plus travel allowances, housing, and a bonus of US$500 for each Japanese plane shot down.

The US recruited one hundred pilots and assigned a hundred P-40 fighters to Claire Chennault, a retired army air force captain, to form the American Volunteer Group (AVG). Chennault had recommended the P-40 because of its greater power and speed, which he thought could overcome the high manoeuvrability of the Japanese Zero fighter. The AVG was formally established on 1 August 1941 in Kunming. Large shark-heads with gaping jaws were painted on the snouts of the P-40s, and the AVG was nicknamed "The Flying Tigers" — a term the Chinese used for crack troops.

On 20 December 1941, after bombing Kunming and Chongqing for a year without resistance, the Japanese were taken by surprise when they ran into the shark-faced P-40s in the skies over Kunming. Making use of the impressive diving speed of their heavy planes, the AVG pilots wreaked havoc on the Zero fighters and sent them scurrying back to their base at Hanoi. This was the first victory of the AVG over the Japanese air force. As the war progressed, the AVG was given more planes and personnel, and eventually expanded to become the Fourteenth Air Force of the US Army. This unit continued to be under the command of Chennault, who was promoted to the rank of Major General.

By early 1942, however, Japanese forces were on their way to conquering Burma and shutting down all supply lines to China. Protecting the Burma Road therefore became of utmost urgency, but a weakened China, even with the help of the AVG, would not be able to do this job on its own. Help was needed from the Allied powers. Since a strong Japanese presence in Burma would also threaten India and alter the balance of power in Asia, the US and Britain decided to set up the China-Burma-India (CBI) Theatre of War and join forces with China to counteract the Japanese advance. Lieutenant General Joseph Stilwell was designated the commanding general of US Armed Forces in the CBI Theatre and was simultaneously named Chief of Staff to the Supreme Commander of the China Theatre (Chiang Kai-shek), Supervisor of the Lend-Lease Agreement, and the US representative on any Allied war council. Stilwell, who spoke Chinese, was first stationed in China during 1926–29, and again in 1935–39. Chiang Kai-shek placed the Chinese Expeditionary Force, comprising the Fifth and Sixth Armies, under Stillwell's command. The air was covered by the US Tenth Air Force, based in India, as well as the Flying Tigers.

Despite their concerted efforts the Allied troops lost Burma to the Japanese, primarily because of lack of coordination. By the end of May 1942, the Japanese had completed their conquest and the Allies were forced to retreat in disarray. British and Indian troops hurriedly withdrew to the west of the Indian-Burmese border, while remnants of the Chinese Expeditionary Force either sought refuge in north India or fled home to Yunnan Province. Advancing along the Burma Road, Japanese troops headed eastward to occupy the westernmost part of Yunnan and stopped only when they reached the Salween River, where the retreating Chinese troops had destroyed the main bridge.

Without the use of the Burma Road, providing supplies to Free China became extraordinarily difficult. Gasoline, munitions and many other vital military supplies had to be shipped by air from north India to southwest China, flying over the Himalayas. Lend-Lease supplies were first sent by sea to Calcutta, then by land to Assam in northeast India, and finally by air to Kunming. American airmen called the Himalayas "the Hump". Flying over the Hump was highly perilous because air currents were so turbulent that they could crush an airplane. To make matters worse, Japanese fighters also posed constant threats; together, these two hazards brought down over four hundred US transport planes during the course of the war.

Nevertheless, until the re-opening of the Burma Road the US managed to airfreight a constant supply of much-needed materials to Free China. The

US Air Transport Command initially gave Stilwell only twenty-five transport planes; in October 1943 the number was increased to one hundred, with the goal of transporting 5,000 tons of cargo each month. As the Allies started to regain control over Burma, the monthly airfreight volume soared to 18,000 tons in June 1944, and eventually peaked at 46,000 tons in January 1945.

Towards the end of 1942, Stillwell started to amass his forces for regaining control of the Burma Road as well as counterattacking the Japanese in China. Retaining his faith that Chinese conscripts, if properly fed and trained, could become first-class fighting men, Stilwell began to work on increasing the combat efficiency of the Chinese troops assigned to him. He organized them into three groups: X-force, Y-force and Z-force. The mission of the first two was to re-open the Burma Road and then join up with Z-force to launch a counterattack against the Japanese armies in central, south and east China.

Before that, however, the Chinese forces required extensive training. X-force was based in Ramgarh, about two hundred miles west of Calcutta, while Y-force and Z-force were drawn from divisions in Kunming and Guilin. Rather than train whole divisions at once, Stilwell proposed a system of training by cadres, who in turn would train their fellow soldiers. All cadres had to be trained in military tactics and combat techniques, as well as in the handling of machine guns, mortars, rocket-launchers, anti-tank guns and other equipment for specialized combat duties. Cadres of X-force and Y-force, who would take part in the Burma Campaign, were also required to attend a course in jungle warfare.

Along with the opening of the Assam-Kunming air route, two herculean engineering projects were launched to deliver supplies to China. One was the Ledo Road, which would begin in Assam and cross the mountains, forests and rivers of north Burma to meet the Burma Road at Longling in western Yunnan Province. The other project was a 1,800-mile pipeline from Calcutta to Kunming, which would augment the limited amount of fuel that could be shipped along the Assam-Kunming air route, and thus allow China to expand its air operations. Since, according to the press, it then required a ton of gasoline to deliver a ton of cargo by air to China, these two land projects were critical to expanding the flow of supplies to the country. Construction had to follow closely behind the offensive carried out by X-force, and unless the campaign succeeded neither the road nor the pipeline would be able to reach China.

To ensure the success of his program, Stilwell established a system of American liaison teams or single officers to serve as advisors to Chinese commanders at each level of the military organization. For this system to work effectively it was essential for Chinese and American officials at all levels to overcome the language and cultural barriers between them and fully communicate with each other. This created an opportunity for those who, like me, were bilingual to join the military and serve as interpreters.

The Nationalist government started its interpreter programme in November 1941 when it set up the War Area Service Corps (WASC), headed by Major General Huang Ren-lin, to provide support to the American Volunteer Group then deployed in Kunming. Aside from building hostels and airport facilities, the WASC also employed interpreters to facilitate the AVG's missions in Kunming and other subsequent locations. However, many more interpreters would be needed to support Stilwell's training plan for the Chinese troops. To meet this requirement, the Foreign Affairs Bureau (FAB) under the Chinese Military Commission took charge of coordinating the recruitment, training and assignment of interpreters. The FAB was headed by Lieutenant General Shang Chen who was then in charge of China's military liaison with the Allies.

The FAB launched a massive recruitment drive, aimed primarily at university students and returned overseas Chinese. The best universities of China had moved from the coastal provinces to the Southwest as the Japanese advanced. Some continued to operate as before, while others merged with existing universities in southwest China or amalgamated to form a single university. Tsinghua University and Peking University in Beijing joined with Nankai University in Tianjin to set up the National Southwest Associated University in Kunming, and Yenching University and other Christian institutions relocated to the site of the West China Union University in Chengdu. As the need for English speakers dramatically increased, the Ministry of Education decided that third- and fourth-year university students with a sound knowledge of English would be conscripted to work as interpreters in the armed forces. Even though Hong Kong people in Free China were "overseas Chinese" and thus not subject to conscription, many decided to join as volunteers. The colonial education system in Hong Kong had provided us with a good knowledge of English, and many former civil servants, students, teachers and office clerks who had taken refuge in Free China responded eagerly to the FAB's recruitment advertisements for interpreters.

To recruit people from Hong Kong, the FAB Interpreter Training School held its entrance examinations in Qujiang, Guilin and Liuzhou, the three main cities where the returnees congregated. As I was excited by the opportunity to serve in the army and also saw this as a chance to pursue a different career, I responded to the FAB advertisement in the newspapers and sat for the examination in Liuzhou in October 1943. The examination was divided into two parts. The first was an oral test, and I was interviewed by a professor of English from a Chinese university and an American army officer. The second part was a written test which required two pieces of translation — from Chinese to English and vice versa — and an autobiography in English.

As soon as I received notice that I had passed the examination, I decided to resign from my position at Aunt Rose's auto accessories shop. Tse Kwong and some of my younger colleagues were happy for me, since they too thought that I would have a better future in the army, but Aunt Rose disagreed.

"If I were you I would stay with Uncle Leung," she said. "It's always better to be a businessman than a soldier. Look at Tse Kwong. He's very obedient towards Uncle Leung, and I'm sure Uncle Leung will treat him well."

Tse Kwong listened quietly to Aunt Rose's arguments, but he told me afterwards that I need not follow her advice if I thought that joining the army would give me a better future.

Aunt Rose and Uncle Leung were not at all happy about my choice. Aware of the dangers of war, those of my parents' generation generally believed in the saying, "A good son should never join the army," but since I had already turned eighteen they let me make my own decision. I said good-bye to them and set off from Liuzhou. Aunt Rose and Uncle Leung were sad to see me go, but Tse Kwong was secretly proud of his "patriotic" elder brother.

Some fifteen candidates, mostly young men from Hong Kong like me, passed the examination in Liuzhou. Guided by an FAB officer, we travelled together by train to Guilin, joined another fifteen candidates there, and boarded a US Army C-47 transport plane for Kunming. As the cabin was not pressurized the journey was highly uncomfortable and everyone except the pilot and the cabin crew became air-sick. Still, this did not prevent me from looking through the cabin window at the expanse of mountains and rivers as the plane flew over the vast plateau which spans the provinces of Guangxi, Guizhou and Yunnan. Seeing this magnificent view of my motherland from the air for the first time, I was exhilarated and almost forgot how air-sick I felt.

The FAB Interpreter Training School was located at the western end of Kunming in a large compound with a dormitory, a mess hall, several classrooms, an office, an assembly hall and a parade ground. Major General Huang Ren-lin, the director of the WASC, was the nominal head of the school, but daily administration and training were the responsibilities of three National Southwest Associated University professors, a major in the Chinese army, and several US army officers. The students were called cadets and came under the jurisdiction of the FAB.

We were the first class to enrol in the Training School, and the six-week course started in November 1943 with 150 cadets; ten classes in all were eventually held. Aside from some thirty overseas Chinese recruited in Liuzhou and Guilin, the rest of our class were mainly students from the National Southwest Associated University studying foreign languages or engineering. Our curricula included oral and written translation from English to Chinese and vice versa, the cultural practices of China and the US, information on the organization and weapons of the Chinese and US armed forces, and international affairs. In addition, our schedule included visits to the Y-force infantry and field artillery training centres, as well as daily military drills and training (since we were now part of the armed forces). As military cadets, we were expected to jump up and salute each time our instructors mentioned Chiang Kai-shek or Dr. Sun Yat-sen by name. Despite my patriotism, I was uncomfortable with this flagrant worshiping of authority, and I thought the practice (which I never got used to) must stem from China's feudal traditions.

It also took me some time to adjust to the Mandarin (Putonghua) taught at the Training School. My mother tongue was Cantonese, the dialect of the inhabitants of Guangzhou and Hong Kong, while Mandarin, based on the principal dialect spoken in and around Beijing, was the official spoken language of China. Fortunately, I had attended YMCA Mandarin classes in Hong Kong in the hope that one day I might return to serve my motherland. After I set foot on the Mainland, however, I was dismayed to find that people did not really understand me because of my Cantonese accent. My Mandarin improved a lot after I finished training, but it took me a while to overcome the old saying: "In heaven and on earth, there is no more dreadful din than that of a Cantonese speaking Mandarin!"

The use of different dialects created factionalism among the cadets at the Training School: mainly among those who spoke Cantonese, those who spoke Shanghainese, and the others. Historically, Western influence was greatest along China's coastal regions, especially in cities like Hong Kong and Shanghai. As a result, graduates of the University of Hong Kong and Shanghai's St. John's University, for example, were generally more fluent in English than their counterparts from other universities in China. The same applied to the standard of English among my classmates and, feeling superior to the rest of the class, Hong Kong and Shanghainese cadets formed their own exclusive groups. Both groups would speak their own dialects not only in private but also occasionally in public, and looked down upon those whose English was not as fluent. Some of the other cadets felt insulted and fought back by calling the Hong Kong cadets "running dogs of colonialism" and commented on how poorly we spoke Mandarin. In retaliation, Hong Kong cadets reminded them of their awkward English pronunciation. This factionalism among the cadets made me very unhappy, and I wondered how this could happen at a time when our country was fighting for its survival. No wonder Dr. Sun Yat-sen once said that the Chinese people were like a "heap of loose sand."

Aside from having to work on my Mandarin, I was also surprised to find that I had to adjust to the English taught at the Training School. While I had learned the King's English under Hong Kong's colonial education system, most people at the Training School spoke American English largely because of the Americanization of the country's higher education system starting at the turn of the century. After the Boxer Rebellion in 1900, China had to make significant indemnity payments to Western powers, including the US. In 1908, however, the US Congress decided to allocate half of America's share of this indemnity payment — about US$12 million — for a programme to send one hundred students a year to study in the US, until the funds ran out. Over 1,200 students eventually benefited from this programme. To prepare these students, part of the funds were used to build Tsinghua College in Beijing, which later became Tsinghua University. Also around this time, American missionaries started to set up universities in various parts of China. By the 1940s, thousands of graduates from Tsinghua and these missionary universities had gone to the US to further their education, and those who returned to China after finishing their studies brought with them a strong American influence. As a result, I found that I had to learn American diction in the Training School and use American spelling and grammar to make my writing acceptable to my instructors. I did not mind the effort, however, since I would be working with US military officers after graduation and learning American English would help me become a better interpreter.

Upon completing our training in December 1943 we were commissioned in the Chinese Army with the rank of captain. Most of the interpreters were dispatched to the FAB and sent on assignments to US Army Headquarters in Kunming, which was responsible for all US army activities in Yunnan, including liaising with the Chinese Expeditionary Force Headquarters regarding training, assigning US army liaison teams to various units of the Y-force, and providing logistical support. Except for a few who stayed in US Army Headquarters, most of the FAB interpreters were re-assigned to work with US army instructors at Y-force cadre training centres, such as the Infantry Training Centre and the Field Artillery Training Centre, as well as other smaller training centres for the Signal Corps, Engineer Corps, Medical Corps and Motor Transportation Corps. In the final phase of the war, some FAB interpreters were engaged by the Office of Strategic Services (OSS) (which was reorganized as the Central Intelligence Agency (CIA) after the war) and were often parachuted into Japanese-occupied territories to carry out intelligence activities and sabotage. This must have been the most risky assignment for interpreters.

Those interpreters who were not dispatched to the FAB were sent to the WASC, the Chinese Expeditionary Forces in India, or the Aviation Commission of the Chinese government which handled arrangements with the US government for training Chinese air force pilots in the United States.

Many interpreters like me had originally joined the armed forces as an act of patriotism, but as time went by our patriotism was put to the test. The loss of China's key cities and industrial base had ruined the country's economy, and conditions were made even worse by corruption within the government and the military. Our rations were poor and the Chinese army uniforms (with a high-collared Chinese-style jacket) which we wore in the Training School were coarse and ill-fitting. For the winter, the jacket was bluish-grey and thickly padded with cotton; for the summer, it was field-green with only a thin layer of coarse cotton cloth. Our shoes were made of cloth, and we had to wear puttees (strips of cloth wrapped spirally around the lower legs of our breeches) for support and protection. Each cadet was also issued a cotton padded blanket roll, a canvas field pack, a leather belt and a metal canteen. After we received our respective assignments, in order that we should not look too shabby as representatives of our country in liaison with foreign military advisors, many of us decided to use our own money to buy leather shoes and tailor-made uniforms. To save up enough money we needed to cut down on dining out and other entertainment, and instead ate in the dining hall and stayed on campus during our days off.

Our already meagre salaries were quickly eroded by inflation. Interpreters who worked for the Infantry Training Centre in Kunming once tried to call a strike to demand higher pay. However, they were no match for the Chinese army colonel in charge of the centre's interpreter affairs, who issued ammunition to a platoon of soldiers, assigned them to guard the interpreters' barracks and gave them orders to shoot anyone leaving. When the interpreters sent word the next day that they were willing to negotiate, he had them brought to his office under armed escort, placed a loaded pistol and a prepared statement on his desk, and ordered them to sign the statement which said that they were satisfied with their wages. The interpreters capitulated and news of the pre-empted strike was blacked out by the authorities.

Our conditions improved once the Burma Campaign began. Our pay was increased, we were issued much better quality American uniforms, and we ate the tastier and more nutritious US army rations. We also shared in all the facilities and benefits that our American colleagues enjoyed. American soldiers were called GIs (for "Government Issue") because everything they consumed or used was issued by the US government, and FAB interpreters were in much the same position. We discarded our Chinese uniforms and captain insignia, and became quasi-GIs. Although I was glad to see the marked improvement in our living conditions, I felt somewhat uneasy about the change, as if we had traded national dignity for material well-being.

Ironically, the fact that we were kitted out like the Americans did not mean that we were protected better than the Chinese soldiers once we entered the battlefield. As we found out during the Burma Campaign, Japanese soldiers hated the Americans more than the Chinese, and anyone wearing US army uniform would be their target of first choice. Quite a few of our interpreter comrades were killed by Japanese snipers hiding deep in the jungle.

The Burma Campaign

I was dispatched to the FAB in December 1943, and my first assignment as an FAB interpreter was to work with US army instructors at the Motor School at Qujing where cadres of the Y-force Motor Transportation Corps were trained. Qujing was an important city where the road networks around Kunming, the capital of Yunnan Province, connected with those around Guiyang, the capital of Guizhou Province. The school used the grounds and buildings of a former army barracks. On either side of the main gate was a long couplet exhorting the Chinese Army:

> Join the war of resistance and build up our nation. To build our nation, we must first build our army. The building of our army starts here.
>
> Vanquish our enemies and achieve our goals. To achieve our goals, it is important to follow a virtuous path. With virtues on our side we will be invincible.

I was joined by three other interpreters from Hong Kong and a dozen interpreters who were third- or fourth-year mechanical engineering students from mainland universities. The training facilities at the school were at first appalling. Only two-thirds of the thirty Ford two-and-a-half-ton trucks of 1930 vintage could be used to train drivers; the others had been dismantled so that their components (chassis, engines, transmissions, clutches, axles, wheels, brakes etc.) could be used for teaching. Later, thanks to US aid under the Lend-Lease Act, the school received new vehicles and motor parts, and we were delighted to see Chinese soldiers driving some of the latest-model jeeps, weapon carriers and trucks.

When I started work in the Motor School, the campaign to re-open the Burma Road was already underway. During the Cairo Conference in November 1943, Allied leaders originally agreed to start the Burma Campaign in the spring of 1944, but Stilwell insisted that the campaign could not be delayed further for strategic reasons. He obtained the assurance of Chiang Kai-shek that the Chinese divisions of the X-force in India were "his" army to command "free of interference". He had hoped to open a land route to China with this force and eventually meet with US forces on the China coast.

The campaign was launched in December 1943 when the X-force (named the New First Army), which had three divisions of twelve thousand men each, crossed the India-Burma border into Upper Burma, followed by the Ledo Road construction team comprising fifty thousand soldiers of the US Army engineer corps and thirty thousand Chinese and Indian coolies. In early 1944, two more divisions were merged with the existing divisions of the X-force, which was then split into the New First Army, commanded by Lieutenant General Sun

Li-jen, and the New Sixth Army, commanded by Lieutenant General Liao Yao-hsiang.

One of the prime objectives of Stilwell's war plan was to capture Myitkyina, Japan's northernmost major garrison and air base in Burma. From there the troops would follow a road that led southwards to the old Burma Road at Bhamo, and then eastwards to the border with China. As the troops advanced through northern Burma, not only did they meet with heavy Japanese resistance but they had to brave the suffocating heat and unrelenting rain of the tropical forests and mountains. Diseases and casualties were rampant.

In April 1944, the Chinese Expeditionary Force (Y-force), under orders from the Chief of Staff of the Chinese Army, began its westward advance for its rendezvous with the X-force. Although the training of Y-force soldiers was not yet complete, General Wei Li-huang was able to amass some two hundred thousand troops (divided into the 11th Group Army and the 20th Group Army) and equip them with modern American weapons to carry out the mission. Known as "Hundred Victories Wei", he was assisted by two chiefs of staff — one American and the other Chinese. At the same time, the Allies had reinforced their air force and gained command of the air not only in combat strength but also in the ability to supply and support ground troops, which was an essential part of the Burma Campaign.

In order to join with Stilwell's armies, the Y-force had to regain control over the part of western Yunnan that had fallen into Japanese hands in 1942. To do so, General Wei's armies needed to cross the Salween River and capture the two strategic cities of Longling and Tengchong. The first major hurdle was to get the troops across the river because, when remnants of the earlier Chinese Expeditionary Force retreated to Chinese territory from Burma in 1942, they had destroyed the bridge to stop the Japanese advance. The Chinese call the Salween River Nu Jiang (Angry River) because, as it flows from Tibet through Yunnan to Burma, the river is noted for its spectacular steep gorges, rapid currents and hazardous whirlpools.

When I first heard about the plan to cross Nu Jiang, I immediately thought about the legendary crossing of the river (then called Lu Shui) in the famous historical novel *Romance of the Three Kingdoms* when troops from the Shu Kingdom under Zhuge Liang marched south to "pacify" ethnic minority tribes in Yunnan and Guizhou. To my amazement, some sixteen centuries after Zhuge Liang, General Wei led the Y-force successfully across the river on 11 May 1944, under the cover of night and stormy weather. His advance troops crossed the roaring waters on bamboo rafts and rubber boats, and constructed a pontoon bridge across the river. The next day, some thirty-two thousand men made the crossing together with thousands of pack horses, cows, mules and transport coolies. Then, scaling the formidable incline of the surrounding gorges in the pouring rain, the troops emerged from the cold, cloud-covered mountains before the Japanese even knew of their presence.

The 11th Group Army took Longling on June 10, but was driven out by a determined Japanese counterattack a week later. The forces were re-assembled for another attempt and regained Longling two months later, but it took the 20th Group Army four months of bitter fighting to recover Tengchong. Possession of both cities was essential to open the passage from Burma to China and permitted Stilwell's troops to begin their advance from Myitkyina. To reach the Japanese strongholds, the Chinese troops had to scale the mountains and gorges around the Nu Jiang and fight in some of the highest battlegrounds in the world. The Chinese ground forces outnumbered the Japanese by about ten to one, and American warplanes controlled the sky over Yunnan and Burma, but the twenty thousand odd Japanese troops in western Yunnan were well protected by the rugged terrain, solid bunkers and underground tunnels. It took massive artillery shelling and bombing to destroy the fortifications and, in the final assault, Chinese soldiers had to use hand-grenades and flame-throwers against enemy soldiers in hiding. In November, more than five months after the first Nu Jiang crossing, Y-force was finally able to wipe out the Japanese presence in western Yunnan.

The Qujing Motor School closed down when the Yunnan force began its westward offensive, and I was transferred with its instructors and other interpreters to the Motor Transport Command (MTC) of the Service of Supplies Department of Y-force. The headquarters of the MTC was stationed in the city of Xiaguan on the Chinese section of the Yunnan-Burma Highway, midway between Kunming and Longling. Some seven thousand feet above sea level, Xiaguan was an ideal stopover station for truckers and travellers. With the snow-covered peaks of Cangshan and the expanses of Erhai Lake in the background, Xiaguan and its surrounding areas were full of legends and ruins from Zhuge Liang's southward expedition, and I often thought about scenes from *Romance of the Three Kingdoms* as I worked there.

As Xiaguan was a very small city, the offices and dormitories of MTC personnel, motor repair shops, supply depots and fuel tanks were all housed in tents outside the city walls, and MTC Headquarters was nicknamed "Tent City". Instructors and interpreters transferred from the Qujing Motor School worked under the MTC's principal US liaison officer. He was a mechanical engineer, and the majority of the liaison officers under his command had engineering backgrounds; even the interpreters were mostly engineering students. I was fortunate to have acquired some knowledge of automobiles while working in Uncle Leung's auto accessories shop in Liuzhou. MTC interpreters had various assignments; some, like me, were attached to the headquarters, while others worked with US liaison officers in Y-force motor transportation regiments or battalions.

Those who worked in the headquarters sometimes took inspection tours along the Yunnan-Burma Highway with US liaison officers, and I made several trips between Xiaguan and Longling with Captain Stevenson. Young, tall and handsome, the captain was friendly, approachable and, like most American servicemen I met during the war, had a pleasant and informal relationship with his Chinese colleagues. We addressed each by our first names, and talked about a wide range of topics from family matters to current affairs. This experience was very different from my later encounters with the British in Hong Kong, who often tended to be formal and sometimes condescending.

Together with Captain Stevenson I made some of my most memorable trips, initially reminiscent of my bus ride two years earlier and the charcoal-burning trucks on the Yulin-Liuzhou Highway. However, the situation had changed and petrol-burning army trucks and jeeps dominated the roads. The scars of war were still evident between Xiaguan and Longling. To the retreating Chinese armies in 1942, this twisting stretch of the Burma Road was known as "death alley", and we saw the rusted hulks of countless abandoned army vehicles and artillery pieces, as well as the skeletons of soldiers, horses and mules. It was a terrible sight but, thanks to the Chinese and American engineers, bulldozers and other equipment were already at work and the battered highway was gradually being repaired.

Our assignment was to examine road conditions and inspect ammunition depots, filling stations and various military installations along the highway. We also monitored the many convoys of trucks to make sure that the flow of army reinforcements and military supplies to the front was continuous. Fortunately, the successful landing of the Y-force spearhead on the west bank of Nu Jiang in May and the construction of the pontoon bridge had ensured that troops and supplies could now be transported smoothly.

We drove mostly on high ground with spectacular overviews of winding rivers and deep valleys. In my first journey to the Salween Valley, in mid August, we followed the edge of a cliff that overlooked the Nu Jiang thousands of feet below. The view of the river tearing through the narrow and almost vertical mountain gorges was breathtaking. To cross the river we drove downhill along a seemingly endless zigzag path, crossed the pontoon bridge, and then took another zigzag path uphill. The journey took more than half a day to complete, and when we finally entered the city of Longling we were greeted by cheering Chinese soldiers and civilians who raised their hands, gave us the thumbs-up sign and shouted "*ding hao*" (very good), "hello" and "okay". It was a truly moving scene; I was totally exhilarated and felt, for the first time, that victory might be in sight.

By April 1944, the tide of war had turned against Japan: its defences in Burma were crumbling, its navy and air force had suffered fatal defeats in the

Pacific, and US forces were advancing toward the China coast. However, the Japanese were not ready to let go of China easily. They launched a new offensive to consolidate control over a strategic north-south corridor across the country and, by November, they had taken all the major cities along the Beijing-Wuhan and Wuhan-Guangzhou railways and advanced into Hunan and Guangxi. The Z-force, based in Guilin, disintegrated in the face of the Japanese offensive, and US army liaison officers and FAB interpreters were evacuated to Kunming. After overrunning Hunan and Guangxi, the Japanese advanced to Dushan, a city on the southern border of Guizhou. With the enemy so close to its wartime capital, Chongqing, the Nationalist government considered moving out of the city, but fortunately this did not become necessary as the Japanese army retreated in December.

In response to the Japanese offensive, the US had asked Chiang Kai-shek to use Chinese Communist troops to fight the Japanese and to appoint Stilwell the field commander of all of China's land forces, but Chiang rejected both requests. With the growing distrust between Stilwell and Chiang, the US government decided to replace Stilwell so as to save the face of the Chinese leader and support the joint war effort. Stilwell was recalled to the United States in October 1944 and the theatre of war was divided into two: the Burma-India Theatre and the China Theatre. Lieutenant General Albert Wedemeyer was named Chiang Kai-shek's chief of staff and commander of American forces in China, but his position essentially meant that he was unable to command Chinese troops without Chiang's consent.

In the meantime, the battle to re-open the Burma Road was drawing to a close. X-force and Y-force (still commanded by General Wei Li-huang) met at the China-Burma border in January 1945. The Ledo Road joined the old Burma Road at Bhamo, and was officially opened for through traffic on 25 January 1945. By that time, my service in the Motor Transport Command had already come to an end and I was back in Kunming waiting for a new assignment. Together with thousands of jubilant Kunming citizens, I witnessed history being made as the first convoy over the completed road entered the city. The bloody Burma Campaign was finally over.

China's Miserable Victory

After its defeat in Hunan and Guangxi, the Chinese army was re-organized according to Wedemeyer's plan and a new fighting force was formed in spring 1945 to replace Z-force. Units of the new fighting force were trained in Yunnan, Guizhou, Guangxi and western Hunan.

After the Burma Campaign ended, Hunan became the major battlefield of the Anti-Japanese War. Since the 24th Group Army (under the command of

General Wang Yao-wu) formed the backbone of Chinese forces in this area, its training and equipment became a priority in Wedemeyer's war plan. In order to increase the firepower of the 24th Group Army, plans were made to equip each of its divisions with an artillery battalion and, as training started in earnest, I was assigned to the Kunming Field Artillery Training Centre in February 1945. My job was to help American instructors train artillery cadres of the 18th Division of the 18th Army under General Wang. My American colleagues included a lieutenant colonel, a captain, a first lieutenant, a master sergeant and a sergeant. The first lieutenant was a Chinese-American, the sergeant was a Japanese-American, and both of them spoke the languages of their forefathers. When our training was completed, my American colleagues and I formed a liaison team for the newly formed artillery battalion of the 18th Division.

American-made howitzers were widely used by Chinese forces in the hilly terrain of Burma and southwest and central China because of the steep angles of their trajectories, and our training had focused on the 75-mm pack howitzer which could be towed by a small truck, or disassembled and carried in several loads on the backs of mules. Equipped with twelve 75-mm pack howitzers (four for each of its three batteries), the 18th Division Artillery Battalion left Kunming for Hunan in July and was deployed at strategic points around Zhijiang, an important military base on the western Hunan front. We waited for orders from division headquarters to fire our first salvo as the infantry moved forward to attack the enemy, but by then the Japanese troops in Hunan had been diverted to the coast in east China in anticipation of a possible US landing, and we never saw any action.

The war came to a sudden end in August 1945 after the US dropped atomic bombs over Hiroshima and Nagasaki. On 9 August, the Soviet Union declared war on Japan, and on 14 August Emperor Hirohito issued a decree ordering all Japanese troops to lay down their arms. On 2 September, Japan officially surrendered to the Allied nations on board the USS *Missouri* in Tokyo Bay.

When the commander of Japanese forces in China officially surrendered in Nanjing on 9 September, China's eight-year-long Anti-Japanese War finally came to an end. Now the most urgent task facing the Nationalist forces was to take over the weapons, ammunition, and military supplies surrendered by the Japanese in the various war zones, and American advice was needed to expedite this process. I joined a US liaison team assigned to advise General Hsueh Yueh, commanding the Ninth War Zone, on matters relating to the takeover. Our team consisted of Lieutenant Colonel Caldwell, a former advisor to the commander of the 18th Division Artillery Battalion, and two interpreters — a Japanese-American sergeant and me — so we had plenty of ability as far as languages were concerned. We flew from Zhijiang to the headquarters of the Ninth War Zone in Nanchang, capital of Jiangxi Province, and on landing we were greeted by General Hsueh's adjutant. After a night in a guest house, we had a cordial meeting the next morning with General Hsueh and, to my surprise, I did not have to speak to him in Mandarin since he and many of his staff were natives of Guangdong Province and we could talk freely in Cantonese.

Guided by Ninth War Zone officers, we inspected Japanese military installations in the suburbs of Nanchang and in Jiujiang, an important port along the Yangtze River in northern Jiangxi. We observed as Chinese officers took inventory of weapons, ammunition, vehicles and others types of military equipment that had been handed over by the Japanese army. We also watched Japanese prisoners of war being herded into internment camps and, with the help of the Japanese-American sergeant, we were able to interview some of the prisoners. I had always thought that Japanese soldiers were bloodthirsty killers whom I could never forgive for the crimes they had committed against Chinese civilians during the war. But I was intrigued and moved by the behaviour of the prisoners in Nanchang and Jiujiang who were disciplined, humble and obedient. After this experience, I had a reluctant respect for the Japanese and was not too surprised when Japan re-emerged as an economic power two decades later.

With the end of the war, my commission as an interpreting officer also came to an end. After completing my Jiangxi mission, I returned to Kunming in October to pick up a letter signed by the Assistant Adjutant General of United States Force Headquarters, China Theatre. It read:

> On the termination of your duty as an Interpreting Officer with the United States Forces in China, the Commanding General, United States Forces in China desires to thank you for a splendid job well done. Without Interpreting Officers the mission of the United States Forces in China would have been seriously hampered. The hard work done by the Interpreting Officers has materially aided in accomplishing this mission, and has helped to cement friendly relations between the peoples of the United States and China. It is hoped that you will continue your good work in the future as in the past, and help to build China into the great nation it deserves to be.

I now had the chance to think about my future. Demobilized interpreters were faced with several prospects. The first was to study in the United States. All FAB interpreters were supposedly given this opportunity provided that they could pass an examination held by the Ministry of Education for this purpose, but this proved to be a sham and only the children, relatives and friends of high-ranking government officials were allowed to go abroad. The second opportunity was to continue one's undergraduate education in a Chinese university with the help of government scholarships. Lastly, those who had already entered the workforce were given preference when applying for jobs in US government agencies and

United Nations organizations in China. Many demobilized interpreters became employees of the US Embassy in Nanjing or US consulates in Shanghai and Guangzhou, and quite a number worked in major cities for offices of the United Nations Rehabilitation and Relief Administration (UNRRA).

I decided to go back home, however, as did most of the FAB interpreters from Hong Kong. After our discharge in Kunming, a group of us boarded (free of charge) a US C-47 transport plane for Liuzhou, from where we took a bus to Wuzhou, sailed down the West River on a flat-bottom river junk to Guangzhou, and took the Kowloon-Canton Railway train to Hong Kong. Many of my colleagues resumed their pre-war posts in government departments, banks and commercial firms, while others took new jobs or started their own business ventures.

In the meantime, the conflict between Nationalist and Communist forces erupted into the open on the Mainland. In January 1946, General George C. Marshall, a special envoy of the US President, came to China to mediate between the two parties, and on 25 February, he worked out an agreement to bring peace to China by merging and consolidating the Nationalist and the Communist armies. Unfortunately, this agreement was undone within a very short time because of the deep hostility and distrust between the two parties and their conflicting political agendas. Fighting broke out in the spring and the US again took the side of the Nationalist government, to which it extended military aid.

With the renewed involvement of the US, interpreters were again needed, first to carry out Marshall's peace plan and later to help the US Army transport Nationalist troops to fight the Communists. Since I was unemployed after returning to Hong Kong, I registered with the Troop Movement Group of the US Army headquartered in Guangzhou, and so did some of my old FAB interpreter comrades. I was assigned to work with a US army liaison officer on board a US navy landing ship. Known as an LST (Landing Ship Tank), it had a displacement of over three thosuand tons and a bow fitted with watertight doors that would open only when the ship hit the beach, allowing tanks, trucks and troops to disembark. From February to May 1946, division after division of Nationalist troops in southern China moved into Hong Kong to board US navy landing ships that would carry them to Qinhuangdao, the seaport nearest to the Shanhaiguan pass — the gateway to the Northeast. Once the Nationalist troops passed through Shanhaiguan they would come face-to-face with Communist troops. I made several return voyages between Hong Kong and Qinhuangdao. At first, life on board a US navy landing ship sailing along the China coast was exciting, but I began to feel guilty about helping my countrymen kill each other and decided to stop working on the LST.

Despite military and financial assistance from the US, Nationalist forces soon started to lose ground in the civil war. Although it had won the Anti-Japanese

War, the government failed to rally the support of the people because of its own corruption and incompetence. I saw widespread discontent in Guangzhou when I stopped there on my way back to Hong Kong in November 1945. The people of Guangzhou had originally welcomed the New First Army which had come to liberate the city with fire crackers and lion dances, but now they were disillusioned and called it the "New Japanese Army". Besides disarming Japanese troops and taking over stocks of enemy weapons and supplies, arrogant officers and rapacious soldiers enriched themselves by confiscating the goods and properties of the local people at will. They also prosecuted many innocent Guangzhou residents as "enemy collaborators" and so, despite its outstanding record in Burma, the New First Army lost its reputation and all its goodwill with the people.

In the meantime, China's economic conditions continued to deteriorate. The mismanagement of the economy by the Nationalist government caused rampant inflation, and corruption made matters even worse. Government and military officials stole property and equipment handed over by the Japanese, and misappropriated relief funds, goods and materiel provided by the US and UNRRA. Many of the stolen goods ended up in the black market, where poverty-stricken civilians had to buy them at exorbitant prices. The standard of living for the ordinary Chinese continued to fall, and many people became destitute.

Most devastating of all was the full-scale war between the Nationalists and the Communists during 1946–49, in which hundreds of thousands of soldiers from both sides were wounded or killed on the battlefields. Even though we had won the Anti-Japanese War after tremendous sacrifices, a unified, prosperous and strong China seemed nowhere in sight. I started to question the meaning of victory.

3

Hong Kong after the War

Liberation

On 30 August 1945, the British Pacific Fleet under Rear Admiral Cecil Harcourt dropped anchor in Victoria Harbour, one day before Chiang Kai-shek ordered his 13th Army to march towards Hong Kong and reclaim the former British colony. The Japanese garrison offered no resistance and British marines soon took over all the strategic points on Hong Kong Island, and in Kowloon and the New Territories. The British established an interim government in the war-torn territory, freeing expatriate soldiers and civilians interned during the Japanese occupation, and rounding up Japanese soldiers for repatriation. Preoccupied with the civil war and giving in to pressure from Britain's ally, the United States, whose support it needed, the Nationalist government decided not to protest. If Chiang Kai-shek had insisted on reclaiming the territory, the history of Hong Kong would have been different.

On 19 September, the Japanese forces in Hong Kong formally surrendered to the British at Government House, the residence of successive colonial governors. The Royal Marine band dressed in Scottish kilts was assembled on the lawn with its instruments, and hundreds of British marine commandos in green berets stood in formation. Inside, Vice Admiral Ruitaro Fujita and Major General Umekichi Okada stood behind a small table bearing writing brushes and an ink slab. Rear Admiral Harcourt read the surrender document. Watched by military observers from the United States, China and Canada, the Japanese officers signed the document, handed over their swords, bowed stiffly from the waist, and were marched away. The band on the lawn struck up "God Save the King" and a seaman slowly hoisted the Union Jack to the top of the flag post. Simultaneously, the warships in Victoria Harbour fired thundering triumphal salutes and the Fleet Air Arm squadron roared overhead at low altitude.

When the Chinese troops arrived in Hong Kong, after the British forces had landed, there was not much for them to do. Awaiting orders, they camped in

Kowloon Tong just north of Boundary Street — the dividing line between the leased New Territories and the ceded areas of Kowloon Peninsula and Hong Kong Island. Kowloon Tong was an upper-income residential district and the soldiers took over many of the large mansions that had been vacated during the Japanese occupation. Since they had no official duties to perform and there was no agreement between the Chinese and British military authorities to confine them to their camps, the soldiers started to roam the streets to kill time. Hong Kong was excited at first about the arrival of the Chinese troops, but quickly became disillusioned by their arrogance and lack of discipline. When I returned to Hong Kong in November, I heard stories about the soldiers bullying local people and getting into fistfights with British sailors and marines. Chinese army vehicles defied traffic regulations, and a junior officer caught shoplifting in an Indian shop in Central was arrested and sent to jail. The Hong Kong people welcomed the Chinese troops as heroes when they first arrived, but saw them off with relief when they were recalled to China towards the end of 1945.

The irony of these events was not lost on those of us who had looked forward to Hong Kong's return to the motherland, and beneath our jubilation at the ending of the war lay a lingering tug of disappointment. The British later proclaimed 30 August as Hong Kong's Liberation Day, an annual holiday.

Home Sweet Home

As our elation subsided, the hard reality of rebuilding our home in a devastated economy started to sink in. Our family had splintered during the war: Tse Kwong and I left home soon after the Japanese occupation; after Father died (in 1943) Mother and Yuan Kwong went to Babu in Guangxi to stay with Aunt Rose; Man Kwong was the only one in our family who remained in Hong Kong throughout the hostilities, and he had to struggle to make ends meet.

Man Kwong's studies at Lingnan University were abruptly terminated when the Japanese invaded in 1941, and he had to support the family as Father's health rapidly deteriorated. Tall and handsome, Man Kwong was groomed to become the head of the family. His education in elite schools, Pui Ching and Lingnan, gave him a broad perspective, a solid personal network and good preparation for the business world. As the eldest son, Man Kwong was pampered by Mother and Father, not to mention *Poh Poh* (our maternal grandmother) who financed his education and showered him with gifts. Among the brothers, he was always the first to wear fine clothes, eat at expensive restaurants and enjoy the luxuries of life, and as he was always away from home as a boarding student he never had to do any work around the house. Unlike me, who had a very Westernized schooling at King's College, Man Kwong was educated in Chinese and was well versed in Chinese history and literature.

During the Japanese occupation, Man Kwong worked at Ming On, the edible oil dealership owned by Uncle Wai Chow. Knowing the firm's connection to Chan Lim Pak, who had collaborated with the Japanese, and remembering Father's unhappy experience working under Uncle, Man Kwong was at first reluctant to work there. However, jobs were hard to come by during the occupation, so he reluctantly took up a marketing and sales position at Ming On. As soon he had learned enough about the edible oil business, he left and set up his own shop — Tin Sang Edible Oil — in partnership with a Pui Ching classmate, Chan Chark Tong. By that time, Chan Lim Pak had died and his edible oil monopoly had disintegrated, so Tin Sang was able to buy and sell oil in the open market.

As the war drew to an end, business was slow and Tin Sang hardly made any profit, so to save money Man Kwong initially used Tin Sang's shop space on Wing Lok Street as both his office and living quarters. When Mother, Tse Kwong, Yuan Kwong and I made our separate ways back to Hong Kong after the war, Man Kwong had to find a place for us to stay, as well as other sources of income to support the family. He started an import-export business with another Pui Ching schoolmate, Hui Ka Wing, and his Eurasian friend William Shea, hoping to tap the strong demand for imported goods after the war. To attract foreign customers, they named the firm William & Co. With little capital, the company could afford to set up office only on the third floor of an old four-storey tenement house at 254 Des Voeux Road Central in Sheung Wan.

The premises were not designed for residential use, but Hui and Shea agreed to let Man Kwong use the back of the office as our family residence and, after some basic renovation work, we set up home in the rear section of the premises. Even though our living quarters were cramped and makeshift, we felt fortunate to have a roof over our heads considering the dire shortage of housing in Hong Kong after the war. The third floor of 254 Des Voeux Road Central was the last place where we lived together as a family.

Given the lack of living space, we had only the most basic furniture: a spring mattress bed for Mother, a small wardrobe, a dresser and a round table with five chairs. To maximize our living space, all my brothers and I slept on canvas cots which were folded up and stored underneath Mother's bed during the daytime. With the exception of Mother, we all had to go to bed late and get up early since the cots had to be set up at night and folded up in the morning.

The office had four desks grouped in pairs. One was for the office manager, Mr. Chiu, who was a retired shipping clerk in his late fifties; he had worked for American President Lines before the war and was familiar with import and export documentation. The other three desks were reserved for Man Kwong, Hui and Shea. Only Chiu's desk had a telephone, but we were allowed to use it when we had to make an urgent call, or if someone called us from outside stating that the call was important. In the evenings and on Sundays and holidays, we had free use of the desks for reading and writing.

Our kitchen had only the barest installations: a concrete sink shaped like a tray to catch tap water, a flat concrete slab used as a counter, and two round firewood stoves made of baked clay on top of a concrete bench. Dirty water from the sink drained through a metal pipe to an open gutter at the edge of the wall. Our cooking utensils were stored on a rack below the counter and firewood was piled up underneath the bench. Since there was no chimney, smoke from burning firewood and vapour from the frying pan were let out of the room through a small ventilating fan fixed on the window. But the fan was not effective, and our kitchen ceiling and walls quickly became greasy and then turned black as time went by. During April and May, when the humidity was high, we could see grease dripping from the ceiling and walls. To keep our food and utensils clean, we put them in a gauze cage the size of a small cabinet, with fresh vegetables, meat and fish on the upper shelves, and chinaware and dried foodstuffs on the lower ones. Refrigerators were not common then, and all the meat and fish had to be consumed within one or two days.

A small brick wall with a flimsy wooden door separated our kitchen from the latrine, which was no more than a trench holding an oblong metal trough which we covered with a wooden lid. For hygienic reasons and to dampen the smell we poured Lysol into the trough regularly, and every night, before going to bed, we would put the trough outside the door on the stairway for the "night soil" collectors. We bathed on the floor space in front of the kitchen sink and the counter, a process that could be very time consuming and cumbersome. We would fill a big wooden basin with water from the tap, place it on the counter, and pour water over ourselves with a small wooden bucket. Piped hot water was unheard of in the neighbourhood, so when the weather turned cold we would have to first boil hot water in a kettle and then mix it with cold water in the wooden basin.

Despite the hardships, we were grateful to have a place to stay. Before the Japanese invasion Hong Kong had a population of about 1.6 million, which dropped to around 600,000 at the time of Japan's surrender, but rose again to about one million at the end of 1945. The war had destroyed an untold number of buildings in Hong Kong, so an acute housing shortfall allowed landlords to charge exorbitant rentals. In an attempt to alleviate the problem, in 1947 the colonial government introduced the Landlord and Tenant Ordinance which placed all pre-war buildings under tight rent control, but landlords would get around the restrictions by collecting a sum of money upfront from the tenant before giving him the key to the leased premises and charging him the "controlled" rent. Those who were desperate for space and could afford it were willing to pay this premium, the so-called "key money", for which no receipt was required since it was not governed by the ordinance. Moreover, if the tenant had to go through a middleman he would have to pay him a commission, commonly known as "shoe money" as the middleman usually had to walk to and fro between the prospective tenant and the landlord in order to conclude the deal. There was no legal requirement for a receipt for the payment of "shoe money" either. We were in no position to pay "key money" or "shoe money", and we might well have been homeless had Man Kwong not started up William & Co. and secured the office space in which the family could live.

Despite the cramped living quarters, we were happy to be together again. We missed Father, but we felt fortunate that the rest of us had survived the war and we were determined to rebuild a normal life. Man Kwong worked long hours at his businesses, but the economy was still recovering from the war and he was barely able to make ends meet. To help with household expenses, both Tse Kwong and I looked for work. Yuan Kwong, who was only fourteen, went back to school, enrolling first at Lingnan Secondary School and later at LaSalle College. As none of us completed our formal education, we were happy that Yuan Kwong at least could continue his studies.

With my wartime training and experience, I had little problem finding a job. I worked for a few months as a junior clerk in one of the government offices of the Colonial Secretariat. Then, hoping to leverage my experience working for the Americans during the war, and remembering Father's wishes for me to enter banking, I wrote to the First National City Bank of New York (now Citibank) on the off chance that they might have a job opening. To my surprise, I soon received a reply — not a job offer, but an introduction to a Mr. Cooper at Dodwell Motors Ltd. Dodwell Motors was part of a large British trading conglomerate — Dodwell & Company Ltd. — and distributed both British and American cars such as Morris, Chrysler and Dodge. Cooper, the general manager, was an American which probably explained why I obtained the introduction and managed to secure a position as his secretary.

Tse Kwong joined Aunt Rose and Uncle Leung's auto accessories company, Kung Lee, which had re-started its operations in Hong Kong. Tse Kwong had to undertake a wide range of tasks at Kung Lee, from clerical and accounting work to unloading goods in the wharfs and delivering them. Like many other lower-level positions in Hong Kong at that time, the hours were long and the pay was meagre. Fortunately, Tse Kwong had the strongest physique among us and was always very independent and self-reliant. At home he would do most of the housework, such as sweeping the floor, wiping the walls and chopping firewood. I helped him whenever I could, but I was slim and had the smallest build among all my brothers. As I was also the only one who wore glasses, Mother was very surprised that I ended up in the army during the war.

Despite our frugal living conditions during those early post-war years, we managed to enjoy life together as a family: Mother kept house, Man Kwong tended to his businesses, Tse Kwong and I were able to support ourselves, and Yuan Kwong continued with his studies. Although Hong Kong's economy was still recovering and the civil war raged on in the Mainland, we were contented with our lives and could have continued to live in peace. But soon, the political situation in China took a sharp turn; Hong Kong was swept up in its throes, and our family was engulfed with it.

Joining the Revolution

By 1948, it had become increasingly clear that the Chinese Communist Party (CCP) was winning the civil war. Although Hong Kong was not directly involved in the war, the presence of the CCP was growing in the colony. The CCP had pursued a United Front strategy during the Anti-Japanese War, forging alliances with people of all parties, factions, classes and walks of life and even, for a period, joining forces with the Nationalist government against the Japanese. This strategy gained it support among the students and intellectuals who had grown increasingly disillusioned with the Nationalist government.

After the war, the CCP continued to pursue its United Front strategy in the fight against the Nationalists, and tried to appeal to a wide range of people by promising social and economic justice and a more democratic society. Its message was particularly well received among students, intellectuals and all those who were critical of the corruption, incompetence and autocratic rule of the Nationalist government. In search of an alternative path to building a strong, more equitable China, many people read Mao Zedong's writings (such as *On New Democracy*) and thought that they had found the answer in the Communist Party.

In this environment Hong Kong became an important centre for the CCP's United Front work after the war. Many intellectuals from the Mainland, including journalists, academics, writers and artists, had taken refuge in the colony to escape the Japanese invasion and, for some, persecution by the Nationalist government. The famed educator Cai Yuanpei and writers Xu Dishan and Xiao Hong lived in Hong Kong for a period but died before the war ended; others who stayed in the colony during the civil war included well-known writers Mao Dun and Xia Yan, renowned scholars Liang Shuming and Guo Morou, and the prominent journalist Xiao Qian. With the presence of such literary and scholastic talents, many magazines, newspapers, cultural centres and educational facilities sprang up in Hong Kong after the war. Quite a number of these publications and institutions reported to the CCP, however, and they often invited well-known writers and artists who were either sympathetic to or affiliated with the CCP to join, hoping to attract a wide audience for the party's United Front and recruitment activities.

In early 1948 Tse Kwong joined such an institution — the Chung Wah Music Academy. Under Man Kwong's influence, he had developed a passion for Western classical music and wanted to study music theory and composition under Ma Sicong, an internationally known violinist and composer, who headed the academy. (Ma later returned to China in 1950 to head up the Central Conservatory in Beijing, but left the country for the US in 1967, at the start of the Cultural Revolution.) Ma's presence at Chung Wah at that time attracted many music lovers, including Tse Kwong, to the school, but the academy was actually a fringe organization of the Cultural Committee of the underground Communist Party.

Tse Kwong began to stay at Chung Wah later and later each evening, and at first we thought that he was just catching up with his lessons and friends. Then he told us that teachers and students at the academy had formed "study groups" and he would be staying late on a regular basis to attend their meetings. Tse Kwong was active and well liked, and quickly became the president of the student union. Although he completed only three years of secondary school, Tse Kwong read avidly and became very proficient in written Chinese; he also possessed strong analytical abilities and was an extremely persuasive speaker.

I became curious about what Tse Kwong did in his "study group". As we had always been very close, Tse Kwong had no reservations in telling me what they read and would even bring home some of the materials to show me, starting with newspaper articles and editorials. The newspapers they read most often were *Hwa Sheung Po* and *Cheng Bao* — which were both affiliated with the CCP. *Hwa Sheung Po*, which boasted a star-studded list of editors and contributors, including many well-known writers and scholars from the Mainland, was particularly popular among young intellectuals. Later, Tse Kwong started bringing back books on philosophy, social development, communism and "New Democracy". He would share his readings and thoughts with me before we went to sleep, and under his influence my reading habits started to change. As well as my regular English newspapers and magazines such as the *South China Morning Post* and *Time Magazine*, I started to read *Hwa Sheung Po* and some of the books that Tse Kwong brought home.

Tse Kwong had the least formal education among all the brothers and only completed Year Three at King's College. At that stage, Father could no longer afford the ten dollars a month that he had to pay for tuition at King's, so he took Tse Kwong out and enrolled him at the Junior Technical School at Morrison Hill which cost only three dollars a month. Tse Kwong learned carpentry and frequently had to work as an apprentice boat maker along the wharfs.

"I had to interact daily with day labourers and coolies on the wharfs," he told me one night as we lay on our cots, "and that was when I first came into contact with people from lower-income groups."

It was a hot summer night and neither of us could sleep. Since his cot was next to mine, we started whispering to each other and I asked him how he first became interested in socialist ideas.

"I was struck by how hard life was for the labourers and how privileged we had been," he said. "Then when I went to Guangxi with Aunt Rose, I was shocked to see that so many people in the countryside were dirt poor. Many were starving and some could not even afford clothes for their children. I'm sure you saw that too."

Tse Kwong left home at sixteen to follow Aunt Rose and Uncle Leung to Liuzhou, Guangxi soon after the start of the Japanese occupation, and later worked in Fook Lee (their auto accessories company). Business was good since auto parts were scarce during the war, but the company operated for only a few years. In 1944, the Nationalist army retreated from Guangxi as the Japanese army advanced towards Guilin and Liuzhou, the province's major cities. The retreat was disorderly and as everyone in the two cities tried to flee many families were split up and lost contact. Aunt Rose and her son Nai Hei took refuge in Babu, a small city to the east of Liuzhou, where they were later joined by Mother and Yuan Kwong who came to live with them after Father passed away.

Tse Kwong stayed with Uncle Leung. After selling his business, Uncle Leung acquired some gold bars which he wanted to sell in Guiyang, the capital of neighbouring Guizhou Province. Since bandits regularly roamed the Guizhou-Guangxi border and attacked trains at will, Uncle Leung did not dare to carry the gold with him on the train, so he asked Tse Kwong and another Fook Lee employee to take them to Guiyang for him.

"We strapped the gold bars to our waists underneath our shirts," Tse Kwong said with a laugh. He still seemed to be thrilled by their bravado. "We then spent days travelling to Guiyang, catching rides on trucks whenever we could and spending our nights in the countryside."

"Uncle Leung paid me a big bonus after he sold the gold bars," Tse Kwong said, and I could almost see his grin in the dark.

Tse Kwong used the money to start up a bookstore in Liuzhou selling books and newspapers. Soon, he noticed that he was receiving an unusually large delivery of *Xinhua Ribao* (New China Daily) everyday, free of charge; this attracted his attention and he began to read the newspaper more closely.

"The paper gave good up-to-date coverage of the war," he said, "but I was also attracted by its editorials and commentaries which called for national unity against the Japanese and greater social justice. They often exposed the plight of the poor while criticizing the corruption of the Nationalist government."

"I really liked what they had to say," Tse Kwong said excitedly, forgetting to keep his voice down.

Xinhua Ribao was then run by the CCP out of Chongqing, the Nationalist government's wartime capital. The United Front formed between the Nationalists and the Communists during this period allowed the paper to be published and circulated in unoccupied areas.

Tse Kwong used up all his money on the bookstore, and made his way back to Hong Kong as the war ended. He went to work again for Aunt Rose and Uncle Leung, who had also returned to Hong Kong, but managed to keep up his interests in socialist ideas. He was always eager to share his thoughts with me, and I was a sympathetic listener since I had experienced similar disappointments with the Nationalist government during the war. I too was shocked at the vast disparity of wealth on the Mainland, and could understand how Tse Kwong felt.

Tse Kwong participated enthusiastically in the activities of Chung Wah Music Academy. After he was elected student union president, he became imbued with a sense of mission and wanted to share his vision with his relatives and friends. He spoke with me often about his ideas and lost no time in involving our youngest brother, Yuan Kwong. One of Tse Kwong's friends from Chung Wah ran the Rainbow Chorus, another fringe organization of the underground CCP. When the group started recruiting new members, targeting secondary school students, Tse Kwong introduced Yuan Kwong to his friend.

Yuan Kwong had always been the dreamer of the family, and was often spoiled by Mother since he was the youngest child. Of all the brothers, he resembled Father most in his physique and facial features: tall and slim, with large, dark and deep-set eyes. Unlike Father, however, he was talkative and impulsive — an easy target for youth groups with a political agenda.

Rainbow Chorus met almost nightly at Sham Shui Po in Kowloon. Yuan Kwong, then studying in La Salle College in Kowloon, was attracted by the chorus and its various activities. Every weekday he would first come home from La Salle and then, after dinner, take the ferry back to Kowloon to attend the Rainbow Chorus activities. It was a long journey but Yuan Kwong was an enthusiastic participant who soon joined the chorus' "study group" and became a regular reader of *Hwa Sheung Po* and other publications sympathetic to the Communist cause.

Yuan Kwong's participation in the Rainbow Chorus was further encouraged by the activism of one of his close friends, Uncle Leung's nephew Leung Nai Ying. Yuan Kwong and Nai Hei (who were around twelve) and Nai Ying (who was one year older) were playmates when they lived in Babu, Guangxi during the war. After the war ended, Nai Ying followed Uncle Leung to Hong Kong, where he also worked at Kung Lee. Nai Ying soon became an active member of the Rainbow Chorus, left Kung Lee and devoted himself full time to the group's activities. His role in the Rainbow Chorus became so prominent that he caught the attention of the Royal Hong Kong Police Special Branch, the arm of the police dedicated to monitoring political activities. Nai Ying was not born in Hong Kong and, like many other active members of the underground party and its fringe organizations who were not Hong Kong citizens, he was arrested, charged and deported to the Mainland in mid-1949.

Although I did not belong to any formal organization, I attended lectures and concerts with Tse Kwong and Yuan Kwong, and joined in many of their activities. Some of the most impressive talks I heard were by Qiao Guanhua — a brilliant journalist fluent in both German and English, with a German doctorate degree. His lectures on journalism and on political and economic developments in China and the world captured the hearts and minds of many Hong Kong students and intellectuals. Qiao subsequently left his teaching job to become the director of the Hong Kong Branch of Xinhua (New China) News Agency — the Chinese Communist government's *de facto* representative office in Hong Kong. Later, he was re-assigned to the Ministry of Foreign Affairs and eventually became foreign minister. Qiao's first wife Gong Peng was with him in Hong Kong at that time; she was the editor of the bi-weekly English publication *China Today*, which enjoyed a wide readership.

In order to learn more about New China — a term that the CCP used for the country now undergoing "socialist construction", I followed Tse Kwong and Yuan Kwong to bookstores to look through books and magazines published by Xinhua Bookstore and the Foreign Language Press of Beijing. *China Today* and *China Reconstructs* were popular among those of us who were trying to catch a glimpse of New China. When we were in a more serious mood we would look for books on social theories and development, and the most studious readers would tackle the works of Marx, Lenin, Stalin and Mao Zedong. The bookstores we frequented included Commercial Press, Joint Publishing Company, Hwa Sheung, New Democracy Press, and Apollo (Chi Yuen), all of which were either affiliated with the CCP or sympathetic to the Communist cause. We would take books down from their shelves and read them while standing in the aisles, and often returning the next day (and even the day after) to finish where we left off. We were not the only ones, and as long as we kept the books in good order and returned them to the shelves the bookstore staff did not seem to mind. Only after we were sure we really wanted to keep the books would we buy them.

During this period, books and newspapers of various descriptions and ideologies flourished in Hong Kong, mirroring the civil war on the Mainland and amplifying messages from both sides. Aside from *Hwa Sheung Po* and *Cheng Bao*, the socialist camp was bolstered by *Wen Wei Po* and *Ta Kung Pao* where staunch pro-communist viewpoints had replaced previously more moderate positions.

The pro-Communist newspapers also quoted widely from Xinhua News Agency, and would use terms such as "progressive", "democratic", "revolutionary" and "patriotic" in line with their United Front strategy.

Newspapers in the Nationalist camp, on the other hand, relied on the Central News Agency for their news reports and often emphasized their side as representing freedom: thus Free China, free labour unions, free merchant associations and free schools. The *National Times* was a mouthpiece of the Nationalist government. Its views were echoed by *The Kung Sheung Daily News* published by Nationalist General Ho Sai Lai, the son of Robert Hotung who had been the former chief comprador of Jardine Matheson and one of the richest persons in Hong Kong. The Nationalist camp was reinforced by a growing number of refugees from the Mainland, many of whom were staunchly anti-communist. Starting in the late 1940s and throughout the next two decades, Nationalist flags were often hoisted in makeshift squatter huts on the hillsides or in the "resettlement" housing estates throughout Kowloon where many of the refugees lived.

In the middle of the spectrum were a host of supposedly more objective, "neutral" newspapers appealing to those who did not want to take either side. Prime examples were *Sing Tao Jih Pao* and *Wah Kiu Yat Po*. *Sing Tao* was published by the Aw family, which made its fortune in Singapore and Malaysia. *Wah Kiu*, the second oldest newspaper in Hong Kong, was noted for its conservative stance and support of the "establishment": at first the British colonial government, then the government of the Occupied Territory of Hong Kong, and again the colonial government after the war.

With this myriad of publications competing for our attention, I tried to read a wide range of newspapers and books and attempted to keep an open mind. What later struck me as strange was that the pro-communist camp which called itself "democratic" never saw the need to uphold individual freedom, while the Nationalist camp which prided itself on representing "freedom" never thought to advocate democracy.

Aside from my many reading sources, I was also deeply affected by some of the realist and more progressive Chinese films shown in Hong Kong during this period. Pictures such as *Eight Thousand Miles of Cloud and Moon* and *A River of Spring Water Flowing to the East* depicted patriotism and sufferings during the Anti-Japanese War and the economic plight and disappointment among the middle class and intellectuals after the war ended. Other films were based on the writings of well-known authors such as Lu Xun's *The True Story of Ah Q* and Ba Jin's *Family, Spring,* and *Autumn* trilogy. These movies, which challenged feudal traditions and criticized social and economic injustice, captured the hearts and minds of many cinema-goers and made a deep impression on me, helping to shape my thoughts concerning China.

On balance, given the patriotism that the Anti-Japanese War instilled in me and my deplorable experience with the Nationalist government on the Mainland, I was sympathetic to the views of the pro-communist media. Man Kwong was less in favour, but he understood the feelings of his brothers and refrained from interfering in our activities. He did remark to me, however, that Tse Kwong was becoming less and less enthusiastic about his work at Kung Lee, and Yuan Kwong was increasingly distracted from his schoolwork.

None of us knew then the extent of Tse Kwong's convictions, or that he was so strongly committed to his beliefs that he had decided to join the Communist Party. Only much later, as we reminisced about that decisive period in our lives when ideologies and destinies were shaped, would Tse Kwong tell me about his dramatic encounters.

"First I had to write a detailed autobiography about my family, my education and my work experiences, and what I did during the war," he said. "Then I had to write about my thoughts and how I came to believe in Communism."

"It was all done in secrecy, like in the movies," he recalled with a smile. "I met up with a middle-aged senior member of the underground party in Central. We walked around the block several times, strolling along Queen's Road and Des Voeux Road Central and the small lanes in between. We talked about what I wrote and he would ask me questions, while looking around from time to time to make sure that we were not attracting too much attention. Finally, we ended up having afternoon tea at On Lok Yuen Restaurant and he told me that I would be accepted into the Party."

As a new party member, Tse Kwong was so eager to commit himself to the revolution that when his teachers and schoolmates started to leave for Guangzhou in mid 1949 to prepare for the Communist takeover, he decided to join them and declined Chung Wah's request for him to stay behind in Hong Kong to take charge of the school.

One early September evening when we were setting up our cots for the night, Tse Kwong announced that he would be leaving for Guangzhou to join the revolution. Man Kwong and I were speechless and could only stare at him blankly. We were not at all sure whether or not he was doing the right thing, but at the same time we did not know what the right thing was. We were definitely disappointed with the Nationalists and wished that they would be replaced, but we were not convinced that Communism was the right answer. Although the CCP was active during the Anti-Japanese War and seemed to be effective in rallying the people, we felt that its policies were untested during peacetime. Besides, all we had learned about socialism and communism was from books, and not from experience in real life.

"Don't rush into this," Man Kwong said, trying to hold down his quick temper and reason with Tse Kwong. "You don't really know what will happen once the Communists take over."

"Why don't you wait and see," I hastened to add.

"The Communist Party fights for greater justice and equality among the people," Tse Kwong said calmly. "Isn't this what we want for China? Most people are behind the Party. If it doesn't have the people's support, how come it's winning the civil war?"

"I support Fourth Brother's move," Yuan Kwong said excitedly. "If everyone just waits and sees, who's going to rebuild China?"

"Our country needs us now, not later," Tse Kwong insisted.

"My mind is made up," he said finally, trying to put an end to the argument. "I'll be leaving soon."

Mother was angry at first, then she burst into tears and begged him to stay. We stood by helplessly and did our best to console her.

In early September 1949, soon after his twenty-third birthday, Tse Kwong resigned from Kung Lee and told Aunt Rose and Uncle Leung that he was moving to Tianjin for further studies. Seeing that Tse Kwong's mind was made up and there was not much we could do, Man Kwong and I gave him a watch and whatever money we could spare, and sent him off with words of caution and encouragement.

Tse Kwong left home and made his way to Ma Liu Shui in the New Territories, where he boarded a small boat and landed in Huizhou on the coast of Guangdong Province before making his way to Guangzhou under cover. As the Fourth Field Army of the People's Liberation Army entered Guangzhou in October, Tse Kwong became part of the Takeover Committee.

Yuan Kwong followed in his footsteps. Through his involvement with the Rainbow Chorus, he was recruited into the New Democratic Youth League of the underground party in early September the same year. Towards the end of the month, a few weeks after Tse Kwong had left, Yuan Kwong told us about his decision to follow suit. We probably should have expected this but were nevertheless taken aback.

"You're still too young," Man Kwong said. "Why don't you finish your studies first and go to university."

"I can't miss this opportunity to serve my country," Yuan Kwong insisted. "Besides, I can always go to university on the Mainland. Many people have done so, including you."

When Yuan Kwong broke the news to Mother, she became almost hysterical. If she were upset at Tse Kwong's departure, she was completely devastated by Yuan Kwong's decision.

"Do you all know how hard we have tried to keep this family together after the war?" she shouted, bursting into tears. "Your father's passing already pierced my heart. The four of you are like my bone and flesh. And now you want to tear them apart too?"

Man Kwong and I were paralyzed by her words. We tried to go through all the arguments with Yuan Kwong again, until there was not much more we could say. I felt sad and completely helpless. In the end, we also gave him a watch and some money and saw him off with our blessings.

Yuan Kwong "smuggled" himself back to Guangdong along a similar route and joined the South China Art Ensemble — a troupe of 129 youths from Hong Kong and Southeast Asia. Their mission was to prepare the people for the "liberation" of Guangdong. On 14 October 1949, when Communist troops entered Guangzhou, Yuan Kwong was among the troupes that performed dances and songs on the city streets to welcome them. He was only seventeen.

Mother wept for days and refused to be consoled for many weeks after Yuan Kwong left. Man Kwong and I tried to keep an open mind; even though we were both worried and sceptical, the political situation on the Mainland was so confusing that we were not entirely convinced that Tse Kwong and Yuan Kwong were taking the wrong path. In fact, we were not even certain that Communist troops would not march across the border and take over Hong Kong.

By October 1949, the CCP had taken control of the Mainland and established the People's Republic of China (PRC). The defeated Nationalist government moved to Taiwan and continued to call itself the Republic of China (ROC). Hong Kong in the meantime remained a British colony — the CCP reportedly, and correctly, saw some strategic value in keeping the status quo — and Macao remained a Portuguese colony. The Chinese people in their homeland were thus divided into four parts along geographical, historical, political and ideological lines.

Despite our anguish at the departure of our younger brothers, it later became apparent that our family was among the more fortunate ones; although we had differences in our political views, we respected each other's beliefs. Many other families in Hong Kong would be tragically torn apart by the ideological differences between couples, among siblings, and between parents and their children, many of whom would never speak to each other or see each other again.

My other relatives in Hong Kong were also caught in the growing ideological divide. Some of them took the path of Tse Kwong and Yuan Kwong and went back to the Mainland to join the revolution, including Aunt Rose's son Nai Hei and two of Uncle Wai Chow's sons, Sai Kwong and Hung Kwong.

After returning from Babu after the war, Nai Hei completed his studies at Lingnan Secondary School and went on to attend Queen's College. After passing the Hong Kong Government School Leaving Examination in 1950, however, he enrolled in Lingnan University in Guangzhou, which was then already under Communist rule. Like Tse Kwong and Yuan Kwong, he was attracted by the vision of a strong, egalitarian and independent China under the Communist Party and decided that he no longer wanted to live under British colonial rule.

Sai Kwong, Uncle Wai Chow's eldest surviving son, was also attracted by the promises of the CCP and went back to Guangxi in 1958. After the war, Uncle Wai Chow started up his banking business once again, trading gold under the Ming On name while continuing his edible oil business under another licence, Ming Fat. Sai Kwong helped out with his father's businesses after he returned to Hong Kong at the end of the war, but during his stay in Guangxi he too had become disillusioned with the Nationalist government. Under Tse Kwong's influence, he started to attend the activities sponsored by the underground party, such as the lectures by Qiao Guanhua and studies of Mao's *On New Democracy*, and took writing classes taught by well-known mainland writers who were often affiliated with the CCP. After Uncle Wai Chow's gold trading business collapsed in 1957, again from over-speculation, Sai Kwong moved with his family to Nanning, Guangxi (his wife's native city) and found work in the finance department of the city's Chinese medical hospital.

Under Sai Kwong's influence, many of his younger siblings studied at the pro-PRC Hon Wah Middle School, which was constructed on the site of our old mansion on Ching Lin Terrace. His younger brother Hung Kwong went on to attend university on the Mainland and was assigned to Hunan Normal University in Changsha, Hunan Province.

Thus we all took different paths. Over the next three decades, during the course of China's numerous political campaigns and social and economic upheavals, I often became frustrated in thinking how different their lives would have been if my brothers and cousins had remained in Hong Kong. The image of their hardships on the Mainland and my thoughts of what could have been would haunt me for many years to come.

Starting Life in New China

Yuan Kwong began his revolutionary career on the Mainland by playing small parts in such well-known plays as *The White-Haired Girl* and *Wang Xiu Ying*, both depicting the plight of peasants under the old society and their new lives after the revolution. After the liberation of Guangzhou, the South China Art Ensemble split into three smaller groups and spread out to different parts of the province. The favourite slogan of the Ensemble at that time was: "Work hard. Study hard. Go to where our motherland needs us most." Yuan Kwong was assigned to the Xijiang Art Troupe and worked in Zhaoqing for six years.

At first he continued to act in plays publicizing the new government's policies and intended to educate the masses, and one of his more prominent roles was in November 1951 as South Korean President Syngman Rhee in a play about the Korean War. In 1952, he was assigned to a new position as manager of the People's Cinema of Gaoyao County, which mostly showed Soviet and Eastern European films.

Even though he was only a junior cadre, Yuan Kwong could not avoid being embroiled in political campaigns during his six years in Zhaoqing. During the Three-Anti and Five-Anti Campaigns targeting government officials and capitalists in 1951–52, he was criticized for employing a former Nationalist official in his cinema. Yuan Kwong tried to defend himself, but much to his disappointment he was re-assigned to a cloth factory during the subsequent Cooperatives Campaign of 1953–54.

"I really saw nothing wrong with what I did," he insisted when he told us about this ordeal much later. "That person was fully capable and did his job."

On the whole, however, Yuan Kwong was not seriously affected by the numerous political campaigns of the 1950s since he was relatively junior and had a "clean" family background. Nevertheless, when he finally wrote to us in 1956 that the Gaoyao County leadership had recommended him to attend Peking University under the government's "Outstanding Young Cadre Education Scheme", we collectively heaved a sigh of relief and heartily congratulated him on this opportunity to enrol in the country's most prestigious university. Yuan Kwong first studied Russian at the university, but switched to the Department of Chinese Literature during his second year when he discovered that there was a surplus of Russian language students. He graduated in 1961 and was the only university graduate in our family.

Since Yuan Kwong had left home as a teenager, Mother, Man Kwong and I continued to worry about him much more than about Tse Kwong. When he graduated, we hoped that he would be assigned to Guangzhou so that he could be near Tse Kwong and closer to Hong Kong, but unfortunately the quota for new postings to Guangzhou was full. As his second choice, Yuan Kwong decided to go to Nanning to be near our cousin Sai Kwong, where he was assigned a position at the Drama Research Department of Guangxi's Cultural Bureau. We were truly happy that he finally seemed to be well settled and launched on a career; but we had no inkling of the dangers ahead.

Tse Kwong also worked in the cultural field after the liberation of Guangzhou. At first he helped the new government take over and manage a cinema and an art institute; then he was assigned to the Provincial Cultural Bureau and given the important task of leading the reform of Cantonese Opera. Working as a political instructor at the opera troupes under the provincial government, he met and later married Lee Yim Sheung, a handsome opera singer from Hong Kong who specialized in playing young male roles.

In the summer of 1955, Tse Kwong suddenly came back to Hong Kong. By that time I was the only family member still in the colony as Man Kwong had married and moved to Singapore with his young family, and Mother had joined them. I was then living alone in a bachelor's apartment in Causeway Bay, and going to work at Dodwell Motors. One hot humid evening, as I was preparing to go out for dinner, there was a quick knock on the door. I opened it and was overjoyed to find Tse Kwong standing in the doorway.

"Shh…" he said, touching his lips with his finger. "Don't tell anyone I'm back."

He had returned to Hong Kong on a PRC government–issued return permit to carry out an undercover mission to persuade two of China's best-known Cantonese Opera singers, Ma Shizeng and his wife Hong Xiannu, to go to the Mainland and help reform Cantonese Opera. Tse Kwong was to accompany them, and this was probably the most dramatic assignment that he ever undertook.

I knew very little about his mission at the time. Tse Kwong would leave my apartment early in the morning and return late in the evening, so we had time for a quick heart-to-heart talk only when I could catch him for dinner or before we went to bed. He told me the details of his mission only much later.

"Xinhua had a small office above a photo studio on Nathan Road," Tse Kwong recalled with a shine in his eyes. "I knocked on the office door. When it opened, I gave the receptionist my password: 'I want to buy books'. He then handed me five hundred dollars for my expenses in Hong Kong."

Tse Kwong met Ma Shizeng over an elaborate dinner hosted by Dr. Liu Yan Tak who was well known for his PRC connections. Liu was the family doctor of He Xiangning, the widow of Liao Zhongkai, a key figure of the Nationalist Party, and maintained close relationship with her son Liao Chengzhi who was a high-ranking PRC official. (Liao headed the CCP's United Front Department and later took charge of Hong Kong and Macao Affairs at the central government.)

"We discussed the government's vision for Cantonese Opera reform and how much he could contribute if he were to go back," Tse Kwong said. "Ma was initially quite hesitant."

They negotiated terms over the dinner table until late in the evening. Tse Kwong eventually persuaded Ma to move to the Mainland and to leave with him via Macao within a few days. Unfortunately for Tse Kwong, Hong Xiannu was at that time performing in Singapore and he could not speak with her. On the morning of the agreed departure date, Tse Kwong arrived early at Ma's house on Shan Kwong Road in Happy Valley to pick up his luggage and take them by car to the Macao Ferry. In the afternoon, however, Ma got in touch with Tse Kwong and said that he wanted to think things over, so Tse Kwong had to move the luggage back to Ma's house. After waiting in vain for a week, Tse Kwong returned to Guangzhou through Macao.

Several weeks later, Tse Kwong came back to Hong Kong to talk to Ma again. This time, Ma made it clear that he wanted to wait for Hong Xiannu to come back before making a decision. So again, Tse Kwong had to go back to Guangzhou empty-handed. The breakthrough finally came in October that year, when Premier Chou Enlai invited both Ma and Hong to the National Day celebration in Beijing and greeted them with great publicity and fanfare. With such high-level persuasion, Ma finally made up his mind to move to the Mainland. After Ma and Hong returned to Hong Kong, Xinhua officials made arrangements for their entire family (including their two sons and daughter) to take the train to the border with Shenzhen, where Tse Kwong was on hand to greet them when they walked across the border.

The return of Ma Shizeng and Hong Xiannu to the Mainland caused a big stir in Hong Kong and scored a major victory for the PRC. Ma was given the post of Head of the Guangdong Cantonese Opera Troupe and Hong continued to perform as well as teach. Ma dedicated himself to opera reform until his death in 1964; Hong's career lasted much longer. Despite persecutions during the Cultural Revolution, her expert performance and contribution to Cantonese Opera remained widely recognized. Admitted to the CCP in 1963, she became Guangdong's representative to the Chinese People's Political Consultative Conference and the National People's Congress during various periods.

After his two visits to meet Ma Shizeng, Tse Kwong came to Hong Kong one more time to meet and accompany another well-known Cantonese Opera singer, Gui Mingyang, back to China. That was the last time I saw him for almost twenty years.

A committed party member, Tse Kwong's career was relatively smooth in the early years. During the Three-Anti and Five-Anti Campaigns he was falsely accused of stealing some fluorescent lights from a room in the cinema he managed and was "isolated for investigation" for several months, but his name was later cleared. During the Anti-Rightist Campaign in 1957, which incriminated over five hundred thousand intellectuals and officials, Tse Kwong also managed to steer clear of various accusations against him. Even after the Great Leap Forward in 1958–60, when China's economy collapsed, Tse Kwong and his family were able to pull through, with food and clothing that Mother and Aunt Rose carried across the border to them by train.

Despite the political turbulence and economic hardships of the 1950s, Tse Kwong had remained fully committed to his work and the Party. He was promoted to deputy chief of the Cultural Bureau's Arts Section in 1960 for his work with the Cantonese Opera troupes and his missions to Hong Kong. It was not until the start of the Cultural Revolution in 1966 that he and his family were swept up in the nationwide political turmoil and he had to re-evaluate his beliefs.

Of all my relatives who went back to mainland China after the war, only Nai Hei left before the Cultural Revolution and managed to escape its ravages. In the midst of the Korean War in 1952, Nai Hei was selected to attend the People's Liberation Army (PLA) Air Force Cadre Training School and served in the air force until 1955, when he went back to Lingnan University to continue his studies. He came back to Hong Kong briefly in 1957 when Uncle Leung passed away. After the funeral, Aunt Rose tried to stop him from returning to the Mainland by hiding his travel documents and begging him to stay, much to his consternation. Nai Hei finally agreed not to go back when Aunt Rose promised to send him to study overseas. He left for Europe and enrolled in the National University of Ireland in 1960. Later he moved to England, obtained a PhD in biochemistry at Bradford University and stayed on as a researcher with Unilever. He was one of the few fortunate ones.

At the Crossroads of Life

After Tse Kwong and Yuan Kwong left for the Mainland in the autumn of 1949, I felt inspired by their patriotism and revolutionary zeal and started to think that I too ought to contribute to China's "socialist construction". Hoping to find a way, I spoke with friends and acquaintances who I knew to be patriotic and progressive, including some of my wartime interpreter comrades and former King's College schoolmates. On their recommendation, I enrolled in the Foreign Language Department of Nan Fang College to study Russian — the foreign language then most in demand in New China.

Nan Fang catered mainly to white-collar workers who could attend classes only in the evenings, after work, and those who could not enter university because they had not completed secondary school or achieved the necessary grades. There were four departments: Literature and Arts, Journalism, Economics and Accounting, and Foreign Languages. Nan Fang was also affiliated with the CCP but, unlike at Chung Wah and the Rainbow Chorus, its activities were not overtly political. Moreover, even though it was founded by mainland educators, the school also had strong local participation. Two prominent local academics sat on the school board: Professor Ma Kam and Senior Lecturer Chan Kwan Po, both of the Department of Chinese at the University of Hong Kong. Ma Kam's son, Ma Lin, was the vice-chancellor of the Chinese University of Hong Kong from 1978 to 1987.

The principals and many of the lecturers at Nan Fang were noted academics who were disillusioned with the Nationalist government and sympathized with the Communists. Many had come to Hong Kong to escape Nationalist persecution on the Mainland. My Russian teacher, Mr. Liu, for example, was a member of the CCP and had been sent by the Party to study at the University of Moscow. I attended classes in Nan Fang in the evenings, after a day at work at Dodwell Motors, and met many like-minded students with whom I would often discuss developments in New China after class.

Towards the end of 1951 Nan Fang had to close down because many of its teachers and students had gone to the Mainland and the colonial government was increasingly wary of the underground activities of the CCP. Some of the students went on to enrol in Nan Fang University in Guangzhou, which was a cadre training school. I was tempted to join them but had some reservations. Employment was not easy to find during the post-war years and I was not keen to give up my job at Dodwell. Also, while I wanted to serve my country, I did not possess the strong faith in the Communist Party that guided both Tse Kwong and Yuan Kwong. I discussed my options with my friends at Nan Fang, and they convinced me that since I had a good command of English and worked well with both the British and the Americans, I would be more useful to China if I were to stay and monitor international affairs from Hong Kong's vantage point. The time to contribute to China would come, they said. I accepted their reasoning and stayed, thereby taking a separate path from those of Tse Kwong and Yuan Kwong and headed toward an entirely different destiny.

That same year, Man Kwong took yet another path and decided to pursue his career overseas. He had closed down his businesses at the end of 1949 and joined Dah Chong Hong, a local trading company affiliated with Hang Seng Bank, through the introduction of a Pui Ching classmate. Assured of a good job and steady income, Man Kwong rented a flat at 3 Mosque Junction on the Mid-Levels and married Wong Wai Ying (Amy), our neighbour and childhood friend from Ching Lin Terrace. Mother and I moved in with them. The flat was a major upgrade from the back office space at 254 Des Voeux Road Central, but we did not live there for long as Man Kwong soon had an opportunity to work overseas.

In early 1951, Dah Chong Hong decided to send Man Kwong to set up a branch in Singapore in order to expand its business into Southeast Asia. Leung Kau Kui, the managing director, asked him to apply for a British passport so that he could travel freely within the region. Man Kwong was greatly excited by the opportunity, but he immediately stumbled upon an obstacle: Mother had lost his birth certificate during the war, and without it he could not qualify for a British passport. In desperation Man Kwong appealed to Fourteenth Uncle Tang Shiu Kin who, in his capacity as a Justice of the Peace, would be able to certify that he was indeed born in Hong Kong. Unfortunately, Uncle Shiu Kin's response was lukewarm. Then Aunt Rose, after consulting with a friend at a law office, came up with a daring idea. Mother had found the birth certificate of our eldest brother Iu Kwong, who died in infancy, so Aunt Rose suggested that Mother take an oath to say that Man Kwong also went by the name of Iu Kwong; Man Kwong could then use this birth certificate to apply for a British passport. The scheme worked and Man Kwong was thereafter known in all his legal documents and business dealings as Iu Kwong.

Man Kwong left Hong Kong for Singapore in the summer of 1951, accompanied by his wife Amy and their new-born son, Cheuk. Mother also went with them and stayed in Singapore until 1958 when she returned to Hong Kong to live with me. Before they left, Mother took Man Kwong to call on Uncle Wai Chow to pay their respects and take leave. Uncle Wai Chow was by then getting old and fragile, but his eyes and voice were as sharp as ever.

Uncle Wai Chow looked steadily at Man Kwong for some time and said: "The higher you climb, the more heavily you'll fall."

Man Kwong was livid and would have retorted had Mother not tugged at his sleeve and pulled him away. Fortunately, Uncle Wai Chow's prediction never came true. With hard work and good business acumen, Man Kwong went on to a successful career in Singapore trading sugar, rubber and other commodities as well as developing real estate. After ten years, he moved on to head up the company's operations in Japan and had another highly successful career there in commodity trading and real estate development until he retired back to Hong Kong in 1985.

So of all my family I alone stayed on in Hong Kong, standing at the crossroads. I could not keep my younger brothers' patriotism and dedication to rebuilding China out of my mind, but I was not ready to follow in their footsteps. While I remained undecided on what to do with my future life, I did start something very personal for myself: I began courting.

When Mother left with Man Kwong for Singapore, she told me not to forget to visit our elder relatives and pay respects to them on her behalf. She specifically mentioned my sister-in-law Amy's parents, Mr. and Mrs. Wong Hing Kwong, our old family friends and neighbours. I started calling on them on Chinese New Year Day and on their birthdays as Mother instructed. Mr. Wong had a big family, which included his wife, his concubine and thirteen surviving children (seven sons and six daughters). Amy, who was my classmate in primary school, was his sixth child. Mrs. Wong and her eldest daughter Wai Sheung used to come over to our house on Ching Lin Terrace to play mahjong with Mother and Grandmother, and I had known the Wong family since my childhood. When I visited them in the 1950s they had moved to a new residence at No. 1 Glenealy — a short steep street leading up to the Botanical Gardens at the Mid-Levels in Central. Almost all of Amy's older brothers had gone overseas to study and only the younger siblings were living at home.

Mr. Wong belonged to the early, elite Chinese upper-middle class. He attended Diocesan Boys' School, a well-known English secondary school, and read economics at the University of Hong Kong, graduating in 1918. He first inherited a Chinese wine business on Wing Lok Street under the name of Wong Kwong Sin Tong (the Wong Family Hall of Great Charity), and later operated the Chung Wah Distillery in Stanley and the Tung Ah Pharmacy on the ground floor of the Entertainment Building on Queen's Road Central. Both these businesses were well known and prosperous before the war.

After the Japanese swept into southern China, Mr. Wong anticipated correctly that Hong Kong would soon be invaded. He stockpiled rice, salted fish and kerosene in various locations on Hong Kong Island, and was thus able to sustain his large family during the Japanese occupation. His three oldest children — daughter Wai Sheung and sons Man Shun and Man Hung — were all studying at the University of Hong Kong when the Japanese invaded. To enable his two sons to continue their studies, Mr. Wong found ways of sending them overseas. Man Shun went to Chongqing through Guangzhouwan and left for the US via India; he continued his studies at the University of Wisconsin and eventually settled in California. Man Hung made his way across land through Qujiang to Chongqing and left for Scotland where he continued his medical studies at the University of Edinburgh; he eventually settled in Vancouver, Canada.

During the Japanese occupation, however, Mr. Wong was deeply affected by the hardships of survival and nearly died during the bombing of Wanchai. He never fully recovered from his war experience. After the war, he became obsessed with the dangers of the Cold War and, convinced that he had to prepare for a third world war, he again started to stockpile rice and other foods. He was also highly critical of the Nationalists, the Communists and the Hong Kong government. His disillusionment with politics and anxieties about an impending war took his attention away from his businesses and almost resulted in a nervous breakdown. To recuperate, during the weekends Mr. Wong would often retreat to his distillery in Stanley or his villa in Macao, and I would miss seeing him when I visited.

No. 1 Glenealy was an old, spacious four-storey apartment building. The Wongs lived on the top floor; the kitchen and the maids' quarters were on the rooftop. During my visits, I would mingle with the younger siblings who were still living at home. Wai Sheung helped Mr. Wong with the family business while keeping an eye on the household. All her siblings called her "Big Sister", and so did I. After a few visits, I became friendly with Josephine, the seventh child, as she was about my age. A top student at Sacred Heart School, one of the best English girls' schools in Hong Kong, she was good natured and intelligent. Noticing my interest in her younger sister, Wai Sheung encouraged me to go out with Josephine. I did so with pleasure, and eventually felt that our relationship could be developed further from just being friends; but the day never came. Josephine left Hong Kong in 1955 to further her studies and later settled in Vancouver, Canada. We saw each other again in Vancouver more than thirty years later, by when we had both raised our own families. Still later, we were delighted to meet again in Toronto, and by then both of us had grey hair and grandchildren.

At the same time that I was seeing Josephine, I also went out with Chan Wing Kin, who would become my wife.

I met Wing Kin through her older sister Chan Hang Chuen whom I met at Nan Fang College, which both she and her husband Man Sing attended. At that time, we regarded ourselves as patriotic and "progressive", sharing the same ideals and beliefs, and we soon became good friends. I was working at Dodwell Motors, a British firm; Hang Chuen and Man Sing were employed by the San Miguel Brewery, the colony's biggest beer producer, owned by Filipino interests. For nationalistic reasons we did not like our employers, but we hung on to our jobs for the sake of earning a living.

Hang Chuen and I were also connected in other ways. Before the war, my cousin Lin Chee (Uncle Wai Chow's eldest daughter), Hang Chuen and her elder sister Shook Ling were classmates at Sai Nam Middle School, a Chinese school registered with both the Hong Kong Education Department and the Ministry of Education of the Nationalist government. The Chan sisters often visited Lin Chee at Uncle Wai Chow's mansion on Ching Lin Terrace and they spent much time together in the house and the beautiful garden at the back. After graduating from Sai Nam, Hang Chuen and Shook Ling attended Sun Yat-sen University in Guangzhou. Wing Kin, who was much younger, remained in Sai Nam to finish middle school and later attended St. Clare's Girls' College — an English secondary school. Lin Chee stayed in Hong Kong but switched to Belilios Public School, one of the top English government schools for girls. She graduated before the fall of Hong Kong and left with me for the Mainland at the beginning of the Japanese occupation.

Hang Chuen was attracted to socialist ideas, but she was not ready to live under a communist regime and decided to return to Hong Kong when Communist troops took over Guangzhou. In the terminology we then used, Hang Chuen was more of a "petit bourgeois" than a revolutionary. While she avidly read newspapers, journals and books with a socialist leaning, she also liked fancy dresses and going to dance parties. She was very sociable and adopted the English name Rosina in order to make friends with foreigners.

After learning that I was Lin Chee's cousin, Hang Chuen lost no time in renewing her acquaintance with her former Sai Nam classmate. Lin Chee, who was married in Guilin during the war, had returned to Hong Kong with her husband. The couple lived in Uncle Wai Chow's mansion while Lin Chee taught at Tak Yan College, a private English school. When visiting Lin Chee at Ching Ling Terrace, Hang Chuen would often ask Wing Kin and I to go along. Then she and Lin Chee would make excuses to stay away from us, so that we had the opportunity to be alone and to get to know each other.

Like Wai Sheung, Lin Chee was another "Big Sister" to me. After Wing Kin and I made a few visits to her house, she encouraged me to start going out with Wing Kin. I was at first embarrassed and reluctant, since I was already seeing Josephine, but I was also attracted to Wing Kin, who impressed me as being very kind-hearted and frugal. When we went out together, she would discourage me from ordering fancy dishes or buying expensive movie tickets. She would also be upset if I did not give money to beggars on the sidewalk or forgot to tip the waiters at the restaurant. After Josephine left Hong Kong in 1955, I started to devote all my attention to Wing Kin, although we went through another year of courtship before getting married.

Every Saturday afternoon for over a year, Wing Kin and I would meet up at the Star Ferry terminal after I finished work at Dodwell Motors. Dodwell's office and showroom were on the ground floor of Queen's Building — an elaborate four-storey arcaded building topped by a small tower in the middle and a turret at each of the front corners. Occupying the current site of the Mandarin Hotel on Connaught Road, Queen's Building was just across the street from the Star Ferry terminal, which comprised a small white building with a clock tower and a long pier covered by a pitched white roof. The building and pier were replaced in the early 1970s by a large two-storey U-shaped terminal building to its east, which in turn was demolished (under protest) in 2006 to make way for highway construction. As the only transportation link between Central District and Kowloon Peninsula at that time, the Star Ferry enjoyed a busy flow of traffic. We would often find long queues in front of the turnstiles of the ticket offices. The passengers were divided into two distinct groups. In the queue for the upper first-class deck of the ferry would be European and Chinese business executives in well-tailored western suits, European ladies with fancy hats and colourful handbags, Chinese ladies in tight-fitting *cheongsam* (*qipao*), and casually dressed tourists with cameras. In the queue for the lower third-class deck would be Chinese white- and blue-collar workers, housewives, and elderly people, who would have to endure the noise and fumes from the engine room of the ferry throughout the voyage. I always thought it curious that, similar to the tram cars on the island, there was no second class. This was perhaps the British way of making an unmistakable distinction between the classes.

When the clock on the Star Ferry terminal struck one, I would be rushing across the street to meet Wing Kin. We would usually start off the afternoon with a light lunch in a small, inexpensive but tasteful Western restaurant where we could enjoy the quiet and privacy. On Hong Kong side we usually preferred Jimmy's Kitchen, which was located in a small lane beside Queen's Theatre on Queen's Road Central and served typical English food on checkered table cloths. On Kowloon side we would often go to Cherikov on Nathan Road, where we would order their signature Russian borscht. After lunch, we would either watch the matinee show at a cinema or just window-shop in Tsim Sha Tsui or Central. Later in the afternoon, we would sometimes go for a "tea dance". A popular Hong Kong pastime during the 1950s and 1960s, "tea dances" were usually held in the ballrooms of major hotels where customers could take their English afternoon tea and dance to a live band. We used to go for "tea dances" at the ballroom on the top floor of the Metropole Hotel on Queen's Road Central; the more up-market "tea dances" at the Hong Kong Hotel and Gloucester Hotel on Pedder Street in Central, and the Peninsula Hotel in Tsim Sha Tsui were too expensive for us. Since Wing Kin's parents preferred that she stayed home in the evenings, we seldom dined out or stayed out late except when we were both invited to dinner parties.

Since Mr. Cooper, my boss at Dodwell Motors, was highly demanding, I was often swamped with work even on Saturdays. Sometimes I would have to work overtime and skip my Saturday afternoon date with Wing Kin, who was never shy in expressing her displeasure. To make up, I would rush to her home as soon as I finished work and apologize profusely. I would also take the opportunity to pay my respect to her parents, and they would often ask me to stay for dinner.

Like me, Wing Kin came from a big traditional family. Her father Chan Yue Chik lived with his wife and their twelve children in an old five-storey building at No. 7 Bonham Road at the Mid-Levels. Wing Kin was their eleventh child and Hang Chuen the eighth.

The Chans' family values were *yee* and *yeung* (righteousness and humility), so their household name was Chan Yee Yeung Tong (the Chan Family Hall of Righteousness and Humility). The antique blackwood furniture in the living room and the scrolls covered in Chinese calligraphy on the walls reminded me that Wing Kin's father came from a scholarly family, just like Father. Wing Kin's father engaged in the so-called *Nam Pak Hong* entrepôt trade between China and Southeast Asia, trading such traditional Chinese products as silk and herbal medicine for rice, spices and sea products from Southeast Asia. He operated his business under the name of Lung Tai Hong, in partnership with some of his clansmen and friends. However, both Father and Chan Yue Chik were better scholars than businessmen since Father's bank went bankrupt and Lung Tai Hong closed down after losing a lot of money. Honest and trusting, Chan Yue Chik was cheated of his investments and shareholdings by his partners, and spent his retirement years reading Chinese classics and writing poems.

"I am sorry that your father passed away so young," Chan Yue Chik said when I first paid him a visit. "He was a good friend."

Father and Chan Yue Chik were acquainted with each other through their dealings with Chan Lim Pak, the ex-comprador of the Hongkong and Shanghai Bank and a notorious Japanese collaborator during the war. Chan Yue Chik was actually Chan Lim Pak's uncle, even though he was younger, because Chan Yue Chik was the ninth son of the family while Chan Lim Pak's father was the third and there was a considerable difference in age between the two brothers. This anomaly was not uncommon in large families at that time. My sister-in-law Amy was the sixth child and her son Cheuk is actually one year older than her fourteenth and youngest sister Wai Sum.

Differences in political ideology split the Chan family just as they did ours. Four of Wing Kin's older siblings had gone to Guangzhou to attend university after the war. Sisters Hang Chuen, Tse Kiu and Shook Ling studied at Sun Yat-sen University and brother Tsok Po attended Lingnan University. When the PLA's Fourth Field Army took over Guangzhou in October 1949, Hang Chuen and Tsok Po returned to Hong Kong, but Tse Kiu and Shook Ling stayed on since both of them had become sympathetic to the Communist cause and Tse Kiu had already joined the CCP. Risking the danger of being caught and imprisoned by the Nationalist government, the two sisters and other pro-communist students called on Guangzhou citizens to welcome the PLA by putting up posters, distributing leaflets and making speeches. The CCP gave Tse Kiu great credit for her underground work and appointed her as the Deputy Chief of the Bureau of Education in the new People's Government of Guangdong Province. Shook Ling was politically less ambitious; her interests were in the fine arts and classical Chinese literature, and she stayed on in Guangzhou as a painter. She later married a railway engineer, Ho Ling Fai, and moved to Bejing where they raised three children. Tse Kiu married relatively late, to a veteran of the Fourth Field Army who liberated Guangzhou.

After graduating from Lingnan's Agriculture Department, Tsok Po returned to Hong Kong to take up a position in the government's Agriculture and Fisheries Department. After a few years he resigned and returned to Guangzhou to continue his studies at Lingnan University. Fired up by patriotism during the war, Tsok Po never felt at ease working in the colonial government and told us that he resented the superior attitudes of the British officials he reported to. At Lingnan, Tsok Po taught in the Sericulture Department, first as a lecturer and later as a full professor.

Another brother, Po Kwong, attended the Teachers' College of Hong Kong before the war, went on to study and practise Chinese medicine, and eventually settled on the Mainland. He went to the Mainland at the start of the Japanese occupation and enrolled in the medical services of the Nationalist government.

He later became the superintendent of the Lodong County Government Health Clinic on Hainan Island where he met his wife. Po Kwong became disappointed with the corruption and incompetence of the Nationalist government. After the Communists took over Hainan, he and his wife returned briefly to Hong Kong but later moved to Guangzhou where he continued his medical practice.

Like my younger brothers who joined the revolution, those of Wing Kin's siblings who went back to mainland China would find their lives following a completely different trajectory from ours in Hong Kong. Over the next two decades, the colony generally enjoyed peace and prosperity, while China was convulsed by continuous revolution. When we met Wing Kin's siblings on the Mainland almost twenty years later and heard about their experiences, we were amazed at how different our fates could be.

Wing Kin and I got married on 4 February 1956 at the office of the Marriage Registry at the Supreme Court (in what is now Hong Kong's Legislative Council Building). We exchanged vows with Uncle Wai Chow and Wing Kin's mother as our witnesses. Uncle Wai Chow and both my parents-in-law were too frail to host our dinner reception that evening, but Aunt Rose came to our rescue. As always, her cheerful and outgoing personality made the occasion a very colourful and joyful one.

Once we had settled into married life, Wing Kin started to teach in Tak Yan College following an introduction from Lin Chee. At first we lived in a rented room in a house on a small lane near the Peak Tram line and Kennedy Road. When we later moved to a two-bedroom apartment on Ying Fai Terrace, off Caine Road, Mother was able to move back from Singapore to live with us. Mother was happy to meet her new daughter-in-law and was looking forward to having more grandchildren, but she was disappointed since we were not able to have children for some time. When Wing Kin suffered a miscarriage a few years after our marriage I finally suggested that she should stop working and stay at home. She succeeded in giving birth to a baby girl in 1962, but the baby died of leukaemia a year later. Mother's wishes were finally granted when Yvonne was born in 1964 and Elaine in 1965 and, thank goodness, our daughters have grown up healthy and strong.

The Decline of Traditional Families

The large family in which I grew up had started to decline toward the late 1930s, and the war and the Communist revolution precipitated its dissolution. Many large traditional families in Hong Kong suffered a similar fate. When the war ended, many of the second-generation children either went back to the Mainland, such as in the Kwan and Chan families, or went overseas, as in the Wong family. For other families, such as the Tang family, economic decline also contributed to their disintegration, and many stately family mansions had to be either sold or demolished.

Uncle Wai Chow was forced to sell our mansion on Ching Lin Terrace before the war so that he could repay his debts when his business failed. In order to "save face", however, he and his family continued to live there as tenants until his death in 1957. The number of residents in the Kwan mansion peaked immediately after the war because both Lin Chee and Sai Kwong had returned home from the Mainland with their families and had to stay in Ching Lin Terrace until they could find a place of their own. In the meantime, however, the ongoing feud within the family intensified, accelerating its dissolution. First Aunt was the first to leave and spent the last years of her life in a nunnery in Sha Tin (in the New Territories). Then, Hung Kwong left for university in Changsha, Hunan Province. After Uncle Wai Chow passed away, the family was quite broke, so Sai Kwong and his family went back to Guangxi; and Lin Chee and her husband moved to a government housing estate in Kowloon, bringing Third Aunt with them. When Sixth Aunt and the rest of her children finally left Ching Lin Terrace for a small apartment in Wanchai, the disintegration of the family was complete.

The Tang family suffered a similar fate. Even though all my maternal uncles and Aunt Rose stayed on in Hong Kong after the war, their respective financial difficulties led to the family's decline. Among my four maternal uncles, only Fourteenth Uncle Shiu Kin was able to build on his inheritance from *Gung Gung* Tang Chi Ngong and reap the benefits of his massive fortune. In 1955, *Gung Gung's* majestic mansion on Gough Street, which had once housed all his children and their families, was sold to developers who tore it down to build high-rise apartments.

The Wong family moved from their Ching Lin Terrace mansion to a large apartment in Glenealy before the war. Highly critical of the colonial government and distrustful of political developments on the Mainland, Mr. Wong encouraged his children to go abroad. After his wife and eight of his thirteen children emigrated, Mr. Wong gave up his Glenealy residence and retired instead to a villa in Macao until he died in 1985.

The Chan family was also splintered. In the late 1950s, my father-in-law Chan Yue Chik decided to tear down his house on Bonham Road and build a modern eight-storey apartment building for his family on the site. While this was a fine idea, my father-in-law was not an experienced builder and was cheated by his contractors. Construction work was delayed, building materials were more expensive than expected, and the financing scheme was full of loopholes. By the time the project was completed, my father-in-law was in debt and had to sell four of the eight apartments in order to pay off his creditors. He and his wife lived in one of the apartments he still owned, but none of his children who were living in Hong Kong at the time chose to move into the other three. In his will, the four apartments that he still owned were shared among eight of his children, but Chan Yue Chik disinherited his four other children because they had disappointed him by going over to the Mainland. Like the patriarchs of other large traditional families, Chan Yue Chik had to give up the tradition of keeping "three generations under one roof". Hong Kong was moving on to a new era.

The 1950s

Political, economic and social life in the colony during the 1950s was greatly affected by developments in mainland China. In January 1950 the British government recognized the People's Republic of China (PRC) on the Mainland, but at the same time it maintained diplomatic relations with the Republic of China (ROC) — the Nationalist government — and set up a consulate in Taiwan. The relationship between Britain and the PRC was, needless to say, uneasy. Beijing was well aware that, for ideological and political reasons, Britain could hardly be a true friend, and neither the British nor local Hong Kong residents doubted China's desire to recover the colony as soon as the time was ripe. Hong Kong thus became a political hot spot — a "borrowed place" living on "borrowed time".

During this period, Hong Kong was flooded with refugees who had fled the Communist regime on the Mainland. Some foreign journalists described this mass movement as people "voting with their feet" and, aware of the political implications, the colonial government felt that it had to give the refugees resident status. Hong Kong's population soared from around 1 million in 1945 to slightly over 2 million by the end of 1950 and to 2.5 million by 1955. The already acute housing shortage after the war was thus further aggravated, and makeshift houses constructed from wooden boards and corrugated metal sheets sprang up all over the hills of Kowloon and Hong Kong Island. After a massive fire burned down a large shanty town in Shek Kip Mei in 1953, leaving over fifty thousand homeless, the government decided that it had to step in to provide basic public services and maintain social stability, and a large-scale government housing programme was launched.

With the burgeoning population, law and order also became a top priority. To maintain order and boost morale, the British government sent massive troop reinforcements to the colony, strengthened the police force and gave it greater discretionary powers, and revitalized and reorganized the auxiliary services that had been dissolved after the war. Several services, including the Air Raid Precaution (ARP) Service in which I had served during the war, were amalgamated to form the Civil Aid Services (CAS) in 1950. The CAS provided a wide range of services, including assisting during emergencies and disasters and helping the police in crowd control at public events. I had taken off my ARP uniform when Hong Kong fell into the hands of the Japanese, and in 1950 I put it back on again, but this time with a different set of insignia. Because of my work experience during the war, I was assigned to the Motor Transport Unit of the CAS.

The colonial government, which had revised or introduced new ordinances to strengthen internal security periodically in the past, set up the Persons Registration Department in August 1949 in anticipation of the flood of refugees from the Mainland. Before the war, Chinese nationals enjoyed freedom of movement in and out of Hong Kong, with the residents of Guangzhou, Hong Kong and Macao treating the three cities as a single community irrespective of the differences in government jurisdiction. This changed after the department was set up. Every Hong Kong resident over twelve years old had to possess an Identity (ID) Card as proof of his or her resident status, and this ID Card soon became essential for obtaining regular employment, opening a bank account, enrolling in school or receiving social benefits.

The Special Branch within the Police Department also stepped up its efforts to monitor political activities in the colony. As a precaution, those found to be politically active would be shadowed and eventually rounded up, whether they were pro-PRC or pro-ROC. They would then be detained in prison, or deported if they were not born in Hong Kong. Detainees and deportees included labour union leaders, teachers, school principals, members of the press, artists and film stars. With these harsh measures, political activities became restricted and the basic freedoms of belief, speech, assembly and association were much curtailed, leading to protests from the more liberal press. Even these restrictions, however, could not entirely prevent political violence from erupting. During preparations for the ROC's national day on 10 October 1956, pro-ROC residents in Kowloon clashed with pro-PRC residents over the hoisting of the ROC national flag, leading to riots and a significant loss of lives and properties.

By then many Hong Kong people had become weary of political violence. When they contrasted the turmoil on the Mainland with the overall stability and business opportunities that Hong Kong had to offer, many chose the lesser of two evils and adapted to life (albeit with restricted freedom) under colonial rule. The fear of mainland politics was accentuated after the Great Leap Forward in 1958–60 when long queues formed outside post offices as people waited to mail parcels to their mainland relatives containing such daily necessities as rice, flour, sugar, edible oil, dried meat, powered milk, vitamin pills, soap, toothbrushes and towels. With such hardships on the Mainland, the people of Hong Kong became even more convinced of the importance of political stability and the need to make money while they could in this "borrowed time" in a "borrowed place". This belief would increasingly take root within the local community and permeate people's collective consciousness over the next few decades.

One of the earliest opportunities to make money was during the Korean War, which lasted from 1950 to 1953. In response to the UN embargo on the shipment of arms and strategic materials to North Korea and China, the Hong Kong government introduced the Importation and Exportation Ordinance, requiring importers to certify that their goods were for local consumption. As Hong Kong was one of China's key trading posts, local businessmen soon found numerous ways to circumvent the embargo and make huge profits. Some of them entered into tacit dealings with Guangdong officials, and elaborate smuggling systems were set up. These usually involved the use of motorized junks from both sides to transfer goods on the high seas, and marine police and customs officers were often bribed to look the other way.

Other businesses just continued to trade with local companies that they knew were associated with the Chinese government without enquiring where the goods were destined. Dodwell Motors was one of them. I remember typing a sale and purchase contract for the sale of fifty Dodge trucks to the China Mutual Trading Company which, though registered as a Hong Kong company, reported to the PRC's Ministry of Foreign Economic Relations and Trade (now Ministry of Commerce); in all likelihood the trucks were then shipped to the Mainland. Indeed, I soon found out that some of my King's College schoolmates and wartime interpreter comrades were working for China Mutual. Out of patriotism, they wanted to help New China acquire much-needed strategic materials, and found that their English language skills could be put to good use there. China Mutual closed its offices in the late 1950s and many of its operations and personnel were taken over by China Resources Company, an official arm of the Ministry of Foreign Economic Relations and Trade.

Eventually, some of the businessmen who smuggled goods to China were prosecuted, and others were blacklisted by the colonial and American authorities. They were banned from doing business with American companies and their US assets were frozen. To the PRC government these "patriotic merchants" were heroes, but to more cynical observers they were the "fat red cats". After the Korean War, many of these businessmen were awarded sole distributorships for valuable Chinese products in Hong Kong and made big fortunes, and those making the greatest contributions were even elected to the People's Political Consultative Conference or the National People's Congress.

For Hong Kong as a whole, the UN embargo was a blessing in disguise. While it caused a period of economic stagnation, many Hong Kong businessmen were forced to look overseas for business opportunities and to start manufacturing for export. When Communist troops started to take over the Mainland during the late 1940s, many Chinese entrepreneurs fled to Hong Kong and brought capital, machinery, management skills and technical know-how to the colony. It was estimated that during 1946–50 some US$500 million in merchandise, securities, gold and foreign exchange poured into Hong Kong from Shanghai alone. After the PRC was established in October 1949, however, many former industrialists who had taken refuge in Hong Kong realized that they would not be returning to the Mainland, and decided to set up factories in the colony instead. Manufacturing activities therefore started to flourish, starting with textiles and garments and diversifying later to toys and plastics. By this time over a million refugees had fled to Hong Kong, and this provided a steady source of cheap labour for the nascent manufacturing industry. This led to the colony's rapid industrialization in the latter half of the 1950s, and changed its main economic focus from entrepôt trade with the Mainland to manufacturing for export. With this new development, the economy took off and people's living standards rose.

My American Connection

Before the war, it was commonly said that the institutions that mattered most in Hong Kong were "the Jockey Club, the Bank and the Governor, in that order". The Jockey Club was one of the earliest establishments in the colony and grew into an enormous business. The Hongkong and Shanghai Banking Corporation, known as "the Bank", was the leading bank and issuer of bank notes in the colony for over a century and acted as Hong Kong's central bank despite its private ownership and non-government status. As for the Governor, he was influential, of course, but governors came and went whereas the Bank and the Jockey Club were as permanent as could be (as they still are to this day).

However, after the war a fourth power emerged: the United States, which had surpassed Britain as a global power at the end of the war. As an international port and manufacturing centre, Hong Kong was highly exposed to the enhanced political, economic and military presence of the US in the region. The powerful Seventh Fleet which patrolled the Taiwan Strait and the South China Sea frequently dropped anchor in Victoria Harbour; the US was the top destination for Hong Kong exports; and American corporations quickly became the biggest group of foreign investors in the colony.

American products invaded the market. Right after the war, Hong Kong received large quantities of relief materials including food, medical supplies and other daily necessities from the US. Then, as trade resumed, American products such as fuel oil, motor vehicles, machinery, household appliances, chemicals and all kinds of attractive consumer goods flooded the market. People in Hong Kong were so impressed by the power of the atomic bomb that they started to attach the name "atomic" to all new consumer products: "atomic pen" for ballpoint pen; "atomic cloth" for synthetic fabric; "atomic radio" for transistor radio; and "atomic watch" for quartz watch. The "atomic fever" was on.

American culture also conquered Hong Kong. Movies from Hollywood exposed people to the American lifestyle, and the new culture captured everyone's imagination. American films became highly popular; I was particularly enchanted by such films as *Casablanca*, *Gone with the Wind* and *Fantasia*.

One of the highlights of Hong Kong's "love affair" with the US was the visit of the battleship USS *New Jersey*, the epitome of American might at that time. At 887 feet long with a displacement of forty-five thousand tons, the *New Jersey* was the largest man-of-war Hong Kong had ever seen. Since Hong Kong harbour could not accommodate a ship of such size, she had to drop anchor in Junk Bay, the inlet just outside the harbour entrance of Lei Yue Mun Pass. To impress the might of the US military upon the people of Hong Kong and to emphasize the country's role in defending the "Free World", the American Consulate General and the US Navy Liaison Office made arrangements with the Hong Kong and Yaumati Ferry Company to transport people to visit the battleship. Thousands took the special chartered ferries and crowded aboard the mammoth ship, myself included (needless to say). The visit was indeed an eye-opener for military machine enthusiasts like me who marvelled at the ship's long deck and her sophisticated superstructure bristling with search lights, anti-aircraft guns, range finders and radar antennas. I was particularly impressed by the main armament — nine huge sixteen-inch calibre guns mounted three at a time in three heavily armoured turrets. From then on, US warships from the Seventh Fleet frequented Hong Kong for procurement and refuelling as well as for the "rest and recreation" (R&R) of the sailors. The bars of Wanchai where the sailors went onshore were often crowded with US servicemen during the Korean War and, later, during the Vietnam War. It was the setting for the movie *The World of Suzie Wong*.

The American way of life had captivated me since my school days; I was attracted to the "Four Freedoms" articulated by President Franklin D. Roosevelt: freedom of speech, freedom of belief, freedom from fear and freedom from want. I also had good experiences with my American colleagues during the war. When I heard about the political upheavals and increasing hardships that my brothers and relatives suffered on the Mainland, I started to think about emigrating to the US.

By 1955, in light of the large number of refugees applying to emigrate, the American Consulate General in Hong Kong had set up an office to screen them and process applicants under the Refugee Relief Program (RRP). A friend who served as a wartime interpreter with me worked at the RRP office and suggested that I might stand a better chance of emigrating if I could get a job there and obtain a recommendation from the officer-in-charge. After eight years at Dodwell Motors I was becoming bored with routine office work and wanted a change, so I decided to send in an application. At the interview the head of the RRP liked my wartime record of working as an interpreter for US forces and hired me on the spot, so I started my new career at the American Consulate General.

The Consulate General in Hong Kong was at that time the largest of the consulates in the US diplomatic service. It was larger than the US Embassy in Taiwan, and would have acquired the status of embassy had Hong Kong been an independent country. The Consulate General had an imposing presence on Garden Road, with a large L-shaped five-storey building, a parking lot at the back and a beautiful fountain and garden in front. The compound was United States territory, and if a political dissident escaped from the Mainland, succeeded in sneaking onto the premises and was offered asylum by the US government, there was nothing the Hong Kong police could do. Inside the garden stood a tall flag post flying the Stars and Stripes, and uniformed US marine guards would come out early in the morning and at sunset to perform the flag-rising and flag-lowering ceremonies. These guards would be fully armed in case of emergencies such as the riots in 1956 and 1967.

My work at the Consulate General was far from pleasant, however. At the RRP we had to screen thousands of applicants and determine as best we could whether or not they were genuine political refugees. I felt uncomfortable with having to cross-examine people and decide their fate. The questions were primarily related to mainland politics: Did they have any involvement with the Communist Party? What were their impressions of the Chinese government and the People's Liberation Army? How did they think about China as whole? We also asked them for details of their experiences in political campaigns (such as the Land Reform and the Three-Anti and Five-Anti Campaigns), and the reasons why they were being persecuted. All applicants had to supply information regarding their relatives and friends in China, Hong Kong, the US and other parts of the world. We would then crosscheck the information with their families and relatives, and with any unrelated acquaintances that were given as references. Finally, we would evaluate each applicant based on his or her level of education, technical or professional skills, financial status and health, and then write up our report.

Since the RRP was only a temporary programme and I grew increasingly uncomfortable with the work, soon after I joined I started looking for other job openings within the Consulate General. At that time, the American Consulate General in Hong Kong was one of the largest and most important US diplomatic posts in the world. Aside from the regular consular and commercial sections, there were the Political Section, the Economic Section, the United States Information Service (USIS), the army, navy and air force liaison offices, the

RRP office, and other specialized offices such as Treasury which monitored the embargo on the PRC. To them, Hong Kong was not just a small British colony — it was the contact point between the "Free World" and Communist China, and thus a strategic focus of US intelligence and propaganda activities. The USIS in particular was actively engaged in propaganda work, and its publications (such as the magazine *Today's World*) were mailed free-of-charge to schools, institutions and households in Hong Kong. Its library was well stocked with books, tapes and films which could be freely rented, and crews were on hand to bring the films for showing in schools, cinemas and community centres. "Voice of America", the USIS radio broadcast, was especially popular and therefore strictly banned on the Mainland.

After working at the RRP office for slightly over a year, I applied for and secured a position as a translator at the Consulate General's US Air Force Liaison Office which, together with the army and navy liaison offices, was responsible for gathering intelligence on mainland China. My job was to gather and translate any information concerning the strength and movements of the Chinese Air Force. This could include any material on individual high ranking officers, the air force's organization and training, the number and types of airplanes, base locations, troop movements and military exercises. On a wider scope, I was also charged with gathering information on the development potential of the Chinese Air Force, including advances in science and mathematics; aerospace research and discoveries; aircraft, rocket and missile manufacturing and testing activities; improvements in transportation and telecommunications; and national economic planning. Other useful information included the location of major infrastructure such as harbours, power stations, oil fields, roads, bridges and railway lines.

To gather all this information, the first thing I did at work in the morning was to read major newspapers from three categories: (1) the pro-PRC camp: *Ta Kung, Wen Hui, New Evening Post* and *Cheng Bao*; (2) the non-PRC camp: *South China Morning Post, The Standard, Wah Kiu, Sing Tao, Kung Sheung,* and *Hong Kong Times*; and (3) mainland papers: *People's Daily, Guangming Daily, PLA Daily* and local papers such as *Nanfang Daily*. During the early 1950s, no mainland paper could be exported since much of the news was considered to be state secrets. The only mainland papers available in Hong Kong were smuggled out, and the liaison office was willing to pay as much as hundreds of Hong Kong dollars for them.

As well as the newspapers, I also looked for books that would give me the information I needed and quickly resumed my old habit of browsing in bookstores after work, but this time for a different purpose. Magazines such as *People's Pictorial* and *PLA Pictorial*, scientific textbooks and journals, and local maps and telephone directories could all prove useful for my work. At first I would pay for these publications and obtain reimbursement from the liaison office, but eventually the office itself would order directly from the bookshops. Our business became so important that even the PRC-affiliated Joint Publishing Company would send us their monthly catalogues and give us a discount. The amount of material available became so overwhelming that in the end I could only translate the index or provide a brief summary before the publications were shipped back to the US to be translated and analyzed.

In 1961, the air force, army and navy liaison offices merged into one, and I left the following year, having worked a total of six and a half years at the American Consulate General. In the end, I never leveraged my position to apply for emigration to the US. I was concerned about how I would adjust to life in a new country, and perhaps I was not yet ready to leave my home country; most probably, it was a mix of both.

By the turn of the 1960s, I had grown weary of China-watching and wanted a change away from politics. Remembering Father's attempt to introduce me to banking one summer long ago, I decided to try and follow in his footsteps.

4
Hang Seng Bank

New Career

On a clear Monday morning in early December 1961, I took a two-hour leave from my job at the American Consulate General and walked down Garden Road to Queen's Road Central for an interview with Lee Quo Wei, manager of Hang Seng Bank. Wearing my best dark-grey suit with a red tie and buoyed by the cool morning breeze, I was in a good mood and felt quite confident about my chances.

The consulate compound was on "Government Hill" and on stepping outside I was in the heart of the colonial government. Behind the consulate was the Government House, the office and residence of the Hong Kong governor. Down the road to my left were the two grey office blocks of the Central Government Offices, the former Colonial Secretariat. Adjoining the offices and surrounded by trees and shrubs was the neo-Gothic St. John's Cathedral, the cathedral of the Anglican diocese of Hong Kong since 1849 and the venue where the colonial government held all its official religious services. Across the street on a small hill overlooking the harbour was Flagstaff House, a Victorian mansion built in 1846 which was the official residence and office of the Commander of the British Forces. (In 1978 the headquarters moved to a new building at the former site of HMS *Tamar* on the harbour front, and Flagstaff House became the Museum of Tea Ware for the display of antique Chinese teapots.)

As I walked further down the road, however, I started to notice significant signs of the changes taking place in the colony's political and economic landscape. Down the slope from St. John's Cathedral was the site of the new twenty-six-storey Hilton Hotel, the first truly modern international hotel in Hong Kong and a major US investment. The hotel site was the former Murray Parade Ground where the British Empire used to show off its military might with pomp and circumstances. Turning left into Queen's Road Central, I passed the three tall granite buildings which housed the key financial powers in the colony. The first was Bank of China's soaring tower-like structure, completed in 1952 as a show of strength by the new PRC government and designed to be slightly taller than the Hongkong and Shanghai Bank Building next door. The massive Hongkong and Shanghai Bank Building was built in 1934 and had previously dominated the Central District. Further down the road was the tall, narrow headquarters of Chartered Bank (Hongkong Bank's colonial rival) which was completed several years after the Bank of China Building and, in turn, was designed to be the tallest of the three bank buildings.

Along Queen's Road Central I passed a mixture of Victorian and pre-war buildings with arches and columns, and the tall, new multi-storey office buildings with plain facades and large windows which housed the offices of British and international companies. Up-market retail shops, restaurants and cinemas lined both sides of the street. However, once I passed the four-storey Central Market — the colony's main retail wet market — the scenery suddenly changed. The road narrowed markedly, and low-rise Chinese tenement houses stretched down both sides of the street as far as I could see.

As I rubbed shoulders with the shoppers and workers along the street I became increasingly anxious as I realized that I really wanted the job with Hang Seng Bank. All my previous jobs had been associated with war and politics: interpreting for US forces during World War II, selling vehicles which I knew were smuggled to China during the Korean War, processing refugees for the American Consulate General, and most recently "China watching" — a euphemism for intelligence gathering — for the Americans. I longed for a change that would free me from war and political intrigues, and thought that this was my best opportunity to escape from it all. Little did I realize then that politics would continue to follow me in one form or another for the next twenty-two years of my career.

Hang Seng Bank was located at 163–165 Queen's Road Central, in a white five-storey Western-style building with aluminium windows and an elevator. The tall modern building stood out from the three- and four-storey pre-war Chinese tenement houses in the neighbourhood. Shops selling garments, leather goods, pharmaceuticals, watches and clocks, jewellery and stationery lined the street, alongside several noisy Chinese restaurants and Hong Kong style cafes. A number of Chinese-owned banks, including Kwong On, Dao Heng, Wing Hang and Wing Lung, were also in the vicinity.

Inside the banking hall, some twenty employees were busy talking to customers or doing calculations behind the counters under a flood of white fluorescent light. The steady clatters of the abacuses mixed with the rhythmic churning of modern calculating machines. This meeting of East and West was also reflected in how the staff dressed: some wore ties and dark grey or blue Western suits, while others wore loose-fitting grey Chinese suits with high stiff collars. This mingling of different periods and cultures, I would later find, permeated the entire bank all the way up to the senior management.

Lee Quo Wei, who wore black-rimmed glasses and a well-tailored dark-blue Western suit, was the modern Westernized face of the bank. In contrast to the white painted walls and small wooden or metal desks in the banking hall, Lee's second-floor office had brown teak wall panels with a large rosewood desk at one end and a dark brown leather sofa set at the other. It was unmistakably a bank manager's room, which only the more important clients would enter. Standing close to six feet tall, with a high forehead and dark complexion, Lee (or Q.W. as many called him) did not resemble the average southern Chinese. We sat opposite each other and, as he glared at me through his large black-rimmed glasses and started to speak rapidly in a slightly high-pitched voice, I saw Lee as the assertive and demanding boss that I had expected.

"Why do you want to join Hang Seng Bank?" he asked me point blank.

Fortunately, I had come prepared. My brother Man Kwong, who worked in Dah Chong Hong (which was affiliated with the bank) and knew Lee as a colleague, had sent me a detailed letter describing Lee and advising me how to handle the interview.

"My father was a traditional Chinese banker," I said. "He expected me to continue the family tradition and I would like to carry out his wishes."

Lee did not comment, but I felt that I had hit the right note.

"Besides," I quickly continued. "Chinese employees in foreign firms are considered 'second class' and my promotion prospects are limited. I want a change so that I can advance my career."

Lee still glared at me with little expression on his face but his stern looks seemed to have softened somewhat. I hastened to deliver my punch line.

"Hang Seng Bank is a fast growing bank and I believe there will be many opportunities for me if I work hard."

Lee slowly nodded his agreement, but he was not about to let me off so easily.

"It will take you a long time to adjust here," he said. "You only worked for foreigners in the past, but Hang Seng is a Chinese company."

He paused for emphasis before continuing.

"However, there may be an opportunity for you. We are expanding our business and need to know more about Hong Kong and the world market. We will need someone fluent in both English and Chinese to do some research and analysis. Can you do this?"

"Yes I can," I replied emphatically before he could think of any more questions. Lee had already seen my résumé and he knew that I was qualified for the position.

"I will do my best to live up to your expectations," I quickly added.

Lee finally seemed satisfied.

"Remember this," he added before letting me off the hook. "To be a good banker, a good education is necessary but not sufficient. Experience and human relations are more important." To emphasize his point, Lee quoted a well-known couplet from *A Dream of Red Mansions*, a classical Chinese novel: "A grasp of worldly affairs is genuine knowledge; the understanding of human relations is true learning."

"Don't let me down," he said, looking at me hard. "Report to work as soon as you can."

I was elated at the opportunity to start a new career, but I also realized that I would be facing a new challenge since I had never worked in a Chinese-run business before except for my very brief apprenticeship at Tang Tin Fuk Yinhao before the war. I would have to learn how to interact with Q.W. Lee and the other senior managers in Hang Seng Bank. Moreover, my new bosses would expect me to be totally conversant with both Chinese and English, and I needed to polish up my Chinese, which I had neglected since leaving school. Nevertheless, I was eager to start my new job. When I resigned from the Air Force Liaison Office my boss, Colonel Daniel Tatum, was reluctant to see me go, but he eventually sent me off with a highly complimentary letter of recommendation.

I started work at Hang Seng Bank in February 1962. My "office" consisted of a dark brown wooden desk about three feet wide, a wooden chair, a Smith-Corona typewriter and some stationery. This was to become the Research Department of which I would be the head and, for some time, the only member of staff.

My first assignment was to translate articles from English economic and financial journals into Chinese for the top management: Chairman Ho Sin Hang, Vice Chairman Leung Chik Wai, General Manager Ho Tim, and other senior officials of the bank. Q.W. Lee, who was the only senior manager educated in English, did not need the translations.

Then, perhaps to put me to the test, I was asked for a report on the motor car industry in Hong Kong which Q.W. Lee needed because Hang Seng's affiliated trading company, Dah Chong Hong, was thinking of acquiring the distributorship for General Motors in Hong Kong and needed information on the market. I drew heavily on my previous work experience at Dodwell Motors, which distributed the American- and Canadian-built Dodge and the British-built Morris in Hong Kong and south China, and spoke extensively with my contacts in the industry. My report was well received. Dah Chong Hong proceeded with its acquisition and later acquired Japanese vehicle distributorships as well, making it one of the leading vehicle distributors in Hong Kong.

The real test during this initial period, however, was writing the bank's 30th anniversary report which was planned for release in December 1962. Digging deep into the bank's archives in a dark corner of the building, I sifted through piles of documents, almost choking from the dust that they threw up. The crackling pages were yellowed at the fringes, and the Chinese ink-brush writing on some of the documents was barely discernable. I gathered what information I could and then tried to find out more by interviewing older bank employees. I did not get a chance to interview Chairman Ho, but Ho Tim, who was general manager, agreed to talk to me. For a young, new employee of the bank this was almost unheard of, but it reflected Ho Tim's truly congenial relationship with his staff and colleagues.

Ho Tim was slim, fair and slight in built, but beneath his dark, slightly tilted eyebrows his bright sharp eyes exuded the energy of a quick and active mind. Having joined Hang Seng at its founding in 1933, he was one of the most senior bank officers and his reputation for maintaining good customer relationships and bringing in business was legendary. As I sat down on the sofa opposite him to explain my mission I started to stammer, but he quickly put me at ease. "Very good. So you're going to write the history of the bank," he said with his characteristic broad smile. "It's always good to see young people taking up important tasks. Now where shall I begin?"

So Ho Tim talked away, his eyes dancing and his hands gesturing lightly in the air. He talked about how the Nationalist government trucked crates of Yuan notes to Hong Kong to exchange for foreign currency during the Anti-Japanese War, and how Hang Seng profited from the exchange. Then he recalled how he applied to import 20,000 taels of gold one day after the war, instead of the usual 2,000 taels, which enabled Hang Seng to corner the market when the Hong Kong government subsequently stopped all gold imports. I was awe struck and could not take notes fast enough.

After many drafts and revisions, Chairman Ho finally reviewed and cleared the 30th anniversary report. It was published as a brochure in both Chinese and English and distributed to the bank's friends and customers as well as to the media in a gala event on 24 December 1962 to mark the bank's anniversary.

The report was a success. Soon afterwards, Lee obtained the Chairman and Ho Tim's approval to officially set up the Research Department and for me to head it.

Humble Beginnings

In many ways, Hang Seng's 30th anniversary marked its coming of age as a modern commercial bank. Starting from its humble beginnings as a small *yinhao*, the bank's remarkable growth and development over three decades bore the unmistakable stamp of its chairman Ho Sin Hang.

Hang Seng first opened for business in Hong Kong on 3 March 1933 and the firm's original founders were Ho Sin Hang, Lam Bing Yim and Sheng Tsun Lin who both had businesses in Shanghai, and Leung Chik Wai who, like Ho, started his own business in Guangzhou. Each was a successful financier in his own right during the 1920s, but civil war and the threat of Japanese invasion in the early 1930s forced them to leave the Mainland in the hope of finding a safe haven in Hong Kong. The British colony was then politically stable and allowed private businesses to operate on a laissez-faire basis with minimal restrictions, an advantage which was not lost on the founders. After arriving in Hong Kong, Ho, Lam, Sheng and Leung came to know each other through their gold trading and soon became friends and business partners.

Hang Seng started business as a *yinhao* at 70 Wing Lok Street, a narrow street in the Sheung Wan area lined with traditional Chinese tenements and bustling with the business activities of bankers, traders and retailers of all description. Lam was the chairman, Ho the general manager and Leung his deputy. About eleven staff crammed into the bank's eight hundred square foot premises. There was so little space that a customer had to take only three steps from the entrance to the bank counter. The four characters of the bank's name — Hang Seng Yin Hao — were boldly written in black on a large wooden panel hanging across the front of the building, and on the two pillars supporting the upper floor balcony on each side were smaller Chinese characters describing the bank's services: remittances, exchange and gold trading. The Chinese Gold and Silver Exchange Society, the focal point of local Chinese banking activities, was nearby in Mercer Street.

In the tradition of its founders, Hang Seng quickly became an active gold trader, but it also expanded into the lucrative remittance and currency exchange business between Hong Kong and the Mainland. Like other *yinhao*, it provided these services to Chinese traders in textiles, pharmaceuticals, rice and dried sea products, and performed a role that foreign international banks were reluctant to play. Foreign banks at that time transacted primarily with foreign companies, and dealt with the Chinese community only through their compradors — English-speaking Chinese who would guarantee the banks' loans to the *yinhao* and handle all local Chinese business.

Hang Seng was started up as a precaution against war, but paradoxically the company made its first major fortune from the start of the war. When the Japanese invaded China in 1937, everyone who could afford it rushed to buy and hoard gold, and a flurry of remittances came to Hong Kong from Shanghai, Hankou, Guangzhou and other major cities in China all looking for a safe haven. Hang Seng benefited handsomely from these activities. Thanks to the partners' business connections on the Mainland, the bank also secured an active role exchanging Yuan for foreign currencies on behalf of the Nationalist government, which needed foreign exchange to finance its war against Japan. According to Ho Tim, Yuan banknotes used to arrive in Hong Kong by the truckloads, and the profits to be made were enormous.

After the Japanese occupied Hong Kong in December 1941, the founding partners and their staff sought refuge in Macao and continued to trade gold in a small office under the name of Wing Wah Yinhao. They moved back to Hong Kong after the war ended in 1945, and re-started Hang Seng's operations at 181 Queen's Road Central, which were larger premises that the bank had purchased before the war.

Q.W. Lee, who had worked with some of the founders in Macao, joined Hang Seng the following year. After leaving his native village of Kaiping for Hong Kong at a young age, Lee attended St. Joseph's College, a Catholic English secondary school. He left school a year before he was due to graduate in order to support his family and joined China State Bank as a trainee. With his knowledge of English and commercial banking, Lee was assigned the specific task of dealing with foreign gold traders at Hang Seng, and soon became an indispensable member of the management team.

The intensification of the civil war between the Nationalist government and the Communists again brought the bank great opportunities for trading gold. China's economy was still recovering from the devastations of war and the Nationalist government needed to raise funds to fight the Communists. Inflation skyrocketed and to stabilize the currency the government instituted the Gold Yuan in 1948, valued at four Gold Yuan to one US Dollar. All Chinese National Currency (CNC) previously in circulation in the market had to be turned over to the government at an exchange value of one Gold Yuan to three million CNC. By 1949, the Central Bank of China was issuing bank notes in denominations of one hundred thousand Gold Yuan for everyday use. Completely losing faith in the national currency and the Nationalist government's ability to control inflation, many businesses and individuals resorted to holding gold, against regulations. Some tried to speculate in the Hong Kong gold market through the *yinhao*. With its founders' business connections and trading expertise, Hang Seng executed many of these transactions and quickly became the doyen of the Hong Kong gold market, so practically all gold traders had to follow its lead. Ho Sin Hang won recognition as the authority behind Hang Seng's success and was elected as chairman of the Chinese Gold and Silver Exchange Society, serving from 1946 to 1949.

At the height of the firm's success, however, historical events again intervened and forced Hang Seng to take a new course. When the Korean War started in 1950, the United Nations imposed an embargo on all trade with the PRC; all gold trading, currency exchange and remittances involving the Mainland came to a halt, and the bank lost the mainstay of its business overnight. The founders realized that the business must adjust to the new political situation.

Ho, who became the group's new leader after Lam Bing Yim passed away in 1949, was acutely aware that times were changing for the *yinhao* and wanted to explore the alternatives. Between 1950 and 1952, Ho toured the US, Canada, Southeast Asia, South Africa and Europe, and visited banks and financial institutions in seventeen cities (including New York, Los Angeles, Havana, Lima, Tokyo, London and Paris) in search of new ideas and business opportunities. Q.W. Lee accompanied Ho and his wife on these tours and acted as Ho's personal secretary and interpreter. At the end of his tour, Ho decided that Hang Seng should still concentrate its business in Hong Kong but would have to become an international commercial bank.

On 5 December 1952, Hang Seng was incorporated as a limited-liability company. Ho Sin Hang was elected chairman of the board with Leung Chik Wai as vice-chairman, and Ho Tim was appointed general manager. After its incorporation, Hang Seng upgraded itself from a *yinhao* speculating in gold and currencies to a full-fledged commercial bank that could finance international trade, take deposits from the general public and make loans. The change was timely. Mainland industrialists sought a safe haven in Hong Kong after the communist takeover, over a million refugees fled to the colony, and the conditions were ripe for the manufacturing industry to take off. As factories sprang up throughout Hong Kong the demand for financing soared.

International banks such as The Hongkong and Shanghai Bank (later known as Hongkong Bank, and now HSBC) and Chartered Bank (now Standard Chartered Bank) abandoned their comprador system and started to deal directly with the larger and better-known Shanghainese textile groups such as Windsor, South Sea, Nanyang and Nan Fung. Hang Seng, on the other hand, mainly took care of smaller businesses within the Guangdong community, including the manufacturers of garments, toys, plastics, metal products and electronics that would later spearhead Hong Kong's economic growth. As most of these small businesses did not have a proper balance sheet and could offer little financial data to support their loan requests, many of the bank's initial loans were based on personal relationships and trust. Many of these small businesses later grew into large corporations and formed the backbone of the bank's corporate customer base. In the late 1960s, real estate developers also became clients and start-up firms such as Sun Hung Kai, New World and Henderson remained loyal customers of the bank when they later became major corporations.

With an expanding business, Hang Seng soon outgrew its second location at 181 Queen's Road Central and in 1953 it moved down the road to numbers 163–165, the five-storey building where I was interviewed by Q.W. Lee. The new headquarters prominently displayed the bank's name in English — "Hang Seng Bank Ltd." — across the main entrance. Hong Kong's Chinese financial district as a whole had shifted east from Wing Lok Street, moving closer to the Central District as commercial banks and Westernized enterprises replaced *yinhao* and traditional Chinese shops. Compared to Wing Lok Street, this part of Queen's Road Central was wider, with more traffic and a number of new multi-storey buildings on either side of the road. In 1960, the bank went public and officially changed its Chinese name from Hang Seng Yin Hao to Hang Seng Yin Hang ("Hang Seng Bank"). The change in that last character was the milestone marking the company's re-birth as a modern commercial bank.

To enhance Hang Seng's new social status further and expand its business network, the founding partners also invited a number of dignitaries to join the board. Among them were Kwok Chan, ex-comprador of Banque de L'Indochine and a member of the Legislative Council, and Tang Shiu Kin, chairman and managing director of Kowloon Motors Bus Co Ltd.

Kwok Chan inherited the post of comprador from his father Kwok Siu Lau and was the last generation of Hong Kong's compradors. He was married to the daughter of Chan Lim Pak, the once prominent comprador of The Hongkong and Shanghai Bank, who was a cousin of my wife Wing Kin, albeit much older.

Tang Shiu Kin was, of course, my maternal uncle, and he was not a little surprised to see me working at Hang Seng. I spotted him in his hallmark grey Chinese gown during the bank's 30th anniversary celebrations and went to greet him. At first he did not seem to recognize me, but when Q.W. Lee came over and introduced me to him as the bank's newly hired research officer, Uncle Shiu Kin quickly broke into a smile and shook my hand. "Sze Kwong is my nephew!" he said to Lee. "I hope he will serve the bank well." I immediately thought of Father. He alone would appreciate the bitter-sweet irony of this encounter.

When Hang Seng celebrated its 30th anniversary on Christmas Eve 1962, it also celebrated yet another move, to a brand new building facing the harbour at 77 Des Voeux Road Central. The new building, twenty-two storeys high with a steel frame, aluminium trimming, and grey and green glass curtain walls, was the tallest and most modern in Hong Kong at the time and a fitting symbol of the bank's successful transition to modern banking. By this time, Hang Seng had total assets of HK$355 million and a staff of four hundred, making it the largest Chinese-owned commercial bank in Hong Kong. Echoing Confucius, Chairman Ho said at the celebrations: "At thirty, we stand on our own feet."

The Teachings of Chairman Ho

Hang Seng was one of the few *yinhao* which succeeded in making the transition to commercial banking and continued to thrive after the war. Uncle Wai Chow and Father's banking businesses went bankrupt successively during the 1930s because of over-speculation. *Gung Gung* Tang Chi Ngong's Tang Tin Fuk Yinhao thrived on the strengths of the property market during the 1930s, but then had to close down during the 1950s due to increased competition from new Chinese commercial banks.

Hang Seng's success in continuously adapting and expanding its business was in many ways due to the vision and business acumen of Chairman Ho. Short and stocky with a large head and a kindly round face, Ho did not fit the stereotype of an awe-inspiring bank chairman. He had started to wear Western suits but it was clear that, unlike Lee, he was not too particular about the tailoring.

Despite his unassuming and often folksy appearance, Chairman Ho commanded great respect among his staff, and not only because of his business success. He treated his employees not as subordinates but as his pupils, giving talks and sharing with them his banking knowledge, philosophy and vision. A firm believer of the philosophy of Confucius, Ho tried to live up to the great teacher's ideals: "He who wishes to be established assists others to be established; he who wishes to be successful assists others to be successful." This teacher-pupil relationship between him and his staff was one of the defining influences behind Hang Seng's drive towards commercial success. Aside from giving talks, Ho would often stroll through the bank and speak with the staff, making use of every opportunity to teach them something. Everyone in the bank called him Uncle Sin, both out of respect and because of their genuine appreciation.

Chairman Ho wanted to build Hang Seng into a modern commercial bank, but at the same time he also placed great emphasis on traditional Chinese values. A native of Panyu in southern Guangdong, he attended only four years of *sishu* — traditional Chinese schools which taught the *Four Books* (the classical teachings of Confucius and Mencius). Although he had to drop out of school at fourteen to become a shop attendant in Guangzhou, he seemed to have taken the classical teachings to heart, and used them freely to formulate his own moral outlook and business philosophy. Ho tried to impart his philosophy to his employees and, in so doing, created a unique Hang Seng culture.

Chairman Ho's teachings were summarized in a booklet entitled *A Talk about My Life Experience* which was distributed to all staff members. I remember some of the teachings to this day:

> Your success or failure in life depends upon the strength of your will. A strong will allows you to overcome difficulties and succeed in your undertakings. However, knowledge and experience are also important, and a lack of either would be a major weakness. You will become susceptible to outside influence or material temptations, and will waver and become indecisive. This is the major cause of failure in one's career.

> Young people lack experience and are therefore more impulsive and easily offended. When they encounter setbacks, which are inevitable in life, they become angry and will often resort to verbal abuse or even physical violence. This not only upsets the people around them but also harms their relationships with other people. In human relationships, therefore, one must start by cultivating oneself; the keys to success are patience and forgiveness.

Ho also taught himself most of what he knew about banking and customer relationships. As a result, he was a firm believer in life-long learning as the key to success, and promoted it enthusiastically within the bank. When Hang Seng was a small *yinhao* with only a dozen employees, Ho used to talk to them individually at the beginning of each Lunar New Year, reviewing their performance and telling them in detail where they needed to improve. Later, as the bank expanded, he would talk at length to all staff as a group. When Hang Seng became a commercial bank in 1952, Ho set up regular training courses to teach the staff modern banking skills, and some of these courses were opened to the public starting in 1963 under the bank's "Elementary Banking Programme". The programme, which was free, was subsequently expanded and culminated in the opening of the Hang Seng School of Commerce in 1980. With funding from the bank, Chairman Ho and other Hang Seng directors, the school was able to offer free tuition to its students.

For Chairman Ho learning was not confined to acquiring banking skills but also involved constantly improving one's moral values. He held seminars for his managers and staff on topics like honesty, integrity, trust and health, and above all on how they could improve themselves. Standing proudly under the spotlight on the red carpeted platform of the bank's auditorium, Ho would often quote from the Classics: "If you can one day renovate yourself, do so from day to day. Yea, let there be daily renovation"; or "Is it not pleasant to learn with a constant perseverance and application?"

After attending his seminars, like many other bank employees I would be touched and encouraged by his words and would secretly resolve to work harder and improve myself.

Regardless of our background or position, Chairman Ho treated all of us as his students and played a pivotal role in helping the bank build a highly motivated, rapidly expanding and increasingly professional staff. To support its growth, Hang Seng hired many trainees from English secondary schools during the 1950s, and later started to employ university graduates in the 1960s. In addition, the bank also hired many mid-career professionals as "special officers" for their expertise in areas such as electronic data processing, public relations, personnel training and public security; I was hired as a "special officer". Despite this infusion of new talent, however, the bank did not lay off any of its employees. Some of the older staff from the bank's *yinhao* days who did not receive much formal education, but who had developed valuable business experience and contacts, were assigned to the Public Relations Department; others stayed behind the counters and worked as cashiers or vault-keepers.

Chairman Ho was also instrumental in building Hang Seng's unique market image as a modern bank caring for and servicing the Chinese community. Hang Seng was faced with two obstacles in its transition to commercial banking: the lack of modern banking knowledge and a relatively small market share. Ho decided to overcome the latter hurdle by making full use of the bank's biggest strength, its Chinese culture. The bank targeted as its customers traditional Chinese merchants and lower-middle working classes who spoke little or no English and knew less about banking — in short, those who were likely to be turned away or feel intimidated by the larger international banks.

To win over these customers, Chairman Ho wanted Hang Seng to provide the best services that a bank could offer, so he wrote these instructions for us to follow:

> Greet your customers with an amiable smile,
> And salute them by calling their names out loud.
> Perform your duties expeditiously,
> And be sincere when rendering your services.
> Always be humble towards your customers,
> And be brief and concise when answering their questions.
> Be considerate of the needs of your customers,
> And bow and thank them for their patronage.

This motto was publicized widely within the bank and disseminated in leaflets, broadcasts and talks at all levels from the chairman on down. It became known as Chairman Ho's Motto and every member of staff knew it by heart. The policy proved highly successful and within a short time Hang Seng had built a reputation for its courteous staff and the quality of the services it provided to Chinese customers. All forms and brochures were clearly printed in Chinese, and staff stationed in the banking hall would bow and greet all customers, big and small, who walked in, help them fill in the forms, answer their questions and walk them to the door when they left.

"We may not be the bank that makes the most profit, but we must be the bank that provides the best service," Ho would often say.

He firmly believed that by providing good service and helping its customers prosper, the bank would prosper too. His prophecy came true, and by the 1970s Hang Seng had grown to become the second largest bank in Hong Kong in terms of customer deposits.

A Bank with Chinese Characteristics

Although I took Chairman Ho's teachings to heart and admired him for his vision and leadership, I never felt entirely comfortable with his methods. Perhaps my discomfort was due to my Western education and experience of working with the Americans, or perhaps it was because his methods resembled too closely the political practices on the Mainland.

During the 1960s, particularly during the Cultural Revolution, people on the Mainland had to recite Chairman Mao's quotations almost every day. Party cadres and workers were urged to study Mao Zedong Thought and hold regular "criticism and self-criticism" meetings to discuss their mistakes and rectify them. Similarly, during the same period the staff of Hang Seng Bank had to learn Chairman Ho's Motto by heart and recite it from memory. They were also encouraged to study the teachings of Chairman Ho and to hold regular "work improvement" meetings to review their work and performance.

Perhaps the Chinese tradition of loyalty to the emperor translated readily into loyalty to a supreme leader, as was the case with Chairman Mao. Within Hang Seng, many employees (including young recruits) listened faithfully to Chairman Ho's teachings and would obey his orders unconditionally. The Communist Chinese slogan "Whatever Chairman Mao says is right" was echoed by Hang Seng's own slogan "Whatever Chairman Ho says is right." While some used the slogan in a light-hearted way, others took it seriously, which made me feel uneasy; I could take comfort only in the thought that if Ho were the equivalent of an emperor, he was at least a benevolent and enlightened one.

While the culture of Hang Seng Bank was not exactly despotic, it was unmistakably patriarchal. Starting from its early days as a *yinhao*, many of the staff came from the extended families of the four founding partners: Lam, Ho, Leung and Sheng. Later, when Leung Kau Kui and Q.W. Lee joined the board, many of their relatives also came to work for the bank. In its early years, especially, Hang Seng was a congregation of princelings, siblings, in-laws, cousins and clansmen. This nepotistic circle then expanded to include former schoolmates, former colleagues and good friends.

I myself was part of this expanded group. My elder brother Man Kwong attended Pui Ching Middle School in Hong Kong and Guangzhou with Chairman Ho's son Ho Tse Cheuk, Mrs. Ho's brother Lee Chiu Po, and Lo Hung Kwan who would later become Chairman Ho's son-in-law. Lee Chiu Po, who was Man Kwong's best friend in Pui Ching, gave Man Kwong the necessary introduction to join Dah Chong Hong, Hang Seng's affiliated trading company, in 1948; many years later, Man Kwong in turn introduced me to Hang Seng's management.

To emphasize the close relationships found in a large family, the staff addressed each other and even their superiors in intimate terms. As with members of an extended family, when addressing another employee who was more senior or older, we would call him "uncle". When addressing a peer or another co-worker of about the same age, we would call him "brother". Following this rule, I called Ho Sin Hang "Uncle Sin",' Leung Kau Kui "Uncle Kau", Leung Chik Wai "Uncle Chik", and Ho Tim "Uncle Tim". As for Q.W. Lee, who belongs to my generation, I called him "Brother Quo Wei" although he is much older, and likewise Man Kwong and Lee addressed each other as brothers.

True to Lee's admonition during our job interview, it took me some time to adjust to the bank's traditional Chinese mode of operation. Fortunately, I had the help of Man Kwok Lau, my schoolmate at King's College and now my immediate superior, to show me the ropes.

Having joined Hang Seng soon after the war, in 1946, Man was already a sub-manager reporting to Lee by the time I joined. Quiet, thoughtful, soft spoken and extremely cautious, Man never replied to any question immediately, preferring to give the answer thorough consideration before committing himself. It could be quite frustrating to speak to him over the telephone since there would often be long periods of silence before I could get any response out of him.

Man was slight in build and his fair, bespectacled and scholarly appearance belied the weight he bore in modernizing the bank. While Q.W. Lee played a key role in introducing the concept of modern commercial banking to senior management, Man was primarily responsible for much of its implementation and designed the operating systems for most of the bank's departments, including accounting, auditing, personnel, customer services, deposits, mortgage loans, trade finance, foreign exchange and credit control.

Intelligent and hard working, Man had a reputation as the "walking dictionary" of Hang Seng. He supervised the drafting of most of the bank's important documents, including business letters and contracts, to ensure they always met with the board's approval. So pleased was he with Man's performance that Uncle Sin used to say: "Kwok Lau is my best pupil ever!"

Man also oversaw economic research, although I answered directly to Lee in actual practice. Perhaps because of this relationship, Man saw me as a colleague rather than a subordinate and counselled me on how to navigate my way within the bank. Over the years, he had learned to survive within the bank's patriarchal structure by being patient and, most of all, tactful in dealing with senior management. "It's very important that the seniors do not lose 'face' in front of juniors," he said. "The boss has to call the shots, not the subordinate."

Man was particularly instructive in helping me handle demands from Lee, since he knew from hard experience that Lee wanted only positive responses from his staff. "When Mr. Lee gives you an order, you should try to carry it out immediately and in the way he wishes," he said. "Don't hesitate, and don't argue with him. Never say 'it can't be done'. Instead, you should say 'I'll try' or 'I'll give it thorough consideration and give you an answer later'."

This was all good advice, but having worked only for foreign bosses in my previous jobs I was used to expressing my own opinions and was either too proud or too naïve to suppress them. As a result, I always got into trouble and Lee would give me a solid scolding whenever I contradicted him, to the extent that I became so frustrated that I seriously considered resigning. "I really can't take this anymore," I blurted to Man one day. "Lee is too unreasonable. Nothing I ever do is good enough. I'm going to quit."

Ever dependable, Man calmed me down and made me see my troubles in a new light. "If your boss scolds you all the time but keeps on giving you assignments, that means he knows that you are capable," he said. "He actually cannot spare you and he expects you to continue to serve him. If this is the case, you are on your way to success."

Sure enough, Lee continued to assign me new projects. My confidence returned and, true to Man's prediction, my banking career steadily took off.

Hang Seng Newsletter

After successfully completing the 30th anniversary report in 1962, my next project was to publish a weekly newsletter in Chinese. Having established a firm foundation for Hang Seng in Hong Kong, Chairman Ho started to look for greater business opportunities overseas. Before the war, remittances from overseas Chinese had played a critical role in the development of the Chinese economy by providing much needed capital and foreign exchange, but after the Communist takeover many overseas Chinese had stopped sending their money to the Mainland. Ho believed that the bank should try to capture these remittances in Hong Kong, where the prospering economy should offer attractive investment opportunities for overseas Chinese.

Soon after celebrating its 30th anniversary, Hang Seng decided to launch an "Overseas Chinese Friendship Mission" to develop this business. To support the mission, Chairman Ho suggested publishing a weekly Chinese newsletter, to be called the *Hang Seng Newsletter*, to inform overseas Chinese about business opportunities in the colony and promote the services that Hang Seng could provide. My research department was tasked with producing the newsletter.

Although I was excited by the opportunity, I was somewhat at a lost how to proceed since I had little experience in news gathering, feature writing or editing. However, both Q.W. Lee and Man urged me to accept the challenge, promising to assign more staff to assist me.

"We had no knowledge and experience in modern banking when we joined Hang Seng twenty years ago," Lee said, "but look what we have achieved!"

"Don't belittle yourself," Man said to me in private. "Your translation and report-writing work in the American Consulate have already proved that you can be a good journalist."

At first I thought that they were just trying to be polite and encouraging, but upon further reflection I felt that they had a point. To show his support, Man offered to act as the newsletter's editor of last resort, and thanks to his commitment the newsletter came off the press with little hitch.

Thousands of copies of the *Hang Seng Newsletter* were airmailed free of charge to the homes and shops of overseas Chinese all over the world to herald visits by the "Overseas Chinese Friendship Mission". General Manager Ho Tim led the mission, which covered major cities in North, Central and South America, Australia, Europe and South Africa. However, the mission left out Southeast Asia countries, since overseas Chinese in this region were mainly from Fujian Province and their banking needs were already well serviced by financial institutions owned by their fellow Fujianese. The mission was an overall success, and Ho Tim was able to make friends and sell Hang Seng's services in many parts of the world. After returning to Hong Kong, he recommended setting up an Overseas Chinese Department to service the investment and financing needs of overseas Chinese clients, and to help them handle their travel needs and immigration formalities.

Unfortunately, the interest of overseas Chinese in Hang Seng Bank waned after the bank runs in Hong Kong in 1965, and especially after the PRC economy opened up towards the end of the 1970s. In the end, the results of Ho Tim's odyssey fell short of expectations, the Overseas Chinese Department was dissolved, and publication of the *Hang Seng Newsletter* was discontinued. Another publication, the *Hang Seng Economic Quarterly*, took its place in 1979 with a new focus on developments in China.

The 1965 Bank Runs

By the time I joined Hang Seng Bank in 1962, the commercial banking industry had just recovered from the bank run of the previous year and the market had started to boom again. Little did I suspect that within a few years we would face another, even bigger crisis.

When Hang Seng converted itself into a commercial bank in 1952, Hong Kong had already started to industrialize rapidly. The flourishing factories provided more employment, which led to a marked increase in living standards, more demand for property and a rise in equity investments. Financings for home purchases, commercial and industrial developments and share purchases were all in great demand.

Banks in Hong Kong expanded aggressively to take advantage of the rising demand, and competition was keen. Many started to finance margin trading in shares, and some even offered unsecured overdraft facilities to finance the purchase of newly issued shares. Even in normal times, new share issues would often put a temporary squeeze on the money market. On 14 June 1961, two new share issues hit the market, the squeeze on the money market intensified, and one of the local banks, Liu Chong Hing, started to experience a cashflow problem. It had loaned out or invested over 75 percent of the deposits on its books, much of it in real estate which could not be readily converted to cash to alleviate the bank's shortfall in liquidity. When news of its problems hit the streets, depositors crowded around the bank to try to withdraw their money and the two major note-issuing banks, the Hongkong Bank and Chartered Bank, had to step in and declare their support for Liu Chong Hing.

This quickly put an end to the bank run, but the incident caught the government's attention. Hong Kong's regulatory structure needed to catch up with its economic growth, so the Bank of England sent H.J. Tomkins to Hong Kong to study the situation and make recommendations for reform. In December 1964, a new banking ordinance was enacted requiring all banks to meet a statutory liquidity ratio. However, the new ordinance did not prevent a second banking crisis from occurring the following year, and the fate of Hang Seng Bank was irrevocably changed.

Thanks to the teachings of Chairman Ho, Hang Seng Bank had little difficulty acquiring deposits since his emphasis on Chinese culture and service enabled it to build up a large and loyal customer base. The bank attracted many grass-roots customers, including blue-collar workers, hawkers, school teachers, traders, factory owners, stockbrokers, real estate developers and other small business owners, all of whom had prospered from Hong Kong's economic boom. By 1965, Hang Seng had become the largest local Chinese bank in Hong Kong in terms of both deposits and assets.

However, unlike larger international banks such as the Hongkong Bank and Chartered Bank which possessed modern banking know-how, Hang Seng had little experience and expertise in diversifying its loan and investment portfolios. Like other local banks, it concentrated its loans in the sector that it knew best — the property market, which unfortunately was also one of the most illiquid areas. This bias among local banks remains largely true to this day.

After the 1961 bank run and the publication of the Tomkins Report, Hang Seng's management tried to diversify its loan portfolio. My department was tasked with preparing a series of reports on Hong Kong's manufacturing industries and their major export markets (especially the US, the UK and the European Economic Community); we spent many hours gathering statistics and meeting with loan officers to compile the reports. In addition, Hang Seng joined the annual Exhibition of Hong Kong Products sponsored by the Chinese Manufacturers' Association (CMA) in 1964, in order to promote its name among manufacturers. It was the first bank to join the exhibition, and we erected a pavilion in the style of a Chinese palace, ornately decorated in red and gold, where the bank exhibited its collection of rare antique Chinese coins dating back over three thousand years. The public response was highly favourable, and the bank received great publicity from the event.

Hang Seng's efforts to diversify its portfolio were timely, and helped to reduce the bank's losses when the Hong Kong real estate market suffered a set-back in 1964. However, despite its attempts at diversification, Hang Seng's portfolio remained over-exposed to the property sector because property lending was relatively secure and highly lucrative, and the bank's clients had seemingly insatiable demands for real estate loans. The stage was set for another crisis in the banking industry.

January 1965 started in a festive mood. Everyone was shopping, cleaning up their homes and preparing food to welcome the Lunar New Year of the Snake. The demand for funds in the money market rose towards year-end, but this was not unusual since it was customary among Chinese businessmen to settle their outstanding debts before the start of a new year.

Then, in mid-January, rumours started to circulate that Ming Tak Bank, an unincorporated bank which also came under the governance of the newly enacted banking ordinance, was in financial trouble due to its heavy investment in the property market. A run started on the bank on 26 January, and the commissioner of banking stepped in quickly the next day and suspended Ming Tak's business under the provisions of the banking ordinance. However, this did not stop rumours from spreading to other banks.

Tuesday, 2 February was New Year's Day and, as usual, all businesses closed down for three days in celebration. When we returned to work on Friday, 5 February, the newspapers reported that the Supreme Court had granted a receiving order and Ming Tak Bank had to declare bankruptcy by 30 April. This was a bad omen for the start of the New Year, and a feeling of unease spread throughout the bank. The next day, a run started on Canton Trust and Commercial Bank, a medium-sized local bank, again on the rumour that it had become illiquid because of its heavy involvement in property loans.

It was not until the following Monday, 8 February, that I started to feel the panic. I was still feeling the effects of too much food and wine over the holidays, and was sound asleep when friends and relatives started calling and woke me up; they wanted to know whether their deposits with Hang Seng were safe. I tried to put their minds at ease, with little success: apparently, hundreds of people had already lined up outside the bank to withdraw their deposits. I quickly put on my suit and rushed back to my office to find out what had happened.

To get into the bank building, I had to push my way through the crowd, which had by then filled the pavement with depositors clamouring to enter the banking hall. The minute I stepped into my office, I received instructions that all non-business departments had to spare part of their staff to help out in the banking hall. By this time, my department had grown to a total of three: a secretary, a research assistant and myself. I asked my secretary to remain in the office to monitor the telex machine and pass any news relating to the bank runs to senior management as soon as possible. I then sent my research assistant to the banking hall to help the tellers.

By then the banking hall resembled a war zone. The tellers were swamped by requests from customers crowding over the counters to withdraw their money; the supervisors were running back and forth behind the counters checking and counter-checking withdrawal slips; and tens of dozens of cashiers scurried behind them, carrying stacks of banknotes from the vault to the tellers. I joined other bank officers in the hall trying to calm down agitated customers and maintain some semblance of order.

I also had another important mission. Through Q.W. Lee's introduction and my own research work, I had come to know Robert Sun of the Government Information Service and, through him, many members of the press; I now needed to call on this network to reassure the media. To prevent the press from picking up false rumours and publishing derogatory reports on the bank, I made an arrangement with Sun whereby I would deliver to him periodic press releases from Hang Seng, and he would distribute copies of these to the news media. For the duration of the crisis, therefore, I doubled up as the bank's *de facto* public relations officer.

On that same Monday, bank runs had spread widely among most of the local banks, including Kwong On, Dao Heng and Wing Lung. The next day, the Hongkong Bank and Chartered Bank had to step in to show their support for the local banks. Confident of Hang Seng's financial position, the Hongkong Bank pledged its full and unlimited support without examining the bank's books. The next day, the government introduced emergency regulations to limit cash withdrawals to a maximum of HK$100 per account (although there were no restrictions on transfers by check), and made arrangements to air freight sterling notes from England to alleviate the currency shortage. Fortunately, the notes never had to be used; a week later calm returned and the restriction on cash withdrawals was lifted.

Unfortunately for Hang Seng, this relatively brief bank run was merely a precursor of greater calamities to come, and in March rumours regarding the bank surfaced again. A number of major clients quietly began to transfer away their deposits, but this did not escape notice and news of the withdrawals soon leaked out. By the start of April, the rumours were widespread and thousands of small depositors again descended on the bank. At the peak of the bank run, the queue stretched eastward from the bank's head office at 77 Des Voeux Road Central, wound around Connaught Road on the waterfront, and continued all the way to the Star Ferry terminal. "It was like a long snake," one passer-by remarked.

The banking hall of Hang Seng Bank was once again a battle scene of boisterous crowds and hassled staff. The bank's security guards struggled to hold back the crowds and maintain order; loud speakers blared down the hall asking customers to keep calm and assuring them that they would all get their money back. I again joined the ranks of those trying to keep the customers calm. Despite our efforts, however, the siege of the bank showed little sign of being lifted, even after the Hongkong Bank renewed its pledge of unlimited support. Within a few days, Hang Seng's vault was almost empty, and huge volumes of Hong Kong bank notes were transported from the Hongkong Bank in large wooden crates to replenish the supply. I had never seen so much cash being moved in my life.

By the beginning of April, over HK$200 million in deposits had been withdrawn but the crowds kept coming; a record HK$80 million were withdrawn on 5 April alone. All of the bank's employees were visibly exhausted from having to handle thousands of customers around the clock, and morale was running low. Hang Seng's senior management felt that they could no longer control the situation. "Our deposits are being sucked out," said Lee, who was then deputy general manager. "If this continues, we will not only be illiquid, we will be insolvent. We have to do something."

The bank's board debated its alternatives for several days. For Chairman Ho, who had personally nurtured and shaped the bank, the decision that he had to make was probably the most momentous and distressing in his entire life. On 8 April, the board finally decided to sell a majority interest in Hang Seng to the Hongkong Bank and sent Q.W. Lee to negotiate the deal. When news of the talks came out, the bank run came to a halt. On 12 April, Hang Seng reached an agreement to sell a 51 percent equity interest to the Hongkong Bank for HK$51 million.

The bank staff heaved a collective sigh of relief at the announcement of the acquisition, but there were mixed emotions: Hang Seng had by then forged a strong identity both as a top local bank and as a big "family", and selling a majority shareholding was like selling one's crown jewels or part of one's home. Moreover, the acquisition of a majority stake by the Hongkong Bank treaded on the delicate question of national pride. Hang Seng had boasted about its success as the largest local Chinese bank, and the fact that it had to be rescued by a prominent symbol of British colonialism evoked feelings of shame which many, myself included, felt deeply.

Chairman Ho must have felt the pain even more keenly. He once told us that we should not feel inferior to foreigners as we have a long cultural heritage and five thousand years of history. Given the proper leadership and environment, he said, we could achieve in banking whatever the foreigners could do. Unfortunately, events did not develop in his favour.

Ultimately, we did not understand why the customers we served so well ended up not trusting us. Was it because we were, after all, a local bank, and they could have real faith only in international banks? Hang Seng's liquidity ratio (i.e. its cash holdings as a proportion of deposits with the bank) stood at 40 percent at the end of 1964, which was considerably higher than the statutory ratio of 25 percent. After the bank run, Hang Seng's liquidity ratio had dropped to 30 percent, but that was still above the minimum 25 percent mark. We will probably never fully understand the vicissitudes of market sentiment.

Looking back at what was probably the biggest crisis in his long career, Ho Tim said: "My hair turned grey overnight."

Once the agreement with the Hongkong Bank was announced, Chairman Ho called his staff together and we crowded into the auditorium as he stood solemnly on the platform in front of the bank's logo (with its name and an antique Chinese coin inside a golden cogwheel). Those who had to remain at their desks listened through the internal broadcasting system. Ho was barely able to hide his emotions, and tears gleamed in his eyes, but he remained true to his stature, asserted his leadership and lifted our spirits.

"Have absolute faith in me and support me!" he said, his voice rising. "I have every confidence in being able to lead you as we forge ahead once again!"

The other directors tried to assure the bank staff that Hang Seng would retain its autonomy and there would be no significant changes, even though four executives from the Hongkong Bank would be joining Hang Seng's board. "The bank's personnel, administration and management systems will remain unchanged," promised Leung Chik Wai, the vice-chairman. "When all is settled, Hang Seng will move ahead steadily and we will recover all our deposits."

Q.W. Lee was just as adamant that business should continue as usual despite the change in ownership. "All staff should maintain the friendly, courteous and caring business environment which Hang Seng has built up over the years," he said. "If Hang Seng continues to prosper, so will its staff."

The bank did indeed regain its customers and it continued to expand after the takeover, maintaining its position as the top "local" bank. Despite the humiliation and heartbreak we suffered as a result of the acquisition, Hang Seng enjoyed certain advantages as a subsidiary of the Hongkong Bank; the bank's credit rating rose significantly overnight and there was seemingly no limit to its potential growth.

Whether by prior agreement or simply good management, for as long as Hang Seng's original senior management team remained at the helm, the Hongkong Bank limited its presence to the board and gave the team a free hand to run the business. This was a wise decision, since the cultures and clienteles of the two banks were extremely different. The Hongkong Bank's management had always been very British, and its customers were mainly larger corporations; Hang Seng, on the other hand, was managed like a large Chinese family, and appealed to smaller Chinese businesses. In many ways, this was a division of labour harking back to the bank's *yinhao* days.

This "one bank, two systems" approach proved highly successful and passed the test of time. In 2000, when the other subsidiaries of the Hongkong Bank Group changed their names to HSBC and adopted a common logo, Hang Seng retained its own name and unique logo.

Years of Turmoil

For Hong Kong as a whole, the 1960s was a decade of economic volatility and political turmoil. The decade started ominously with the run on Liu Chong Hing Bank in 1961, followed by the collapse of the property market in 1964 and the large-scale bank runs of 1965. To top it all, the violence of the Cultural Revolution on the Mainland spread to Hong Kong in 1967, and the economy went into a tailspin.

At the turn of the 1960s, unending political campaigns and persecutions on the Mainland had stoked anti-communist feelings among many in Hong Kong and planted doubts in those of us who had supported New China. Mao Zedong's Great Leap Forward campaign during 1958–60, a massive experiment to collectivize and industrialize the country, led to a steep fall in agricultural production; an estimated tens of million of people died of starvation. To escape this countrywide disaster, waves of refugees started to cross over the border to Hong Kong; by the end of 1962, the colony's population had soared to over three million, from slightly over two million in 1950.

The inflow of refugees reached a climax in May 1962, during the so-called "May refugee tide". After this, the Hong Kong government decided to stop the flow by fencing off the colony's border with the Mainland and posting armed soldiers along the fence, leaving only four checkpoints (Lok Ma Chau, Lo Wu, Man Kam To and Sha Tau Kok) for those with valid travel documents to pass through. Many tried to bypass the fences by swimming across the sea to the New Territories, swimming up to five to six hours in the dark and cold and often braving high winds and even sharks. This escape route continued to be used throughout the 1960s and early 1970s, especially by those who later tried to flee the turmoil of the Cultural Revolution.

As waves of refugees poured into Hong Kong, I sometimes wondered whether my brothers Tse Kwong and Yuan Kwong, and my other relatives who had gone to the Mainland, would return. However, they all decided to stay and ride out the hardships. My cousin Hung Kwong was the only one who came back to Hong Kong, but he left again for the Mainland after a short stay. Hung Kwong went to the Mainland to study education at Hunan Normal University in Changsha, Hunan Province, and was later assigned to teach middle school in a remote corner of the province bordering Guangxi. He fell ill from overwork and malnutrition during the Great Leap Forward, and although he went to Changsha for medical treatment he did not fully recover. Knowing that he was from Hong Kong, the authorities granted him special permission to return to the colony for treatment, and gave him a two-way travel permit so that he could return to Hunan after his recovery. Seeing how pale and emaciated he had become, his friends and relatives in Hong Kong entreated him not to return to the Mainland, but Hung Kwong refused to listen and went back to his teaching post in Hunan after regaining his health. He returned to Hong Kong with his family for good only in the early 1970s, after becoming disillusioned with the Mainland when he was accused of being a spy from Hong Kong during the Cultural Revolution.

The only one I knew who did return to Hong Kong with the refugee wave and stayed was Sam Chi Yan, my former classmate at King's College. One of the founding members of the patriotic Xingwu Society, Sam was among the first King's College students who discarded their English-style school uniform and put on Sun Yat-sen suits to demonstrate their patriotic sentiments. During the Battle of Hong Kong, Sam joined the St. John's Ambulance Brigade and later went back to the Mainland to attend Jiangxi Medical College. After the Communist takeover, he served in the Jiangxi Provincial Hospital and was highly regarded by both the hospital and provincial authorities. However, his work was constantly disrupted by endless "criticism and self-criticism" meetings as one political campaign followed another, and in 1962 Sam decided to follow the refugees and returned to Hong Kong to start life anew.

Living conditions in Hong Kong during the 1960s were quite difficult for most people. With the surge in population, both housing and water were in short supply. Despite government efforts to build more reservoirs, a dry spell during 1963 led to a critical water shortage; during the worst months, water was supplied for only four hours every four days, when everyone in the family would try to take a shower and wash our clothes. We would then fill up as many large buckets and barrels as we could fit into the kitchen and bathrooms in order to have enough water supply for the next three days. During those limited hours of supply, water pressure in the pipelines of old tenement houses often became so weak that dwellers on the upper floors would hardly get any water and the cry of "People downstairs, turn off your taps!" was often heard. Those who did not have piped water supply in their homes would queue for long hours on the streets and jostle to fill their containers from standpipes, often leading to squabbles and even fistfights among neighbours. Worried about social unrest, the government finally decided that they had to import water to relieve the shortage, and reached an agreement with the Guangdong government to purchase water from the East River (Dong Jiang). By this time, the importance of water had become so ingrained in the psyche of the Hong Kong populace that the word "water" became a substitute for money or wealth, still used today. Thus, wealthy people would have a lot of "water", and to make money was to "find water".

The 1960s also saw a series of demonstrations motivated by concerns about rising living costs and overall dissatisfaction with work conditions. The first major outbreak was triggered by an increase in the fare for the Star Ferry in April 1966. Inspired by a young man named So Sau Chung, who went on a hunger strike to protest the fare hike, a group of youths demonstrated outside the Star Ferry terminal and then along the main streets in Central. Later, more people joined the protests on both sides of the harbour, with demonstrations continuing in Kowloon for four days. The police eventually used force to disperse the crowds, killing one and arresting many.

Then in the spring of 1967, a series of strikes broke out across a wide range of industries, involving taxi drivers and workers in cement plants, textile mills and artificial-flower factories. Many of the strikes appeared to be supported or organized by pro-PRC labour unions. In May, a dispute over wages and working hours led to strikes and fistfights at an artificial-flower factory in San Po Kong; again, the police used force to dispel the protesters, which resulted in many casualties. In sympathy with the victims, strikes and demonstrations broke out all over Hong Kong.

Nothing prepared us for the violence that subsequently erupted. Inspired by the Cultural Revolution on the Mainland, pro-PRC schools and corporations saw the strikes as legitimate struggles against capitalism and the colonial government, and quickly threw in their support. The ranks of the demonstrators swelled, and clashes broke out everywhere.

During the long hot summer months of 1967, I could often see column after column of demonstrators from the window of my office in Hang Seng Bank, almost all wearing white shirts and blue or black trousers and holding the *Little Red Book* of *Quotations from Chairman Mao Zedong* high in their hands. They often chanted revolutionary songs and shouted anti-British slogans as they marched eastward along Des Voeux Road Central and then uphill along Garden Road to protest in front of the Central Government Offices and Government House. Armed with pistols and billy clubs, and protected by steel helmets, rattan shields and gas masks, the police tried to block the demonstrators' processions at major road junctions and fired tear gas to disperse the crowd. The demonstrators, in return, would pick up rocks and broken bricks on the curb-side and hurl them against the police line-up.

Fanning the flames, the local pro-PRC media vied with each other to urge the demonstrators on. Many of their headlines echoed the political violence on the Mainland, such as: "Organize a courageous struggle against the British; respond to the call of the motherland to smash the reactionary rule of the British." Their propaganda became more inflammatory as demonstrations progressed: ethnic Chinese policemen were called "yellow skin dogs" and Caucasian policemen "white skin pigs". As the violence escalated, arrests became rampant. Then, unable to overcome the much stronger forces of the police, demonstrators resorted to the guerrilla tactics of Communist Chinese fame. They started staging "cat-and-mouse" games with the police, planting home-made bombs in congested streets and narrow alleys with the label: "compatriots stay away". Some of these bombs looked like the pineapple-shaped hand grenades that the British Army used during the war, and were nicknamed *boh loh* (pineapples) by the locals. Even though many of these bombs turned out to be fakes, quite a few exploded, killing or injuring policemen as well as innocent bystanders. Then, in August, a well-known radio broadcaster, Lam Bun, was burned to death in his car, presumably for criticizing the demonstrators on his show. This tragedy, together with the mounting number of injuries and deaths, started to turn public sentiment against the pro-PRC camp.

Another event in 1967 that also helped to change public opinion was the outbreak of fighting at Sha Tau Kok on the eastern end of the border with the Mainland. Across the border from the Hong Kong police post at Sha Tau Kok was a sentry post guarded by soldiers of the People's Liberation Army and the local militia. In early July, after hurling antagonistic slogans at the Hong Kong side, the Chinese guards crossed the border and fired at the Hong Kong police post, injuring and killing quite a few policemen before retreating. When Hong Kong's director of medical services tried to dispatch medical officers to Sha Tau Kok to tend to the wounded, few were willing to go because of the danger involved. Time was running short and Sam Chi Yan, my King's College classmate, volunteered to go even though he was then an unlicensed medical officer (since his mainland qualifications had not been recognized by the Hong Kong government). Sam's mission was a success, earning him the respect and gratitude of the colonial government. When the demonstrations were over, the director of medical services recommended Sam for the award of MBE (Member of the British Empire), but he declined, requesting instead to be sent to the UK to further his medical studies so that he could obtain his doctor's licence. His request was granted, and he eventually became a director within the department.

Whenever people talked about the events of 1967, they would use two markedly different terms, depending upon their political stance. The colonial government and many others in Hong Kong called the incidents "the '67 Riots"; the pro-PRC camp would refer to "the movement to oppose the British and resist violence". In reality, violence was used by both sides. To control the "riots", the Legislative Council passed a series of emergency laws, which allowed the police to make arrests with little regard for freedom of speech or human rights. Around five thousand students, teachers, factory workers and office clerks of pro-PRC or PRC-owned institutions were arrested and locked up in Victoria Prison in the Central District. Those with a higher social status and better known to the public — such as school principals, labour union leaders, businessmen, newspaper publishers, film producers and directors, and actors and actresses — were placed under the close surveillance of the Special Branch of the Hong Kong police. Some fifty of them were eventually rounded up and confined to a special internment camp, an isolated white building facing the sea at the foot of Mount Davis. Many of the prisoners and internees were confined without a fair trial, and quite a few reported being physically abused in prison. Among those detained were two people I knew: my cousin Lun Kwong, the youngest son of Uncle Wai Chow and a music teacher at the pro-PRC Hon Wah Middle School; and Wong Kin Lap, the principal of Hon Wah and my former schoolmate at King's College. Even though I was upset by the growing violence, the imprisonment of people without trial made me feel that Hong Kong was increasingly "ruled by law", even though the British prided themselves on "the rule of law".

As public sentiment turned and Beijing reportedly intervened towards the end of 1967, the "riots" or "anti-British movement" finally came to an end, but Hong Kong paid a hefty price. Innocent people had suffered injuries, some had died, and the economy had almost ground to a halt. Many who qualified for immigration sold their assets, closed down their offices and factories, and left for foreign countries; property and share prices plummeted and unemployment shot up. The PRC side was also adversely affected. During the turbulence, nobody dared to shop for mainland products at Chinese emporiums or use pro-PRC banks, so business at all pro-PRC banks and companies nose-dived. After 1967, the term "Leftist", which was used to describe people from the pro-PRC camp, took on a more derogatory meaning as "Leftists" became increasingly isolated from mainstream Hong Kong society and suffered discrimination.

At Hang Seng Bank, more and more middle- and high-ranking officers took leave to explore career opportunities in the United States, Canada, Australia and Singapore, often with emigration in mind. I, too, was tempted, so I consulted Wong Hing Kwong, Man Kwong's father-in-law, who had already sent his older children overseas after the war. He was then making plans for his eleventh son,

Man Fai, to join his third son, Man Hung, in Vancouver, Canada. Mr. Wong always held a pessimistic view of Hong Kong, and he urged me to emigrate to Canada where, he said, I would find peace of mind as well as employment opportunities since several banks from Hong Kong had already opened up branches there. At his suggestion, I visited his son Man Hung in Vancouver for three weeks in the summer of 1969, and stayed for another week in Winnipeg, Canada where one of my good friends, Dr. Poon Yee Kit, had emigrated the year before.

In the end, however, I did not carry out my plan to emigrate. By 1969, calm had returned to the streets of Hong Kong, and many of the businessmen who had previously fled returned, bringing their capital back with them. Of the ones who had stayed behind in Hong Kong, those who had sufficient daring had made handsome profits from the exodus by buying up properties, plants and shares at bargain prices. This reshuffling of wealth re-shaped the colony's economic landscape, and Hong Kong was ready to move on. I did not take the decision to emigrate until fifteen years later.

Launching the Hang Seng Index

As the Hong Kong economy struggled to recover from the turmoil of 1967, few could foresee that the damage caused to the mainland economy by the Cultural Revolution would actually enhance Hong Kong's position as China's window on the world market. The colony would profit from this role and enjoy unprecedented prosperity over the next three decades.

The Hong Kong economy rebounded quickly after reaching its nadir in 1967–68. Demand for property, goods and services rose as both capital and emigrants returned to the colony. The stock market picked up as the economy recovered, and businesses started to tap the public markets to raise equity capital. Hong Kong's stock market had been relatively small up until then; only fifty companies were listed on the Hong Kong Stock Exchange in 1954, and few individuals played the stock market. However, Hang Seng had been active in the market since the 1950s, and income from securities trading and investments formed an important part of its earnings. The bank's subsidiary, Hang Seng Finance Ltd., underwrote many new issues, and another subsidiary, Hang Seng (Nominee) Ltd., helped small investors buy and sell shares.

As the stock market rose and the bank's securities trading activities and investments grew, Chairman Ho and Q.W. Lee (who had by then succeeded Ho Tim as General Manager) decided in late 1969 that they needed a measure of the performance of the stock market for their own as well as their customers' reference. Ever the visionary, Ho wanted to create an index which would be the "Dow Jones Industrial Average of Hong Kong". Some of the senior managers were sceptical and questioned whether this was not a task for larger, international banks, but Lee convinced them that we should do it. "Chairman Ho believes we should constantly provide new products and services to our customers and the community," he said. "This will bring in more business and profits for the bank. If we create the index, Hang Seng's name will be mentioned over and over again in newspapers, financial journals, and radio and television broadcasts. Can there be any better publicity for the bank?"

I agreed totally with Lee, and threw myself wholeheartedly into the project when he gave me the task of creating a "Hang Seng Index". It proved to be more of a challenge than I had expected. By then I had a staff of seven, including three university graduates, but since none of us had any experience compiling a stock market index, we had to consult statisticians and economists in the government and the universities on all the technicalities, including the computation formula. We finally decided to use a Laspeyre's type price index. Its application was remarkable in its simplicity: the aggregate market value of a designated basket of stocks (the "constituent stocks") on a given day would be compared to the aggregate market value of these stocks on a fixed "base day" in the past, in order to show overall changes in the market during that time period. The aggregate market value of the "constituent stocks" on any given day could be calculated by first multiplying the market price of each stock at the close of the day by the number of shares issued, and then aggregating these amounts.

For the index to reflect market fluctuations accurately, however, we needed an appropriate date for the "base day" — one that would be representative of a normal trading day in the history of the Hong Kong Stock Exchange. We would then use the market prices of our "constituent stocks" on that "base day" to calculate their aggregate market value, on which we set the base index number of 100. Any subsequent changes in the prices of the "constituent stocks" over time would be reflected proportionately in the movement of the index number. We poured through the records of the stock exchange dating back to its establishment in 1947, and eventually decided to use 31 July 1964 as our "base day". The market was generally stable during 1964, turnover was spread evenly over the months, and in July few companies published accounts, declared dividends or altered their capital, all of which could have affected stock prices.

The next question we faced was which stocks to select for our basket of "constituent stocks", but the answer was less straight forward. At that time there were less than one hundred listed companies on the Hong Kong stock exchange so, in theory, the prices of all quoted shares could be averaged out at the end of each trading session to calculate the index. However, we decided that not all share prices should be treated as if they were of equal interest and importance. By including stocks that were insignificant or inactive, we would actually distort the index, which should be a measure of overall price movements. In the end we decided to select as constituent stocks for the index only those stocks which met the following criteria: (1) the principal operational base of the company that issued the stock must be located in Hong Kong; (2) the stock must satisfy a minimum average market value for the past twelve months; and (3) the stock must satisfy a minimum aggregate monthly turnover for the past twenty-four months. In addition, we also evaluated each company in terms of: its current and past financial condition; the earnings record and growth prospects; the quality of the company's management; and the business prospects of the industry sector to which it belonged.

We tried to apply our criteria objectively in selecting the constituent stocks, but this turned out to be more complicated than we had expected. Since any stock chosen for the Hang Seng Index would immediately be considered "blue chip" — a sign of the company's financial strength and stability — once the top executives of some of the larger companies in Hong Kong heard about our preparations for the index, they started to lobby Chairman Ho for their stocks to be included. This put Ho in a bind since he did not want to upset any of his business relationships. The selection debate went on for some time, and some newspapers sarcastically called the Hang Seng Index the "Old Pal Index".

Despite these glitches, we managed to stick to our selection criteria and choose thirty-three companies as our "constituent stocks". In addition, in order to accommodate changes in company fortunes and the emergence of new companies, we allowed for alterations to the list of constituent stocks if the performance or eligibility of any of the companies in the index should change, or if new companies met the selection criteria. In the end, the system worked well. By the time I retired in 1984, the number of companies listed on the Hong Kong Stock Exchange had increased to over 250, but the number of constituent stocks remained 33, and these companies still accounted for about 75 percent of total market value (based on the average for the last twelve months) and over 70 percent of total market turnover (based on the aggregate for the last twenty-four months).

The Hang Seng Index made its debut on 24 November 1969, and immediately, we faced the challenge of computing the index in a timely manner. This was in the days before the electronic age, when calculators had to be cranked by hand and stock prices and transaction volumes were written on a big blackboard on the centre wall of the stock exchange's trading hall. Our index-computing team, which consisted of two "share price copiers", two calculator operators and the team leader, would go to the stock exchange twice a day, at the closing of the morning session and the afternoon session. When the closing bell rang, the copiers would quickly jot down the closing prices of the constituent stocks on specially designed forms, and the calculator operators would then compute the index based on the data in the forms. To make sure that there would be no mistakes, the two copiers would exchange data, and the calculator operators would run their machines for a second time. When everything was done, the team leader would immediately inform the stock exchange manager of the results and telephone the information back to us at the Research Department.

This was undoubtedly a very primitive computation method compared with today's technology. As was to be expected, calculations could still go wrong despite our precautions, and when this happened the news would be splashed across the papers and I would be summoned to Q.W. Lee's office to give him an explanation. If he was still dissatisfied, he would raise the issue at the weekly executive meeting and I would be criticized for "damaging the bank's image". A typical resolution from such a meeting would read like this: "Mr. Kwan to meet with editors of the press with a view to offering them an explanation as well as an apology."

It was not until July 1981, when the index was reported online through computerization, that mistakes were minimized to near zero. By then the index could also be updated by the minute instead of only twice a day. The Hang Seng Index turned out to be so useful and widely accepted that Hang Seng Bank set up a wholly-owned subsidiary, HSI Services Limited, to take over index computation from the Research Department in December 1985. Since then, the company has published a series of new indices, including the Hang Seng China-Affiliated Corporations Index, the Hang Seng China Enterprises Index, the Hang Seng Asia Index, the Hang Seng London Reference Index, and the Hang Seng 100 Index.

The Hang Seng Index started me on the path of public service. Seeing the success of the index, in July 1974 the government invited the bank to compile a new consumer price index (CPI) to complement its two existing CPIs, CPI (A) and CPI (B), which focused on lower- and medium-expenditure households respectively. The new CPI would focus on households in the higher expenditure range. Remembering the favourable publicity that the Hang Seng Index generated for the bank, Lee gladly accepted the invitation and again assigned the project to me. I worked closely with the government's Census and Statistics Department, and we again decided to use a Laspeyre's type price index, measuring changes in the average price level of a fixed basket of goods and services. We launched the Hang Seng Consumer Price Index (HSCPI) in October 1974. When Hang Seng handed over the work of data collection and index compilation to the government in July 1999, the HSCPI was re-named CPI (C).

My work with the government on the HSCPI led to other opportunities for public service. On 21 May 1976, I received a letter from the secretary for economic services informing me that Governor Murray MacLehose had appointed me as a member of the Statistics Advisory Board (SAB) for a term of two years. My role was "to advise the Commissioner for Census and Statistics on all statistical matters referred to the Board by the Commissioner." My term began on 1 June 1976, and I was re-appointed for three more two-year terms until I retired in 1984. During the period of my service, the SAB reviewed new statistics legislation and launched a number of important projects, including: the survey of imports and exports of services, quarterly business surveys, the general household survey, the industrial production index, and the 1981 population census.

So for eight years I worked for both the bank and the government, and although this could be quite a challenge at times, I was glad of the opportunity to work on various economic issues facing Hong Kong in my position on the SAB and to provide public service to the community.

23. A smiling mother at the inauguration of the new Hang Seng Bank Building at 77 Des Voeux Road in 1962.

24. With Mother and my family at the Great Wall, 1973. My first visit to the Mainland in almost twenty years was arranged as part of a United Front effort.

32. Family gathering in Toronto with daughters Yvonne and Elaine (middle row second and third from right), and Man Kwong's children Nicole (middle row second from left) and Cheuk (front row left), and their families, 1993.

33. Ho Tim (left) and Q.W. Lee (right) at the inauguration of the Ho Leung Ho Lee Foundation in Beijing, 1994. They are flanked by the daughters of Chairman Ho and Leung Kau Kui.

23. A smiling mother at the inauguration of the new Hang Seng Bank Building at 77 Des Voeux Road in 1962.

24. With Mother and my family at the Great Wall, 1973. My first visit to the Mainland in almost twenty years was arranged as part of a United Front effort.

25. Launching the Hang Seng Consumer Price Index with Commissioner for Census and Statistics D.S. Whitelegge, 1974.

26. Inspecting a Red Flag limousine at No. 1 Motor Car Factory in Changchun, Jilin, during a tour of the Northeast arranged by Bank of China in 1977.

27. With Fourteenth Uncle Tang Shiu Kin and cousins Wai Han and Pak Hei at a Radio Television Hong Kong (RTHK) event, 1981.

28. With Chairman Ho at Hang Seng's Golden Jubilee in 1983.

29. Man Kwok Lau presenting me with my Hang Seng retirement souvenir, 1984. Man also emigrated to Canada.

30. Emigrating to Canada, Kai Tak Airport, 1984. Aunt Rose gives Yvonne a goodbye kiss.

31. Receiving my MBE from Governor Edward Youde, Government House, 1985.

32. Family gathering in Toronto with daughters Yvonne and Elaine (middle row second and third from right), and Man Kwong's children Nicole (middle row second from left) and Cheuk (front row left), and their families, 1993.

33. Ho Tim (left) and Q.W. Lee (right) at the inauguration of the Ho Leung Ho Lee Foundation in Beijing, 1994. They are flanked by the daughters of Chairman Ho and Leung Kau Kui.

34. Q.W. Lee (right) with Premier Li Peng. The premier officiated at the prize-presentation ceremony of the Ho Leung Ho Lee Foundation in Beijing in 1995.

35. My Alma Mater: King's College, 2006.

36. Hon Wah Middle School at the former site of our family mansion on Ching Lin Terrace, 2006.

37. Playmates reunited: Yuan Kwong and Wong Man Fai in front of Lu Ban Temple at Ching Lin Terrace, 2006.

38. Celebrating our 50th wedding anniversary in Toronto, 2006.

5

New China

Ping Pong Diplomacy

Although my work at Hang Seng Bank did not involve China until much later, I tried to keep up with developments in New China through the news. However, throughout the 1950s and 1960s most of my friends and relatives would avoid talking about politics when we met. We had little to discuss about Hong Kong since the colonial government set all the policies and there were no elections and few dissenting voices. If we talked about mainland China, any discussion would inevitably lead to heated debates, with some staunchly supporting the PRC, right or wrong; and the others, fiercely anti-communist, loudly condemning the mainland government. I harboured mixed feelings since I found it hard to accept the endless political campaigns on the Mainland, but on the other hand I took a certain pride in China's industrialization and independence.

I was especially careful not to talk about China during the monthly lunch or dinner gatherings among my King's College classmates (class of 1942) since I knew that we all held different political views. I attended these gatherings mainly to stay in touch with my old friends, and we usually talked about harmless, typical stag-party topics such as food, wine, horse racing and women. Every now and then, however, someone would comment on the political situation on the Mainland and arguments would flare up. During these often heated debates, our classmate Tam Ting Kwong would speak calmly and eloquently, and kept on smiling in order to cool down the discussion. Since I knew that he was a staunch supporter of the mainland government, I always marvelled at his ability to remain calm and controlled in these situations.

Sturdy and bespectacled, Tam excelled at school both academically and in sports; he led our class soccer team to many victories and was awarded a government scholarship in 1940. Our principal and teachers had high expectations of him, and his classmates loved him. After the Japanese invaded China in 1937, Tam's interests took a different turn and he became one of the founding members of the Xingwu Society, which was dedicated to promoting national and social awareness among Hong Kong students. He also joined the K.C. Boys Chorus, which was formed after the Wuhan Ensemble performed in our school in 1938. Inspired by the ensemble's performance and with the permission of our open-minded headmaster, Mr. Kay, the chorus sang patriotic anti-Japanese songs and often gave performances in school.

Tam and I lost contact with each other during the war. When we met again in 1949, he was working for China Mutual Trading Company, which handled imports and exports in Hong Kong on behalf of the PRC Ministry of Foreign Economic Relations and Trade. During the Korean War, China Mutual Trading bought many Dodge trucks from Dodwell Motors (when I was working there) and smuggled them to the Mainland in violation of the UN embargo. Tam's ties to China ran even deeper than his work since his elder brother, Tam Kon, was one of the earliest officials of the Xinhua News Agency (the unofficial representative of the PRC government in Hong Kong) and eventually became the head of foreign affairs within the agency.

Tam Ting Kwong later changed his name to Tan Zhi Yuan and became a director of Tiantsu Weijing in Hong Kong. Tiantsu Weijing, which started as a Tianjin-based private company producing monosodium glutamate (*weijing*) under its own name, was converted into a state-owned enterprise after the communist takeover. During the 1950s the company expanded its Hong Kong operations to include the production of bleaches and dyes (for the colony's booming textile industry), and later diversified into trading and real estate development. Tam and I stayed in touch with each other throughout his highly successful careers in both China Mutual Trading and Tiantsu Weijing.

At the turn of the 1970s, China's rigid ideological stance began to thaw although the Cultural Revolution had not yet ended. In April 1971, the PRC government launched its "Ping Pong Diplomacy" and invited the American ping pong team to visit the Mainland. This led to President Nixon's milestone visit to China in 1972 and a *détente* in the US-China relationship which paved the way for the PRC to replace Taiwan (a.k.a. Republic of China) as one of the five permanent members of the United Nations Security Council.

I felt encouraged by this turn of events and began to think about visiting China again myself. During the past two decades I had been worried about the political situation on the Mainland and had avoided visiting my younger brothers, Tse Kwong and Yuan Kwong. I had picked up some news about them from Mother and Aunt Rose, who visited them by train from time to time with suitcases full of powdered milk, clothes and other daily necessities, but I had long wanted to see them myself to find out how they were. I was also curious about how China had developed since I was last there during the war, so when more and more overseas Chinese and Americans started to visit China in the early 1970s, I was tempted to make the journey and see the country for myself.

Sensing my change of heart, Tam Ting Kwong urged me to go and promised to make all the necessary arrangements; he had probably been waiting patiently for this moment all along. Tam introduced me to Huang Daoming, who would arrange the journey for me and my family (including our itinerary, transportation and hotel reservations) and who would also serve as our guide. The speed and efficiency with which Tam and Huang coordinated the visit left me with little doubt that I had become a target of the CCP's United Front.

I met Huang with Tam at a restaurant in To Kwa Wan, Kowloon near the Tiantsu Weijing factory and office complex, from where we could see aircraft taking off and landing on the Kai Tak Airport runway. A big sturdy man in his forties, Huang was dressed like a seasoned Hong Kong businessman, with a tailored Western suit and a brightly-coloured tie, but both his northern accent and his manner of chain smoking cigarettes suggested that he was from the Mainland. His knowledge of both Hong Kong and the Mainland made a deep impression on me during the hour we spent over lunch. Huang had learned Cantonese from his wife, who studied Chinese medicine in Guangzhou during the 1940s, and now owned a Chinese herbal medicine shop in the Yau Ma Ti district.

After the meeting, I alternated between excitement and anxiety over the trip. I would be seeing my brothers and my country for the first time in over two decades, but how have they changed? What would I find?

A Pilgrimage

I embarked on what felt like a pilgrimage to New China in August 1973, together with Wing Kin, Mother, my daughters Yvonne and Elaine, and of course our guide Huang Daoming. Huang, who had been attentive to us and answered all our questions regarding the trip, had by this time become almost a family friend; he had started to call me "Lao Kwan" (old pal Kwan) and I called him Lao Huang.

Upon Lao Huang's advice, we decided to enter the Mainland via Macao instead of taking the usual route by train through Lo Wu. Starting out early in the morning, we took a ferry to Macao and then a taxi to Portas do Cerco (Border Gate) across from the PRC checkpoint at Gongbei in Zhongshan County, Guangdong. The advantage of going through Macao was that the Hong Kong immigration authorities would have no record of our visit to the Mainland since both the Macao and the PRC authorities had agreed that neither would stamp our travel documents; the only travel record the Hong Kong authorities would see would be our visit to Macao.

Lao Huang was right to take this precaution. Although Britain was one of the first nations to recognize the People's Republic of China, Sino-British relations were far from cordial during the first three decades of the People's Republic and the Hong Kong government did not encourage its residents to visit the Mainland. Government officials, especially, could not travel to the Mainland without special approval, and very few did. Since Hang Seng was now part of the Hongkong Bank Group, which was close to the colonial government, the bank's senior management toed the official line and discouraged their staff from visiting the Mainland. The bank had an unwritten rule that those taking holidays outside Hong Kong should inform the Personnel Department of their destinations beforehand, and any visit to the Mainland without management approval would be recorded and could jeopardize the employee's career prospects within the bank. In view of my position within Hang Seng Bank, my relationship with the government's Census and Statistics Department, and the fact that I had two brothers serving the mainland government, it was perfectly understandable that Lao Huang decided to escort us through Macao.

After leaving Portas do Cerco on the Macao side, we walked across the border to the PRC checkpoint at Gongbei with dozens of other people. Many of the travellers were older men or women carrying large canvas or vinyl bags filled with great quantities of food, clothing and daily necessities for their relatives on the Mainland. There were also a few businessmen, some traders transporting small goods across the border, and a handful of tourists who, like us, were curious to see New China.

On the Chinese side of the border crossing was a one-storey, yellow brick building, where a large red PRC flag with its five yellow stars flew from a flagstaff on the roof. As I walked towards the flag my heart started to pound, just as it had done thirty years earlier when I first entered Free China and saw the Nationalist Chinese flag. Three People's Liberation Army (PLA) soldiers in olive green uniforms were posted at the border gate. During the Cultural Revolution, Chinese military personnel did not wear any insignia to mark their rank; the only way to distinguish an officer from the ranks was to count the number of pockets on their uniforms — officers would have four pockets and enlisted men two. The three soldiers were enlisted men, with the older man (in his forties with a battle-hardened face and a pistol holstered on his belt) probably a sergeant, and the other two (who were hardly twenty) privates. The latter stood erect outside their sentry boxes carrying AK-47 automatic rifles, the most widely used assault weapon of the PLA infantry, while the sergeant paced the open ground between the sentry post and the brick building. The presence of stern, fully armed soldiers on the border reminded us unmistakably that we were in the People's Republic.

The immigration and customs offices were inside the yellow building. Seated upright behind small wooden desks, several immigration officers were examining the travel documents in their hands carefully, flipping through the pages and occasionally looking up to question the travellers. They seemed oblivious of the long lines in front of their desks. A suspenseful silence filled the room; anyone remotely suspected of being a counter-revolutionary or a foreign spy would be detained for interrogation or sent back to Macao.

After clearing immigration procedures, travellers faced the customs officers who searched through everyone's belongings meticulously, imposed heavy taxes on foreign goods, and confiscated anything they deemed undesirable, including all reading materials that were considered indecent or politically unacceptable. Seasoned travellers would usually discard such matter before crossing the border, and consequently the litter bins on the Macao side of the border were filled with Hong Kong and Macao newspapers and magazines that could not be taken into China.

Thankfully, we were spared the ordeal of going through either immigration or customs. As soon as we entered the building, Lao Huang led us across the hall to a small office where he gave an older official a letter and our travel documents. After reading the letter and glancing at our documents, the official nodded and waved us through.

Once outside, Lao Huang quickly ushered us into a waiting minivan and loaded our bags. As we sped away, I could see a long queue of people at the Zhongshan-Guangzhou bus terminal, waiting patiently with their heavy sacks and suitcases in the uncomfortably warm mid-morning sun. Quite a few of them looked at us curiously as we sped away, and I too was surprised that we had private transportation since there were very few cars on the roads. When I asked Lao Huang about it, he shrugged off my question with a smile; "We are concerned about the convenience and comfort of our guests," he said.

The road to Guangzhou passed through the counties of Zhongshan, Shunde and Panyu in the Pearl River Delta, and was crisscrossed by many waterways. There were very few bridges, and both travellers and vehicles had to be transported on flat-bottomed wooden barges across some of the major waterways. When our van reached a ferry pier we would alight, stand on the roadside with other passengers, and wait for the barge to dock. As the day progressed and the sun became stronger, the waits became longer and more uncomfortable, and many of the passengers from the buses in front would take cover and squat in the shade of nearby trees. Mother usually sat patiently inside our van, but my daughters would fidget and complain about the heat. As we all stood around waiting, Lao Huang tried his best to entertain us with the latest news and stories about China.

Often there was only one barge servicing the river crossing and, as each barge could carry only four or five vehicles at a time, we would have to wait for it to return, dock, unload and take on board the waiting vehicles followed by their passengers on foot. Once we crossed the waterway, the vehicles would again get off the barge first, stop by the roadside and wait for the passengers as we walked up to our van to continue the journey.

I had plenty of opportunity to look at the countryside during our long, slow journey. The green paddy fields on both sides of the road were interspersed with orchards and vegetable plots, and appeared much more fertile than the ones I had seen during the war. Moreover, water buffaloes were no longer the only source of power in the countryside; light tractors drove along the roads towing trailers loaded with farm products or chemical fertilizer. Although I was tired from the journey, I was heartened and excited by the progress I saw.

Since we had to cross five waterways by barge it was dusk by the time we reached Guangzhou. The city seemed little changed since the war, except for a handful of grey, Soviet-style government buildings and a few high-rise hotels, some of which were from the pre-war era. Thanks to Lao Huang we checked into the People's Hotel which, at fifteen storeys, was the tallest building in the city and one of the better hotels in the downtown area. Because of the shortage of good facilities, first-class hotels in Guangzhou (as in other cities in China) were reserved for foreigners, second-class hotels were reserved for Hong Kong residents and overseas Chinese, and PRC visitors to the city had to stay in third-class hotels. Local people could not even enter first- and second-class hotels without approval, but the attentive and ever-reliable Lao Huang had obtained permits for all of my relatives in Guangzhou to visit us at the People's Hotel. More importantly, he had secured the necessary approvals for my youngest brother, Yuan Kwong, to travel from Nanning in Guangxi to meet us in Guangzhou.

The next morning we were taken on a sightseeing tour of the city in a motorcar belonging to the municipal government. Before we started, Lao Huang gave us a long briefing on the geography and history of Guangzhou, and the overall political and economic situation in China. At first I was impatient to leave the hotel and see the city, but then I realized that Lao Huang only wanted to carry out his duty, give us a good impression and make sure we understood New China, so I listened to his talk obligingly.

Guangzhou was hot and humid, like Hong Kong, and full of narrow streets crowded with low-rise tenement houses. Aside from our car, the only other motor vehicles on the roads were the occasional military truck or heavily-packed public bus. During commuting hours the streets would turn into a sea of bicycles, and the din from the ringing of their bells and the honking of the trucks and buses caught in the traffic was almost deafening. We were grateful to be sitting in a motorcar, but we felt rather uneasy as people stared at us through the windows and wondered who we were.

Our tour included the many sites related to China's past revolutions: the Sun Yat-sen Memorial Hall, the Mausoleum of Revolutionary Martyrs, which commemorated the National Revolution of 1911, and the former Whampao Military Academy, which had trained many military and political leaders from both the Nationalist and the Communist camps. Guangzhou was the "Holy Land of Chinese Revolutions", and I had known the names of these memorials ever since I began to learn about China's modern history. Now that I was finally standing at these "sacred sites", I seized the opportunity to reflect on the efforts and sacrifices of these early revolutionaries and pay them my respects. Lao Huang must have been happy to see how impressed I was by these historical sites.

After our city tour, Lao Huang conveniently excused himself and left us alone for the next two days so that we could spend time with our relatives. That evening, I hosted dinner at the hotel for our close relatives: my brother Tse Kwong and his family, my youngest brother Yuan Kwong (who had just arrived from Nanning), and Wing Kin's sister Tse Kiu, her brothers Po Kwong and Tsok Po and their families. They had all gone back to China during the 1950s to join the Communist revolution, and Wing Kin and I had not seen them for more than twenty years.

The Price of Patriotism

Our relatives were very excited when they entered the hotel dining room, and were not only happy to see us but also pleased to be able to enjoy the hotel facilities, which were normally reserved for foreign guests and high-ranking cadres. We rushed to shake hands and hug each other. Tears streamed down Mother's cheeks, and Wing Kin, Tse Kiu and Yim Sheung, Tse Kwong's wife, were also sobbing with joy. We started shouting all at once: "Long time no see!" "How are you?" and "I missed you so much". Some of us even asked, "Why didn't you write or telephone?" even though we all knew that communication between the Mainland and Hong Kong was taboo during the Cultural Revolution.

I grabbed Tse Kwong and Yuan Kwong by their hands and called their names as they, also overwhelmed, called me "Third Brother" repeatedly. Tse Kwong and I had been very close when we were growing up, sharing intimate thoughts and feelings with each other and holding similar views on life, but as we now lived in entirely different worlds we had not seen or talked to each other for the past twenty years. We had both grown middle-aged, but I was surprised to see Tse Kwong looking older than his years; his face was puffed and his hair visibly greying. Although he assured us that he was fine, Yim Sheung later told me that he had developed hypertension from stress and exhaustion during the early years of the Cultural Revolution.

I was even more surprised and saddened by the sight of Yuan Kwong. Unshaven and wearing a worn-out Mao suit, he seemed over-excited and kept on talking loudly, completely oblivious of others around him. I had heard from Mother that Yuan Kwong had suffered severely during the Cultural Revolution, but I was unprepared for this change in my youngest brother. There were many questions I wanted to ask him, but I was too busy talking to our other relatives during the banquet.

I found out more about Yuan Kwong when we visited Tse Kwong's house the next day. Soon after we sat down, Yim Sheung started to tease Yuan Kwong. "You need to find a wife to take care of you," she said. Yuan Kwong stared at the floor and was at a loss for words; it was evident that he was not in a position to start a family, although he had already turned forty.

Rather than worrying about Yuan Kwong's marriage prospects, I was more concerned about his state of mind and his future. As Yuan Kwong had attended the highly prestigious Peking University and was the only university graduate among us, he should have been able to pursue a good, productive career. Instead, like many other young people at that time, he had been deeply embroiled in the violent upheavals of the Cultural Revolution. When we met in Guangzhou, Yuan Kwong had just been released from "isolation for investigation" for his alleged involvement with the "516 Anti-Revolutionary Group". (16 May 1966 was the date of the official notification from the Communist Party Politburo that heralded the start of the Cultural Revolution.) After almost two years of confinement, the party cadres could not find enough evidence to charge him, but neither were they ready to send him back to work. He was able to meet us only because Lao Huang had sent a telegram to the Revolutionary Committee of the Nanning City government asking for special permission for him to travel to Guangzhou.

Yuan Kwong became actively involved in the Cultural Revolution almost from the start. When one of Nanning's high officials came under attack, Yuan Kwong put up a "Big Character Poster" (a wall posting then widely used for expressing political opinions) in his defence, which immediately drew attacks upon himself from the opposing camp. Meanwhile, as the Cultural Revolution escalated, the Guangxi armed forces started to take sides and opened fire on each other; heavy armed conflicts broke out in the streets of Nanning and other cities in the province, killing tens of thousands of people. Fearing for his life, Yuan Kwong asked Tse Kwong for help, and Tse Kwong quickly sent him a telegram: "Mother ill; come immediately." With this in hand, Yuan Kwong managed to board a train for Guangzhou. Our cousin Sai Kwong, who also lived in Nanning, sent one of his daughters to tail Yuan Kwong on the train and make sure that he was safe. By then, however, Sai Kwong himself had come under attack for being a spy from Hong Kong, and was repeatedly paraded in the streets and beaten by Red Guards.

After a brief stay in Tse Kwong's house in Guangzhou, Yuan Kwong decided that it would be safer to move on. He escaped to Wuhan and then Beijing, but was eventually sent back to Nanning, where he was accused of being "anti-party" and thrown into a "study group" with thirteen other cadres, some of them high-ranking city officials. They were kept under "protective confinement" in a small school building from September 1968 to May 1969, and had to undergo "criticism and self-criticism" sessions almost daily. The living conditions in these confinement quarters were generally so poor that they were often referred to as "cow sheds". Yuan Kwong was adamant that he had not been physically abused during his confinement in the "cow shed", but I found this hard to believe based on what I had heard about the Cultural Revolution.

In May 1969, local Revolutionary Committees received new directives from Beijing to send all government officials to "May 7 Cadre Schools" (so called because the directive from Mao Zedong to "re-educate" the cadres was issued on that day). Yuan Kwong was released from the "cow shed" and sent to a cadre school outside Liuzhou, where he laboured for over two years in an orange orchard. Then, in August 1971, his political fate took another turn — he was suspected of being a member of the "516 Anti-Revolutionary Group" and committing "serious political errors". Although later findings reportedly showed that the group never existed, Yuan Kwong was "isolated for investigation" for the next two years and was released only in February 1973, a few months before he came to meet us in Guangzhou.

Despite his ordeal during the Cultural Revolution, Yuan Kwong remained a staunch supporter of the Communist Party leadership. When he recounted his experiences to us in Guangzhou, he insisted that the party was correct and that any mistakes were made by individuals who had wrongly interpreted party policies. More than ten years later, Yuan Kwong finally received a Decree of the Party Committee of Nanning City, dated 20 December 1983, stating that all previous allegations against him were unfounded, and that he was innocent. I heaved a deep sigh of relief when he sent me a copy of this decree but, by this time, Yuan Kwong was fifty-one and his health was faltering; I missed the boy of seventeen who had left home in high spirits so long ago to join the revolution.

Tse Kwong was twenty-three when he left home. He was the first of us to be attracted to communist ideology, but he had always been more analytical and level-headed and, unlike Yuan Kwong, he had already developed some reservations about the party's policies when we met in Guangzhou.

When the Cultural Revolution started, Tse Kwong was the deputy head of the Art Section in the Cultural Bureau of the Guangdong Provincial Government and his wife, Yim Sheung, was a well-known Cantonese Opera singer. Tse Kwong soon came under attack in three areas: (1) following a *heixian* ("black" or subversive line) in cultural policies; (2) belonging to the *heibang* ("black" or subversive gang) of Hong Xiannu, the most famous Cantonese Opera singer at that time (whom Tse Kwong had helped recruit to serve New China); and (3) maintaining "suspicious Hong Kong–Macao connections", a euphemism for espionage. Tse Kwong successfully defended himself against all three charges, but when the "May 7" directive came out in 1969, both he and Yim Sheung were sent to cadre schools along with other officials for "re-education". "We had to leave right away," he recalled. "We barely had time to ask our helper to stay in our house and take care of our two sons, who had just started primary school."

Tse Kwong and Yim Sheung were both "sent down" to labour in Yingde County in central Guangdong for two years. Tse Kwong grew vegetables on a farm while Yim Sheung worked in the kitchen of a tea plantation. Even though they were in the same county, they seldom had the chance to see each other or to go back to Guangzhou to visit their sons, Niandong and Nianfeng. Mother tried to visit her two grandsons in Guangzhou as often as she could, bringing with her canned food, clothing and other supplies that were in severe shortage. Niandong, the elder son, had to join Yim Sheung at the tea plantation a year later because the helper could no longer take care of both boys.

Tse Kwong was able to escape political persecution in Yingde since he had defended himself successfully against the *heibang* label, but he was still not fully trusted by the "revolutionaries". As a result, he was exempt from most political activities and his two-year stay in Yingde was relatively peaceful. By the time we met in Guangzhou, Tse Kwong had re-located back to the city and was ready to move on. "I had some reservations about the party's policies," he said later. "But then I believed that the worst was over. I told myself that we were not the only ones affected; many other families also suffered. I was ready to put this experience behind me." It was not until 1976, when he heard about the bloodshed in Tiananmen Square when a large gathering to commemorate the death of Premier Zhou Enlai was violently suppressed, that Tse Kwong started to seriously question some of the party's policies.

When we visited Tse Kwong and his family in 1973, the Cultural Revolution was still going on and life in the city had not yet returned to normal. Even though Niandong and Nianfeng attended school, classes were often not in session, and they spent a lot of time working in nearby farms and factories. Sometimes they would work as extras in Yim Sheung's opera troupe, playing the role of the soldiers who followed the generals on stage, performed stunts, and waved their spears or sabres in the air while the generals sang arias and displayed their prowess at martial arts.

Despite their political ordeals, however, Tse Kwong and Yim Sheung's living conditions were relatively comfortable in Guangzhou, where they lived in a three-storey brick building on a narrow cobblestone lane close to the city centre. The cement on the surface of the building had turned a patchy grey with age and neglect, peeling off in some places, and the rooms inside had only bare cement floors and sparse wooden furniture. Nevertheless, with piped water, electricity and about a thousand square feet of living space, the house was the envy of many families in the neighbourhood. The biggest drawback was the lack of a flushing toilet, so the "night soil" collector had to come every evening to empty the waste bucket.

At that time Tse Kwong was a Grade 20 official with a monthly salary of 50 yuan, which was higher than the 36 yuan a month paid to the lowest-ranked, Grade 24 officials but still not enough to afford the relative comfort they lived in. Fortunately, as an opera singer Yim Sheung received a handsome monthly salary of 165 yuan, and her mother owned the house they lived in and let them stay free of charge. Yim Sheung was thus able to pay the bus fares and buy us soft drinks and snacks as she led us on a tour of the city over the next two days.

Since we no longer had the use of a car we had to tour the city by bus and on foot. The buses were infrequent and very crowded, so many residents preferred to commute by bicycle regardless of the sometimes long distances involved; as a result all the major streets were over-run by a river of bicycles from dawn until dusk, especially during rush hours.

Walking on the streets gave us a different perspective of Guangzhou. Despite the grime and decay of the city's old tenement houses, I was pleasantly surprised to find that the streets were clean and litter-free. Few residents wanted to discard anything since all daily necessities were in short supply, so everything was recycled: old newspapers were recycled as wrapping paper; empty soya sauce bottles became kitchen containers; and old clothes and shoes were patched, mended and re-used. Moreover, the city had put spittoons and rubbish bins on the street curbs at intervals of about fifty metres. Life in Guangzhou was therefore quite hygienic and environmentally friendly.

I wished for more colour on the streets, however. Against the background of drab, grey buildings, men and women alike wore loose-fitting white shirts and trousers in only two colours: grey and dark blue. Soldiers on leave wore loose olive-green uniforms. The only colours which brightened the street scenes were the brightly-coloured, often floral-patterned skirts of young school girls and the red scarves knotted around the necks of the honour students called "Young Pioneers". The shops had a limited supply of goods for sale, and the window displays were sparse and unattractive. Only designated Friendship Stores carried better-quality clothes, foods and artworks, but they were open only to foreigners and overseas Chinese and accepted only foreign exchange coupons. Officially, I was not entitled to shop at these stores since I belonged to the category of Hong Kong and Macao compatriots but, with Lao Huang's help, I was able to go into a Friendship Store to buy some imported candies, cigarettes and liquor as gifts for my relatives.

At the end of our Guangzhou tour, we visited the home of Tse Kiu, Wing Kin's older sister who had chosen to stay and serve the new regime when Communist forces took over the city in 1949. Tse Kiu and her husband, a veteran soldier of peasant origin from the north, lived with their adopted daughter in a single-storey government flat in the Henan district in the southern part of the city. I was appalled by its dilapidated condition, with cracks all over the roof and walls, dim lamps and leaking taps. The apartment badly needed repairs which the couple could not afford on their meagre salaries, and although Tse Kiu appeared contented enough, I felt depressed after seeing her home. Like my younger brothers, Tse Kiu had gone back to China to participate in the country's "socialist construction", but twenty years later her living conditions were even worse than when she was living in Hong Kong before the war.

I was generally dismayed by my experiences in Guangzhou. My relatives had all gone back to the Mainland with high hopes of building a strong New China. Instead, while Hong Kong had grown and prospered during the past two decades, Guangzhou seemed to have been frozen in time. My relatives had spent some of the best years of their lives working for their country, but they were forced to live in poor conditions and endure repeated political ordeals. I said goodbye to Tse Kwong and Yuan Kwong with mixed feelings when we left for Beijing to continue our tour; I was overjoyed to have seen them again, but my heart ached when I thought about what they had to live through.

My spirits only lifted when we arrived in Beijing Airport. As we climbed down to the tarmac, we were greeted by groups of school children in colourful uniforms holding flowers in their hands and chanting: "*huan ying, huan ying*" (welcome, welcome). They had come to greet the aeroplane's main passengers — delegates from Southeast Asian countries who had arrived to participate in the Asia-Africa-Latin America Ping Pong Tournament in Beijing. The event was an extension of China's "Ping Pong Diplomacy" with the US, which started in 1971 as part of the country's efforts to break out of its political isolation.

Two black Shanghai-brand sedans, which resembled the Mercedes cars of pre-war vintage, waited for us outside the airport building; Lao Huang got into one, and our whole family got into the other. Our destination was the Beijing Hotel — a majestic seven-storey building on Changan Avenue overlooking Tiananmen Square — which, at that time, was reserved primarily for foreign businessmen and tourists. Again, I was sure that we could stay there only because we were targets of the United Front.

At my request, we started our Beijing tour in Tiananmen Square because it best symbolized New China for me. As I stood in the middle of the square, facing Tiananmen Gate, I recalled the black-and-white photograph of Chairman Mao on the gate tower, proclaiming to the whole world on 1 October 1949, "The Chinese people have stood up!" All at once, I was seized by a surge of national pride.

In the middle of the square was the Monument to the People's Heroes, a flat obelisk erected on a stone terrace that commemorated the struggles of the Chinese people against oppression during the past century and a half, including the burning of opium in 1839, the National Revolution of 1911 and the May 4 Movement of 1919. When I described these events to my daughters, I was surprised that they knew very little about them, but Wing Kin, who had taught in schools in Hong Kong, explained that the government's education policy was to avoid talking about modern Chinese history in schools or textbooks. I was also disappointed to see that local tourists who posed for pictures on the monument never bothered to look closely at the reliefs depicting the historical events. Unlike them, I felt strongly that we should study these sculptures carefully, pay our respects to the fallen heroes, and try to learn from history. For me, the search for a strong, modern and democratic China was still in progress; as Dr. Sun Yat-sen said in his *Last Will and Testament*, "The Revolution has not yet been successfully concluded. Let all our comrades continue to make every effort to carry it out."

For my family as a whole, the highlight of our tour was, inevitably, the Great Wall. We began our adventure at Badaling ("Eight Prominent Peaks") Pass, the northern outpost of Juyongguan ("Dwelling-in-Harmony") Pass, which was about fifty kilometres northwest of Beijing and one of the best-known fortifications of ancient China. This section of the Great Wall was a truly magnificent sight. True to the saying, "If you have not been to the Great Wall, you cannot be a brave man", we felt absolutely on top of the world as we completed the steep climb and stood on the highest point of the wall at Badaling, where the undulating mountains and rolling plains stretched out as far as we could see. First built in the seventh century BC, the Great Wall had become the predominant symbol of China's national identity and resistance against foreign incursions. I was totally exhilarated, and as I stood behind the parapet and reflected on China's long history, scene after scene of the countless battles against foreign invading armies flashed across my mind.

On our way back to Beijing, Mother, who did not climb the Great Wall with us, suggested that we stop at Juyongguan. I readily agreed, knowing that this would be her own rendezvous with history. In the centre of the Juyongguan pass, framed by steep mountain slopes on both sides, was an elevated stone platform called Yuntai (Cloud Terrace) which was almost in ruins. According to legend, this was the place where Mu Guiying, a well-known general of the Song dynasty, inspected her troops in preparation for their battle against the Liao armies invading from the north. Mu was one of the legendary "Yang Women Generals" — a group of women warriors from the Yang family who took the place of their brothers or husbands who had died in battle. The story captured the imagination of many generations of Chinese women and was one of Mother's favourite Cantonese operas. Before leaving Yuntai we took a picture of Mother seated on the ruins of a stone foundation, embraced by the serenity of the surrounding woods and the warm summer sun. Mother's radiant smile showed her heart-felt pride and satisfaction, and she later displayed the framed picture on her dresser at home.

We spent the next few days touring the capital's historical sites — the Ming Tombs, the Forbidden City, the Temple of Heaven and the Summer Palace — which gave us an even deeper feel for Chinese history. Towards the end of our sightseeing, we took a break and visited Wing Kin's older sister, Shook Ling, who had moved to Beijing from Guangzhou, where she had chosen to stay when Communist troops took over the city in 1949. Shook Ling and her husband Ho Ling Fai lived in the Dongcheng district in the eastern part of the city; their three children, who were all working, had moved out. Their house was part of a *siheyuan* — a compound bordered on four sides by single-storey houses which opened into a common courtyard — which had been the typical form of housing in Beijing for several centuries. Constructed in the late Ming and Qing dynasties, most of the *siheyuan* were linked to the main streets by winding narrow alleys, called *hutong*, which were often accessible only to bicycles, tricycles and horse-drawn carts. Almost all the *siheyuan* have been demolished in recent years to make way for the construction of high-rise buildings.

Shook Ling's house faced a courtyard which had trees and flowers in the middle and tiny plots of vegetables on each of the four sides. Since it was summer, some families had placed chairs outside their houses to sit and cool off in the evenings. Shook Ling, who was watering her vegetable garden when we entered the compound, rushed over to give us all a big hug without pausing to wipe her hands. Her husband was well paid as a railway engineer so their house had been refurbished and looked quite comfortable, but the three other houses around the *siheyuan* needed major repairs; torn, faded "Big Character Posters" still hung on the walls of the compound.

Gentle and artistic by nature, Shook Ling had never been a fiery revolutionary; and her support for the CCP had cooled down considerably after the Great Leap Forward in 1958–60 when Mao Zedong's industrialization campaign failed and tens of millions starved to death. "The residents of this *siheyuan* had to help construct the Ming Tombs Reservoir during the Great Leap Forward," she recalled. "All able-bodied residents had to go, including women and children, except for Ling Fai, whose job as a railway engineer was considered far more important. For more than a year, my children and I had to dig and carry mud, stones and rocks using only shovels, bamboo baskets and even our bare hands. We toiled from daybreak till sunset with little rest, food or drink, until our hands were bleeding. We had to continue because anyone who complained would be considered unpatriotic or unfaithful to Chairman Mao, which was a crime in those days. We were each awarded a "Labour Hero" medal when the project was completed. Some people felt very proud, but I had really mixed feelings about it."

"It was even worse during the Cultural Revolution," Shook Ling continued, raising her voice. "The whole country was in chaos. People were encouraged to turn on each other; children were told to denounce their parents; and neighbours and colleagues spied on each other. Antiques were smashed or crushed to pieces; books in foreign languages and religious works were burnt. Thousands upon thousands of people were condemned, beaten and dispatched to factories or farms for ideological re-education. Many who could not bear the hardship or humiliation took their own lives."

With the exception of Ling Fai, who was again exempt, Shook Ling and her children had to leave their home for the countryside: Shook Ling went to a Beijing suburb, her two sons went to Inner Mongolia, and her daughter to the southern part of Hebei Province. They did not see each other for three years. "The Cultural Revolution was a nightmare for me, my family and all the people of China," Shook Ling lamented as she leaned back in her chair. Fortunately, she and her family survived.

We listened to Shook Ling's story with heavy hearts, although we were relieved to see that her life was now relatively comfortable. After leaving her house, we tried to relax by strolling around our hotel and doing some shopping on Wangfujing Street. My spirits revived as we mingled with the people on the street. Beijing residents were polite, helpful and generally friendlier than the people we met in Guangzhou, but they were also more curious since they had less opportunity to meet outside visitors. With our colourful shirts and Western-style trousers we stood out clearly in the crowd of people wearing only white, blue and grey, and they would stop on the street to stare at us. Younger people were especially attracted by the Leica 35mm camera hanging around my neck and some of them asked to see it, which usually drew a large crowd around us. When I tried to strike up a conversation with the onlookers I had to struggle with my rusty, Cantonese-accented Mandarin, and often had to use sign language or writing to communicate. Beijing citizens generally had not the foggiest notion about Hong Kong and were immensely curious about the place.

The end of our visit to Beijing coincided with the opening of the Asia-Africa-Latin America Ping Pong Tournament, an important event for the Chinese government intended to convey a message to the international community that China had friends all over the world. The tournament was held at the newly built Capital Gymnasium, one of the most modern buildings in the city at that time. Eager to participate in this historical event, Beijing citizens rushed for tickets and seats were quickly sold out. However, Lao Huang was able to get us five front-row seats right at the centre of the spectators' stand, across from the VIP boxes where Beijing's diplomatic corps and high-ranking government officials were seated. We were delighted to see Premier Zhou Enlai, who officiated at the opening ceremony and spoke eloquently about friendship and unity within the Third World. "Friendship first; competition second" was the big slogan on huge red banners hanging on the stadium walls. In spite of this slogan, the Chinese team won almost every event that day and their achievement filled me with immense pride; I felt for the first time that the days when the Japanese derided China as the "sick man of East Asia" were finally over.

After the ping pong tournament, Lao Huang took us on a ride in the newly opened Beijing underground railway. "Look, Lao Kwan, our country is not as backward as most foreigners think. We already have a subway system!" Lao Huang said proudly as we entered the underground station at the Military Museum. It was truly an eye-opener for us, especially since Hong Kong did not have its underground Mass Transit Railway at that time. The marble walls and platforms, with large chandeliers hanging from the vaulted ceilings, reminded me of photographs I had seen of the Moscow subway. Every inhabitant of Beijing seemed to want to try out the new railway, and all the platforms and carriages were packed with passengers. Although the train, which was made in China, was poorly ventilated and rather noisy, we thoroughly enjoyed our sixteen-kilometre ride from the Military Museum station to the Beijing Railway Terminal station. After we returned to Hong Kong, Yvonne told her classmates that she had travelled on the subway in Beijing but no one, including her teacher, believed her. She burst into tears when she came home and told me; I despaired at her teacher's ignorance which I believed showed another of the shortcomings of Hong Kong's colonial education system.

A United Front Target

The evening before we left, Lao Huang was waiting for us at the hotel lobby when we returned from our last-minute shopping. Apologizing to Wing Kin, Lao Huang invited me to go to the top floor of the hotel to meet someone who he said was very important. I promised Wing Kin that I would return early to help her pack, but it was midnight before I went back to our room and our daughters were already fast asleep.

Lao Huang and I took the elevator up to the penthouse and entered an elegantly decorated meeting room with large glass windows and a panoramic view of the city since the Beijing Hotel was then the tallest building in the capital. Standing in the middle of the room to greet us was a tall, middle-aged man in a dark grey well-tailored Mao suit. We shook hands.

"This is Comrade Yan," Lao Huang said with emphasis. "He is the 'person responsible' at the Overseas Chinese Affairs Office of the State Council who arranged your New China tour."

I never discovered the exact rank or official position of Comrade Yan, or whether Yan was even his real name; all I knew was that one of his duties must have been to recruit overseas Chinese to return and work for the motherland. In this respect, his office and the United Front Department of the CCP seemed to complement each other.

Comrade Yan smiled and asked me to sit next to him on the sofa. A waitress in a bright red ankle-length *cheongsam* (*qipao*) with a stiff collar and high slits on the sides — an unusual sight on the Mainland at that time — offered us tea and Zhonghua (China) brand cigarettes. Lao Huang immediately lit a cigarette, but I declined the offer and took only tea.

"Welcome to Beijing, Mr. Kwan," Comrade Yen began casually. "Has Comrade Huang taken good care of you and your family?"

I thanked him and Lao Huang sincerely for all the services and courtesies extended to us during our visit. Lao Huang smiled modestly but did not join in the conversation.

"Through our sources in Hong Kong, we are well aware of your background and views," Comrade Yen continued. "Like your brothers on the Mainland, you are a patriot. We regard you as a comrade."

"How did you enjoy your trip?" he asked eagerly. "And what is your impression of China?"

I knew that this was the final debriefing for my tour and he wanted to hear my views. I was prepared to be frank with him.

"I learned a lot about China's history on this trip," I replied, "and I am glad for the opportunity to see New China, even superficially. But I am surprised by the poor living conditions of the ordinary people. Beijing is the capital and yet its citizens have to live in old, crowded houses, eat coarse, rationed food, and wear shabby, dull-coloured, unisex clothes. They have to ride their bicycles for long distances or pack into overcrowded buses to go to work every day. I feel guilty that my family and I have been given such good treatment in comparison. To tell the truth, I am quite disappointed by the general lack of economic development in the country."

Yan nodded acknowledgement but tried to draw my attention to the advances that China had recently made on both the domestic and international fronts.

"Premier Zhou Enlai has already announced the Four Modernizations Programme for agriculture, industry, science and technology, and defence," he said. "The country will soon see great progress in these areas."

"The United Nations General Assembly recognized the People's Republic as the sole legitimate government of China the year before, and Vice Minister Qiao Guanhua spoke to the General Assembly," Yan continued. "The voice of New China was heard in the United Nations for the first time!"

"How did you feel when you heard this good news in Hong Kong?" he asked me pointedly.

"That was an exciting moment for me," I said with genuine emotion. "I was greatly moved by Vice Minister Qiao's speech; I felt very proud to be Chinese."

Both Comrade Yan and Lao Huang broke into a broad smile.

"Our Ambassador to the UN, Huang Hua, pronounced that the questions of Hong Kong and Macao were entirely within China's sovereign right," Yan continued, "and the Chinese government has consistently held that these questions should be settled in an appropriate way when conditions are ripe. What do you think about that, Mr. Kwan?"

The phrase "when conditions are ripe" had left many people in Hong Kong and Macao in suspense, albeit with dramatically different reactions: some wished that the settlement date would come as soon as possible; others hoped that it would not occur for a long, long time.

"I don't have any particular opinion about it," I said truthfully, "but one thing is certain: from now on no one can challenge the fact that Hong Kong and Macao must be returned to the motherland, whether they like it or not."

Comrade Yan seemed satisfied with my answer.

"Even though the US has continued to maintain official relations with the government of Taiwan," he said, "it could not ignore us forever, which was why President Nixon came to China and met Chairman Mao."

Obviously excited by the *détente* between the PRC and the US, Yan was eager to talk about President Nixon's visit.

"Vice Minister Qiao Guanhua was the principal advisor to Premier Zhou on US-China relations and the drafting of the Shanghai Communique. He was Henry Kissinger's counterpart during the meetings."

"In case you wondered, the women who spoke such good English and interpreted for the Chairman and the Premier were Tang Wensheng and Zhang Hanzhi. Tang Wensheng, who grew up in New York City, is the daughter of Tang Mingzhao, the deputy to Vice Minister Qiao in the Chinese delegation to the UN. Tang Mingzhao returned to China with his family in the early 1950s to serve the motherland. Zhang Hanzhi is the daughter of Zhang Shizhao."

Zhang Shizhao was a renowned scholar and high-ranking former Nationalist official who had defected to the Communist camp, and Zhang Hanzhi later married Qiao Guanhua. I was not sure why Yan told me all this; perhaps he wanted to show me how overseas Chinese intellectuals and even Nationalist officials supported the Communist cause.

"We need to build a New China," he said enthusiastically, leaning over to put his hand on my shoulder. "With your qualifications — your experience in working with Western military officers and diplomats, your proficiency in foreign languages, and your knowledge about banking and finance — and with relatives already serving the People's Government, you can have a promising career in our Ministry of Foreign Affairs or the Ministry of Foreign Economic Relations and Trade."

"Comrade Kwan, given the right opportunity, you could be a Qiao Guanhua of tomorrow!"

I was startled and embarrassed by his flattery and mumbled a vague reply while I pondered what he had just said.

"Lao Kwan can do it!" Lao Huang, who had remained largely silent during our conversation, chimed in heartily.

Unfortunately, Comrade Yan's prognostication about a new political direction did not materialize, not immediately anyway. As soon as we arrived back in Hong Kong the next day, I read about the startling events at the First Plenum of the Tenth National Congress of the CCP: Jiang Qing, Chairman Mao's wife; Wang Hungwen, a former Shanghai security officer; Zhang Chunqiao, a Shanghai propagandist; and Yao Wenyuan, a journalist, had seized control of the party apparatus. This Gang of Four, as they were later called, tried to discredit Premier Zhou and the Four Modernizations Programme, thus effectively prolonging the Cultural Revolution.

The rise of the Gang of Four seemed to have undercut the United Front's efforts. After my return to Hong Kong, I saw Lao Huang less and less frequently and eventually lost contact with him. Later on I tried to find out what had happened to him from Tam Ting Kwong, who had introduced us, but Tam could tell me only that Lao Huang had been recalled to Beijing for a new assignment. I never saw him again.

The Cultural Revolution finally ended in 1976 when the Gang of Four were arrested following the death of Chairman Mao. The fall of the Gang of Four brought the illustrious career of Qiao Guanhua to an abrupt end; Qiao and his wife, Zhang Hanzhi, were accused of conspiring with the Gang of Four and held under arrest for the next two years. Qiao Guanhua subsequently faded from public view and died in 1983. For those of us who were inspired by him during our youth in Hong Kong and wanted to use our knowledge of Western languages and culture to serve New China, Qiao's distinguished career but ultimate downfall mirrored our hopes, fears and potential destinies.

Self-reliance

When the Cultural Revolution ended, the PRC government resumed its United Front work in order to regain the hearts and minds of the Hong Kong people. Pro-PRC institutions started to organize mainland tours for different sectors in Hong Kong, including banking, trading, shipping, publishing, education and labour unions. The response was enthusiastic. With the end of the Cultural Revolution, the people of Hong Kong began to change their attitude towards the Mainland, and "Return to the motherland to witness her reconstruction" became a popular slogan and almost a fashion. Under this new political climate, Hang Seng Bank had to relax its staff policy regarding visits to the Mainland.

Hang Seng itself became the target of the United Front in May 1977 when the Bank of China's Hong Kong Branch extended an invitation to several officers of the bank, including myself, to visit the Mainland. The visit would focus on the Northeast — the country's main base for heavy industry since its occupation by the Japanese in the 1930s. The region had received heavy investment from Beijing since 1949, as well as intensive technical assistance from the Soviet Union during the 1950s, but it had been closed to outsiders for decades because of its strategic importance and had only recently been re-opened to visitors. Excited by this opportunity, five of us from Hang Seng accepted the invitation for the tour.

We had to register with Kung Yulong, a sub-manager of Bank of China who would serve as our tour organizer. A Shandong native in his late thirties, Kung was fit and energetic, though not as tall and erect as the Hong Kong stereotype for people from that province. (Before the war, Shangdong natives were often recruited by the colony's police force because of their outstanding physique.) He was smartly dressed and a successful young bank executive in all aspects; although he spoke Mandarin with a heavy Shandong accent and his Cantonese was merely passable, he had no difficulty getting along with people in Hong Kong.

We were joined on the tour by more than twenty officers from other banks in Hong Kong. During our introductory meeting, Kung announced that the group needed a leader and spokesman and, much to my surprise, recommended me enthusiastically for the job. So I was elected group leader, and a young woman banker volunteered to be the group secretary and to take notes during our visit. Kung later admitted to me that they had known about me all along and thought that I would make a good group leader; I could see that the United Front was at work again. During the tour, Kung would always defer to me and carefully position himself as my deputy but, in reality, he would prepare the itinerary and make all the travel arrangements and decisions.

We toured northeast China for three weeks, first flying from Guangzhou to Shenyang, the capital of Liaoning Province and the largest city in the region, and then travelling by train to Fushun, Anshan, Changchun, Jilin and Dalian, all major industrial cities. On our way back, we flew first to Beijing and then to Guangzhou to take the train back to Hong Kong. We travelled first class throughout our trip and stayed in government guesthouses that were not open to ordinary tourists.

Unlike Guangzhou in the South, the cities in the Northeast were cool and dry, with wide streets, large plazas and tall, stately Soviet-style buildings. The people seemed better housed, clothed and fed, but their exposure to outside visitors appeared to be almost non-existent. Whenever we strolled on the streets, we were immediately surrounded by large crowds of men, women and children who would often point at our cameras and Western-style suits.

Of all the sites that we visited on our tour, including such well-known industrial complexes as Anshan Iron and Steel and the Beijing General Petrochemical Works, two enterprises held special meaning for me. The first was the Fengman Hydroelectirc Power Station on the Sunghua River in Jilin. The Sunghua River, which surrounded the city on three sides, was made famous by the patriotic song, "On the Sunghua River", which the Wuhan Ensemble sang in King's College in 1938; I was overwhelmed by memories of my school days as soon as I saw the river quietly flowing past me.

The other enterprise that touched my heart was the No. 1 Motor Car Factory of Changchun, probably the best-known car manufacturer in China at that time. I had been fascinated by cars and assembly lines ever since I learned about Henry Ford at school, and how he pioneered the mass production of motor vehicles. I also had a long history of involvement with motor vehicles: working at Aunt Rose's motor accessories firm in Liuzhou during the war; acting as a wartime interpreter in the motor transportation units of the armed forces; and working for Dodwell Motors in Hong Kong. I was therefore thoroughly thrilled to see a vehicle assembly line, for the first time, in Changchun and took detailed notes on its operation. The highlight of the day for me came at the end of our visit, when I was invited by the factory manager to take a ride with him in a finished black "Red Flag" limousine, which was the most deluxe and prestigious of the vehicles produced in China at that time and was reserved primarily for the use of important visitors and high-level officials. We took a test drive along the road next to the factory site, and I thoroughly enjoyed the ride.

All the factory complexes we visited on our tour were model enterprises of China's heavy industry base, of which our hosts were very proud. With tens of thousands of workers and their families living on-site, these large enterprises were like cities, complete with post offices, police stations, hospitals, senior homes, orphanages, schools, recreation centres, parks, theatres, retail shops and government service departments. Each of our visits followed a set protocol. First, we would be greeted by the manager or chief engineer at a reception hall, and he would brief us on the history and operation of the enterprise. This was usually followed by a speech about the set-backs they suffered when the Soviet Union withdrew its assistance, and their subsequent success and pride in becoming self-reliant. Then the manager or chief engineer would lead us on a tour of the plants on the site, where the officers on duty would explain the operation of each unit and answer our questions. At the end of our tour we would return to the reception hall, where I would make a speech and tell our hosts how much we appreciated the tour.

One of the most memorable speeches we heard on our trip was the one delivered by the chief engineer of the Beijing General Petrochemical Works regarding the transfer of technology from the Soviet Union. A stocky man in his early fifties, wearing a loose-fitting short-sleeved white shirt and baggy grey pants, the chief engineer impressed us with his great passion and deep conviction. "China was 'poor and blank'," he said, gesturing emphatically. "It is very important to make full use of foreign technology and equipment and achieve the best results possible. We must follow the guidance of these four words: *yong, pi, gai, chuang* (use, criticize, alter, create). We have to make full use of imported technology and equipment, critically analyze their weaknesses, alter them to suit our needs, and try to create our own technology and equipment."

The PRC was then recovering from its confrontation with the Soviet Union during the 1960s, and the Cold War between the Communist Bloc and the West was still ongoing. Since the country was effectively isolated from the rest of the world, the government had little choice but to emphasize self-reliance in developing the economy. Everywhere we went, factory managers and workers would tell us with pride and confidence that China could develop on its own strength. "Whatever foreigners can do, we can do also," they would say.

Nothing symbolized the Cold War and China's national security fears more than Beijing's Underground City. When Sino-Soviet relations sank to their lowest point and armed conflicts erupted at the border in 1969, Chairman Mao launched a movement to "deeply dig caves and extensively store grains" in anticipation of a nuclear attack. The citizens of Beijing responded enthusiastically and excavated huge underground areas beneath the city. More than 300,000 residents, including school children, dug a massive system of tunnels under the capital which totalled over thirty kilometres in length and covered an area of eighty-five square kilometres at depths of eight to eighteen metres.

We visited the Underground City before leaving Beijing at the end of our tour. Entering through an entrance in the Dazhalan District, which used a garment shop as a front, we walked down a well-lit tunnel to the vast area underground. The city had three levels and offered a wide range of facilities, including a 1,000-seat theatre, a 500-bed hospital, clinics, air-raid precaution command posts, telecommunication centres, arsenals, dormitories, public baths, classrooms, grocery stores and granaries. With elaborate systems for ventilation and electricity generation, Beijing's Underground City was designed to hold a million people for up to four months, while they waited for the air to clear after a nuclear or chemical attack. The country's major cities had reportedly dug enough underground quarters to hold up to 60 percent of their population during the 1970s, and Beijing's Underground City was the largest and most comprehensive of all of them. After the Cold War ended, parts of the Underground City were converted to good use as shopping centres.

Shortly after we returned to Hong Kong, Kung Yulong left the Bank of China to head up Hua Chiao Commercial bank, which later became part of the Bank of China Group. We continued to see each other over the next few years and were able to maintain the friendship that we developed during the trip. After our tour, I was able to express my opinions frankly to Kung, who was receptive since he had been exposed to Western culture and ideas in Hong Kong. I was impressed by China's ability to develop through self-reliance, I told him, but I felt that the West definitely held more advanced technology and management know-how, and self-reliance might not be the most effective way for China to modernize. Kung agreed with me, although he had to give verbal support to the policy of self-reliance during our tour.

In 1979, two years after our tour of the Northeast, Deng Xiaoping announced his Reform and Opening policy which encouraged the import of foreign capital and technology for China's economic development.

Changing Political Winds

Hong Kong had been building the groundwork for economic growth in the more stable political environment of the 1970s, and was therefore well prepared to take advantage of Deng's new policy. Learning from the hard lessons of the 1960s, the Hong Kong government under Governor Murray MacLehose had launched a comprehensive programme to build social and economic infrastructure by investing heavily in housing, education, health and transportation, and by setting up the Independent Commission Against Corruption (ICAC). With this solid foundation, Hong Kong's economy picked up quickly after the global oil crisis of 1973–74; manufacturers expanded rapidly into higher value-added products such as toys, electronics and watches, which gradually dominated world markets and replaced textiles and garments as the colony's top exports.

As the economy grew and living standards improved, however, wages also rose, which led to an overall increase in production costs that threatened to make Hong Kong exports less competitive. Fortunately, the timely opening of the mainland economy provided Hong Kong manufacturers with a solution: they could keep wages low by relocating their factories across the border to the Pearl River Delta, where the labour supply was still abundant and cheap. The early 1980s thus witnessed a massive relocation of production facilities from Hong Kong to the Mainland. By the mid-1980s, the weight of the manufacturing sector in the Hong Kong economy had dropped significantly and was overtaken by the service sector, including finance (and associated services), transportation and tourism. As a result of the opening of the mainland economy, Hong Kong transitioned from being a manufacturing hub to predominantly a financial centre, all within less than a decade.

Hong Kong's prosperity and growing ties with the Mainland could not alleviate the colony's rising concerns about its political future, however. The lease that Britain had signed with China for the New Territories was due to expire in 1997 and, with a little more than ten years to make preparations, Hong Kong could no longer ignore the question of having to return to Chinese sovereignty. In this climate, Hang Seng Bank found itself facing a serious dilemma; although it had tried to minimize contacts with the PRC, it now had to plan for 1997 and also consider doing business on the Mainland, where many of the bank's customers had moved their factories.

Before the 1980s, Hang Seng's political stance had been "pro-Britain, befriend the US, and keep China at a distance." "The British are trustworthy," Chairman Ho used to say, and he thought the Americans were friendly and approachable. However, Chairman Ho and the senior management were wary of the CCP's policies, and were much more cautious in dealing with the PRC. While the bank's management kept in touch with Chinese officials and with the PRC state-owned banks and corporations in Hong Kong, their contacts were primarily limited to the occasional cocktail party or dinner. Many senior officers even ignored invitations to the PRC National Day celebrations held on 1 October every year, which was undoubtedly the most prominent social and political event on the calendar within the pro-PRC community.

In contrast, Hang Seng courted the Americans actively. As both the bank and its affiliate Dah Chong Hong had heavy business commitments in the US, Chairman Ho wanted to win the goodwill of the American consulate officials overseeing Hong Kong–US trade and economic relations. Every summer, Ho would invite the Consul General, key officials and their families to a grand garden party at his villa in Stanley, which had a tennis court, a swimming pool and access to Stanley Beach just across the street. Since Ho hardly spoke any English, Q.W. Lee usually played a lead role in the party, assisted by bank officers who dealt with international clients. Lee would also invite a number of English-speaking female staff from the bank to socialize with the wives of the American guests and keep an eye on the children. Since I had worked at the American

Consulate General and had developed an easy rapport with the Americans, I was often assigned a key role in entertaining the guests. We would play tennis, swim in the pool and enjoy a sumptuous buffet dinner with a wide range of cuisine, including Cantonese barbecued pork and suckling pig, Japanese sushi, American roast beef, Canadian salmon, Australian oysters, and (everyone's favourite American fare) Coca Cola and ice cream.

Hang Seng's senior management also entertained the British frequently, but usually in a more formal and discreet setting. Q.W. Lee would throw small dinner parties for the financial secretary and other senior officials in charge of the colony's financial and economic affairs, usually accompanied by Man Kwok Lau or Ho Tak Ching, who headed the bank's Foreign Division. I would attend from time to time.

One of the bank's earliest senior government official guests was John Cowperthwaite, who was financial secretary during the 1960s and whom Lee came to know when he negotiated the sale of the bank's equity to Hongkong Bank. The deal was concluded smoothly with the government's blessing, and during Cowperthwaite's remaining career as financial secretary, Lee would occasionally take him out to dinner in order to maintain their relationship. Cowperthwaite first formulated the colonial government's policy of "positive non-intervention", which was later popularized by Philip Haddon-Cave, his successor as financial secretary from 1971 to 1981. Hong Kong had always been one of the freest economies in the world, with minimal tariffs and no controls over the movement of capital. To let the free market thrive, the government's policy was to keep regulations and taxes to a minimum, and to intervene only when the market failed (for example, by introducing legislation to strengthen the banks' liquidity positions after the bank runs of 1964). Although this policy of "positive non-intervention" was downplayed and eventually abandoned after 1997, Hong Kong has remained a largely free-market economy.

To consolidate his relations with the government, Q.W. Lee also socialized with other senior government officials overseeing the banking industry, such as the banking commissioner, the secretary for economic services and the secretary for monetary affairs. He frequently hosted them at *Bo Ai Tang* (the Hall of Universal Fraternity) on the top floor of the bank's building, which offered a panoramic view of Victoria Harbour and was famous for serving Chinese delicacies such as sharks' fins, braised abalone and snake soup. The only person Lee was not able to entertain in *Bo Ai Tang* was Haddon-Cave, who would not touch any of these Chinese dishes. Dinner parties in his honour had to be held in a Western restaurant and usually served lamb chops or steak along with Scotch whisky and brandy. Haddon-Cave, who was tall, erect and serious-looking with black-rimmed glasses and greying hair, would often sit back and smoke his pipe after dinner.

As Hang Seng developed closer ties with government officials and its impact on the Hong Kong economy grew, the colonial government decided to give a voice to the bank as the representative of local Chinese financial interests. In 1968, Governor David Trench appointed Q.W. Lee to the Legislative Council (Legco), the colony's legislative body. (Until September 1985, none of the seats in Legco were elected and all appointments were made by the governor.) At the time of Lee's appointment, Legco had twelve "official" members, all top government officials, and thirteen "unofficial" members chosen from the business and professional communities. Ten of the "unofficial" members were ethnic Chinese, from various industries and professions, but Q.W. Lee was the first and only representative from the Chinese financial sector. At that time one of the most prominent Chinese council members was Kan Yuet-keung, a respected lawyer whose father Kan Tong-po was a co-founder of another local Chinese bank, the Bank of East Asia. Of medium build and always immaculately dressed, Kan worked closely with Hang Seng Bank and often visited our offices. He accompanied Murray MacLehose to Beijing in 1979 and met Deng Xiaopeng, who gave them the message that investors in Hong Kong "should be told to set their hearts at ease"; Deng apparently also made it clear that China would re-assume sovereignty over Hong Kong in 1997. Not long after the meeting, Kan resigned his official posts and retired from public service.

Hang Seng's senior management was extremely pleased with Q.W. Lee's appointment. With Chairman Ho's encouragement, the bank became even more active in entertaining important government officials, and every year they filled the halls of *Bo Ai Tang* on two occasions: a few days after the governor's address in Legco in October, and after the financial secretary's budget speech in February.

Although Q.W. Lee had been highly successful in promoting relations with the government, he faced an unprecedented dilemma in his new, unaccustomed role as a legislator. On the one hand, he wanted to affirm his loyalty to the Hong Kong government by supporting its policies; on the other, he felt he was responsible to the general public as one of the few representatives of local Chinese interests in Legco. As I was his speechwriter, I too faced the same dilemma. In order to maintain a balance between these two different interests, we decided to steer a seemingly neutral path: Lee would focus on economic and financial matters, and leave political issues alone.

At that time, Legco was generally expected to "rubber stamp" any legislation that the colonial administration proposed; but twice a year it would hold a wide-ranging debate on government policies. The first debate followed the governor's address at the opening of the new session of Legco in October, and the second was a debate on the proposed budget during the second reading of the annual Appropriation Bill in April. My research department would start preparing economic and financial data for Q.W. Lee's speech more than a month before each event, and I myself would be summoned frequently to his office to work on the content and wording.

Q.W. Lee had a bright, spacious office on the third floor of the bank where he usually sat at a large blackwood desk in the centre of the room facing the door; he could swivel his leather chair around, pull open the embroidered silk curtains at his back, and enjoy a full view of Victoria Harbour. Several small, high-legged tables along the walls held Lee's collection of antiques: porcelain and jade vases and bowls from the Ming and Qing dynasties; ivory and bronze Buddha statues from India and Thailand; and clocks from Europe and America similar to the one that Mother brought with her as part of her dowry. We usually worked on his speech around a small conference table on one side of the room, but Lee would constantly rush over to his desk to answer telephone calls, give instructions in his high-pitched voice or tend to other bank business, while at the same time trying to talk or listen to me. When we came across an issue that we could not resolve between us, Lee would usually ask Man Kwok Lau or Ho Tak Ching to come to his office and join our discussion. Sometimes he would telephone Lee Ming Chak, a distant cousin whom he called "Chak Goh" (Brother Chak). Lee Ming Chak (also known as Richard Charles or R.C. Lee) headed the Hysan group, served as a member of Legco during 1961–66, and maintained excellent relations with the PRC. (I learned, much later, that R.C. Lee had introduced Q.W. to senior officials in Beijing during the early 1970s, and that the two of them were among the first people to hear about China's "one country, two systems" policy for Hong Kong.)

Q.W. Lee's Legco speeches would undergo many drafts before being finalized. First we had to take the views of the colonial government into careful consideration because, as Lee would say, "In dealing with the government, we must be politically correct." Then we needed to make sure that the speech was in line with the thinking of the bank's senior management. As a further precaution, before finalizing his speech Lee would show a draft to his learned friends outside the bank, including noted journalists and university professors. After everyone we had to consult had given their comments, Lee and I would go over the draft one last time and iron out the final wording. I would then translate the speech into Chinese for distribution to the media, with a copy to Chairman Ho.

Q.W. Lee's term at Legco lasted until 1978, but Murray MacLehose (who succeeded Trench as governor in 1971) appointed him to the Executive Council (Exco) during the period 1976–78, and again in 1983–88. The role of Exco was to advise the governor on major policy decisions. At the start of 1984, the members of Exco included six top government officials, Michael Sandberg, the chairman of Hongkong Bank, and David Newbigging, the chairman of the British *hong* Jardine Matheson. In addition, there were eight local Chinese members, including Chung Sze-yuen, who was an industrialist (and at that time the senior member of the council), and Lydia Dunn, who was a director of the British *hong* Swire (and who later succeeded Chung as the senior member of Exco).

Lee's appointment to Exco made it impossible for him to avoid political issues, and he soon stepped squarely on a major political landmine. In 1983 the British and PRC governments had started negotiations for the handover of Hong Kong to China in 1997. Although Hong Kong did not have a seat at the negotiating table, Lee's appointment was probably an effort by the British government to involve the local Chinese business community indirectly in issues surrounding the handover. It would not have escaped the government's attention that Lee had by then started to develop closer ties with PRC agencies and officials.

With 1997 around the corner, Hang Seng's senior management had little choice but to start cultivating their relationships with the PRC. By the early 1980s, Leung Chik Wai, one of the founders, had died, Ho Tim had vacated his general manager seat and became first vice-chairman, and Q.W. Lee had been promoted to second vice-chairman and general manager. The task therefore fell on Lee to develop a closer relationship with the PRC.

Wang Kuang, the director of Xinhua News Agency in Hong Kong (which was the unofficial representative of the PRC government), was the first high-ranking PRC official Lee entertained in *Bo Ai Tang*. On one of the walls of the banquet hall hung a much-prized original calligraphy by Dr. Sun Yat-sen with two large Chinese characters — *Bo Ai* (universal fraternity) — which now seemed to have assumed even greater significance as 1997 drew closer. Xu Jiatun, who succeeded Wang in 1983, also frequented *Bo Ai Tang* and developed an especially good relationship with Lee. One of Xinhua's missions was to develop a United Front with Hong Kong's business community, and Xu was one of the most successful PRC officials in this area. Unusually open-minded and sociable, Xu was very popular among Hong Kong's business elite; but he was also the most senior PRC official to defect to the West after the violent suppression of student protests at Tiananmen Square in June 1989.

I again became a target of attention during this round of United Front work. In 1982, I received an invitation to attend Xinhua's National Day celebration party delivered in person by Wong Man Fong, whose calling card said that he was the chief reporter of Xinhua. Wong was, of course, a high-ranking PRC official, who was at one time in charge of Taiwan affairs at Xinhua Hong Kong and held the position of Deputy Secretary General at the agency when he retired in 1994. (My King's College classmate, Tam Ting Kwong, later told me that Wong had reported to his older brother Tam Kon when he first joined Xinhua in the late 1940s.). Wong said that he had heard about me from Lee and that

Xinhua was interested in the work of my research department. I thanked him for the invitation, but did not attend the party.

After his first visit, Wong often dropped by my office on the pretext of gathering economic information; occasionally, he would invite me out to lunch. Slight in build, Wong had a round, animated face and an intense look behind his black-rimmed glasses, but he always had a big friendly smile and was willing to listen as well as speak his mind. His frankness, warmth and apparent openness gradually put me at ease about being on the receiving end of his United Front mission. We eventually became good friends and were able to exchange views frankly about the future of Hong Kong. In his way, Wong was one of the most successful United Front officials I knew.

Wong had always been very open about the goals of the United Front. "The first thing China has to do is to win over Hong Kong's business elite," he said, "as this will ensure Hong Kong's continued stability and prosperity after 1997." From his perspective, Wong believed that it was necessary to protect the interests of Hong Kong's capitalists so that they would continue to invest in Hong Kong after the handover, and that this would be best for Hong Kong. Although I understood his logic, I still found the idea ironic since the Communist Party was supposed to promote the interests of the workers rather than those of the capitalists.

In any case, I found myself increasingly drawn into the growing interaction between mainland China and Hong Kong's business sector. Deng Xiaoping's Reform and Opening policy had unleashed tremendous interest on the Mainland in the intricacies of a market economy and international trade, and Hong Kong was the ideal place to learn about them. The colony had developed into an international financial centre and was within easy reach of China's major cities. More importantly, it shared a common language and culture with China, making it easier for Mainland officials to communicate and learn new ideas. As a result, a steady flow of Mainland delegations and visitors began to descend on Hong Kong from the mid-1980s onwards. Q.W. Lee frequently received and entertained well-known scholars, party and government officials, and leaders of trade and economic delegations, especially those introduced by Xinhua. Staff from the People's Bank of China (the PRC's central bank) as well as other state banks came to Hang Seng frequently as observers and trainees, and many of our department heads (including myself) had to brief them on the bank's operations and talk to them about international finance.

Hang Seng Bank also needed to know more about China in order to evaluate the feasibility of doing business on the Mainland. In 1980 my research department and the Business Promotion Department jointly set up a China Trade Group to conduct research on China's economic laws and make contacts with PRC-related enterprises in Hong Kong. Later that year, we visited the

Shenzhen Special Economic Zone (SEZ) across the border from Hong Kong, which had been established earlier in August as one of the four "open" areas allowed to experiment with foreign investments and a more "market-oriented" economy. (The other three original SEZs were Zhuhai, near Macao, Shantou, on the southeast coast of Guangdong Province, and Xiamen, a port city in Fujian Province facing the Taiwan Straits. Shenzhen and Zhuhai were chosen for their proximity to Hong Kong and Macao respectively, and Shantou and Xiamen for their historical ties to the overseas Chinese diaspora and to Taiwan.)

When we first visited in 1980, Shenzhen was a relatively quiet town with a population of only seventy thousand; low-rise brick houses clustered in the old residential areas, and a thin layer of dust covered everything in sight. We were greeted by Shenzhen's Party Secretary, a middle-aged man who wore a grey Mao suit but talked and gestured like someone from Hong Kong. He assured us that plans were underway to build a new city with wider roads, expanded sewage and electricity systems, and additional telephone lines. "Nothing can stand in the way of constructing a new Shenzhen in accordance with Comrade Deng Xiaoping's plans," he said enthusiastically.

To prove his point, he took us on a tour of the construction sites on the outskirts of town. We felt quite dizzy at first as our minivan bumped along rugged unpaved roads, but we were soon rewarded with the amazing sight of hundreds of workers toiling under the sun with picks and shovels, and dozens of cranes, bulldozers and steamrollers busy at work. Our scepticism receded after our site visit; with Beijing's strong financial backing, it was quite possible that this once sleepy town could transform itself into a modern city.

When we visited Shenzhen again in April 1982, the SEZ had undergone an astounding transformation; all major roads had been paved or widened, and modern multi-storey buildings had sprung up everywhere. Party cadres and government officials showed us a more detailed development plan for the SEZ, with areas earmarked for industrial, commercial and residential districts, recreation centres, theme parks and container terminals. We also toured a number of new factories where hundreds of women workers, recruited from the poorer parts of the province, assembled electronic parts for export.

Despite the SEZ's progress, however, our investigations showed that foreign and Hong Kong investors still faced a long list of unresolved issues. Many investors complained about the lax attitude of the workers, while others could not find enough workers with adequate industrial experience to staff factories. More importantly, even though the Regulations for Special Economic Zones had been in place since 1980, there was still a lack of detailed rules governing basic business operations such as custom clearance, business registration, employment practices, land use, the availability of foreign exchange, taxation, trademarks and patents, and licensing and technology transfer. We discussed these issues with the officials we met, who then promised to raise them with the relevant authorities.

Soon after we had submitted a report on our visit to our senior management, Chairman Ho decided that the bank should start doing business in China. In 1983 Hang Seng dissolved its China Trade Group and set up a new China Trade Department, and in June 1985 the bank established a representative office in Shenzhen to service customers doing business in southern China. A second representative office was set up in Xiamen in August 1986.

Hang Seng was now going full steam ahead to develop the China market. My department stepped up research on China's economic and political development, and periodically published our analysis in the *Hang Seng Economic Quarterly* (which we started in 1979 and converted to the *Hang Seng Economic Monthly* in 1984 by popular demand). Our reports were well received in both academic and commercial circles, and allowed me to make friends and exchange ideas with the economists employed by all the leading banks in Hong Kong. To enhance the quality of our research work further, the bank retained Leo Goodstadt as an advisor. He was a lecturer in economics at the University of Hong Kong, deputy chief editor of the *Far East Economic Review*, and a colleague of mine on the government's Statistics Advisory Board since 1976. Goodstadt later headed the Central Policy Unit, an administration think tank, under Chris Patten, the last governor of Hong Kong.

In addition to publishing the quarterly, at Q.W. Lee's request I also organized bi-weekly economic symposiums to brief all the department heads on the latest developments in Hong Kong and China. Lee, or in his absence Man Kwok Lau (who had become deputy general manager), chaired the meetings. The department heads talked about their business activities and reported any intelligence gathered from their customers or other banks. At the top of our agenda were the challenges that Hong Kong businessmen would face with the handover of sovereignty in 1997, and whether China would continue to be politically stable and prosperous. We had no choice but to abandon Chairman Ho's earlier dictum, "A businessman should only talk about business, not politics," since a different political and economic reality now confronted us.

Meanwhile, anxiety and tension regarding the handover had started to build up as China and Britain jointly announced the start of formal negotiations on 1 July 1983. The negotiations took twenty-two rounds and lasted until September the following year. The fourth round of the talks, held on 22 September 1983, came to a deadlock over Britain's insistence on continuing to administer Hong Kong after 1997. China reacted strongly and stated categorically that it would both assume sovereignty and take over the administration. This political confrontation shook the entire community; investors withdrew their capital from the Hong Kong markets and converted their Hong Kong Dollars to foreign currencies, thereby driving down the value of the Hong Kong Dollar which, until then, had floated freely.

The public's confidence plummeted and queues started to form in stores and supermarkets to buy up canned goods, dried foods, household items and anything that had to be imported, since the depreciation of the Hong Kong Dollar was expected to drive up the prices of foreign goods. Some shops even refused to take Hong Kong Dollars and accepted only US Dollars. A mad scramble for US Dollars hit all the banks from 22 to 24 September and as the biggest dealer in foreign currency banknotes, Hang Seng was besieged by a horde of customers (including small merchants, office workers and housewives) all desperate to convert their savings into US Dollars. For those of us who had been through the bank run of 1965 it was *déjà vu*, albeit on a smaller scale. Q.W. Lee was away from the colony on a business trip at that time, leaving Man Kwok Lau to hold the fort. To discourage a repeat of 1965, Man gave orders to limit the sale of US Dollar notes to one hundred dollars per customer; this measure worked and the queues soon dissipated.

"That was one of the hardest decisions I ever had to make in my forty years of banking," Man said to me long after we had both retired. He still had a distant, worried look as he recalled those three traumatic days.

By Saturday, 24 September 1983 the Hong Kong Dollar had lost half its value, the exchange rate having plummeted from around HK$4.80 to the US Dollar in August to an all-time low of HK$9.60. That afternoon, the government held an urgent meeting with leading bankers, financial gurus and monetary experts to try to devise a scheme to stabilize the Hong Kong currency. They decided to adopt the suggestion of John Greenwood, the chief economist of GT Fund Management Group, and set up a "linked rate" system. Under this scheme, the government would fix the exchange rate at which it would undertake to buy or sell Hong Kong Dollar banknotes. The beauty of the scheme lay in its simplicity; as long as the government was willing and able to buy and sell banknotes at the stated rate, all other Hong Kong Dollar transactions would follow since no buyer or seller would accept a rate that was significantly different. The big question was to agree the appropriate rate. The group of experts thought that the rate should be pegged slightly above the recent market rate in order to recoup some of the currency's speculative losses, but not so high as to provoke a rush to convert and thus push up interest rates. On 17 October 1983 the government launched the linked exchange rate system at HK$7.80 to the US Dollar and, once the peg was in place, it held as time passed by.

The linked exchange rate system successfully shielded the Hong Kong Dollar from the effects of the political confrontation between China and Britain during this period and contributed to the colony's continued economic growth in the run-up to 1997. Both the colonial and the post-handover Special Administrative

Region (SAR) governments have held steadfastly to the pegged rate, despite some of its drawbacks, in order to avoid destabilizing financial markets and the economy.

With the negotiations over Hong Kong's future at an impasse, many community leaders became worried and decided to voice their views in order to help move the discussions forward. On 23 June 1984, three key Chinese members of the Executive Council — Chung Sze-yuen, Lydia Dunn and Q.W. Lee — met Deng Xiaoping at the Great Hall of the People in Beijing with the hope that, as "unofficial" members of Exco and Legco (Umelco), they could convey the views and interests of the people of Hong Kong.

The meeting attracted much publicity and the initial moments were broadcast over television in Hong Kong. Dispensing with pleasantries, Deng gave the three a lecture in front of the press and immediately declared that, as far as he was concerned, they were there as private individuals and not in any representative role. "We have heard a lot of different opinions," he said, "but we do not recognize that these represent the interests of all Hong Kong people". He also emphasized that China would resolve the question of Hong Kong with Britain and would not be affected by any "external influences".

It was later reported that the three were not given the opportunity to say much during the ensuing closed-door meeting, and Deng ended by giving them another lecture:

> "What you have said can be reduced into one single sentence: you have no trust in the policies adopted by the People's Republic of China and the government here ... If there is no trust, there is little we can say ... Frankly, you do not believe the Chinese are capable of ruling Hong Kong ... You are not representing the Hong Kong people. You are only representing yourselves." (Cottrell, *The End of Hong Kong*, p. 159)

The headline in the *South China Morning Post* the next day was: "Humiliation! Deng turns on Umelco three". That was probably the most embarrassing moment of Q.W. Lee's entire public career.

The End of an Era

For his services, the British government awarded Q.W. Lee the honours of Officer of the Most Excellent Order of the British Empire (OBE) when he was appointed to the Legislative Council, and Commander of the Most Excellent Order of the British Empire (CBE) when he was appointed to the Executive Council. In 1987, Queen Elizabeth II conferred a knighthood upon him.

I myself received the award of Member of the Most Excellent Order of the British Empire (MBE) in 1985, a year after my retirement. I had suffered a heart attack in 1983, decided to retire in 1984 after twenty-two years of service at Hang Seng Bank, and emigrated with my family to Canada. On 25 June 1985, I received a telephone call from the British Consulate General at my house in Toronto informing me that I had been awarded the MBE because of my services to the Hong Kong government as a member of the Statistics Advisory Board. The same day I received a letter from the Consul General relaying a telegram message from Hong Kong Governor Sir Edward Youde which said: "Please accept my warm congratulations on the award to you of the MBE. I wish you well in your retirement."

I arrived in Hong Kong in time for the investiture ceremony at Government House on the afternoon of 15 October 1985. Built on the mid-levels of Victoria Peak overlooking the harbour, Government House is a two-storey white building with tiled roofs and a tower. Home to twenty-five Hong Kong governors and known for the beauty of the azaleas in its gardens, the house also served as the governor's office and a venue for special ceremonies. The gardens are usually opened to the public in April each year, when the red, purple and white azaleas are in full bloom. Tung Chee Hwa, who became chief executive of the SAR government after the handover in 1997, chose not to reside on the premises in order to signal a clean break with Hong Kong's colonial past. However, Donald Tsang, the former colonial government official who succeeded Tung as chief executive in 2005, decided to take up residence in Government House again.

When I entered, the main hall of the House was simple but elegant, with square white pillars, cream-coloured walls and chandeliers hanging from a high ceiling. The Union Jack and the British Hong Kong flag hung in front, facing the dignitaries and guests who filled the seats in the hall. Attending the ceremony as my guests were Wing Kin, Aunt Rose, and Man Kwong's two children, Cheuk and Nicole, who were both living in Hong Kong at that time. I sat in the front row together with some thirty other award recipients; and we all stood up as "God Save the Queen" was played. Sir Edward Youde, who had a moderate build, grey balding hair and a kindly round face, wore a starched white uniform with all the trappings of a colonial governor: a high collar, gold buttons and epaulettes, and a blue-and-red sash across the front. I walked up to him when my turn came and he pinned the medal to my lapel with a soft smile and words of congratulation. The metal cross of the medal was capped by the Royal Crown and hung from a red ribbon with gold trimming; inscribed around the centre of the cross were the words: "For God and the Empire". I was suddenly overcome by a surge of mixed emotions. I had enjoyed a productive and fulfilling life in the colony and was gratified by this public recognition of my services, but I also recalled how deeply I resented the British Empire's exploits in China and how its "gunboat policy" had forced open China's ports for British merchants.

Sir Edward himself had a connection to this "gunboat policy". As a young Third Secretary of the British Embassy in Nanjing in 1949, he had learned about the plans of the People's Liberation Army (PLA) to blockade the mouth of the Yangtze River and prevent the escape of HMS *Amethyst*, a British frigate which had been patrolling the river between Shanghai and Nanjing. The PLA had fired at the *Amethyst* from the north bank but had succeeded only in damaging the ship. Youde passed the information to the *Amethyst*, and the ship slipped through the blockade at night on 31 July and sailed safely to Hong Kong. A few days later, as I rode across Victoria Harbour on the Star Ferry, I spotted the *Amethyst* in the navy dockyards with a big hole in its hull.

The "*Amethyst* affair" marked the end of British "gunboat policy". Youde received the MBE from King George VI in 1949 for his vigilance, and was promoted rapidly within the Foreign Office. He was the British Ambassador to China in the early 1970s and became Hong Kong's 26th Governor in 1982. As governor, Sir Edward was actively involved in the Sino-British negotiations over Hong Kong, but died unexpectedly in Beijing in 1986 during one of the negotiation sessions.

Caught in the tug of war between China and Britain over the past one and a half centuries, Hong Kong had seen its fortunes wax and wane but, overall, the colony had prospered far beyond all initial expectations for the "barren rock". Mirroring Hong Kong's fortunes, the Hang Seng Index saw major fluctuations between 1969 and 1997 but maintained an upward trend overall; the index, which had started at 158 points on 24 November 1969, closed at a historic high of 15,196 points on 30 June 1997, the last day of British rule over Hong Kong. My career had been closely tied to the rise in Hong Kong's fortunes and, more specifically, to the success of the Hang Seng Index which led to my involvement in the compilation of the Hang Seng Consumer Price Index and, in turn, to my appointment to the government's Statistical Advisory Board. Without all this, I would not have stood in Government House and received my MBE from Sir Edward.

I had spent the best part of my productive life in Hang Seng Bank, which celebrated its Golden Jubilee in 1983, the year before I retired. Ho Sin Hang officially announced his retirement during the celebration ceremony, but remained active in many of the bank's functions as its honorary chairman. Q.W. Lee became Hang Seng's chairman and chief executive officer; Ho Tim, who had also retired, became a non-executive director; and Leung Kau Kui (the only other remaining patriarch) continued to be active as a Hang Seng director as well as the head of Dah Chong Hong, the bank's trading affiliate.

Ho Sin Hang, Leung Kau Kui, Ho Tim and Q.W. Lee had been known as the "Four Patriarchs of Hang Seng" for some time, not just because of their seniority or the size of their shareholdings, but also because of their influence over the bank for more than half a century. Ho Sin Hang, who held the largest number of shares, was of course the patriarch of patriarchs. In 1994, the four patriarchs contributed HK$100 million each to set up the "Ho Leung Ho Lee Foundation" to promote the development of science and technology in China. Ho Sin Hang was then ninety-four years old, and Leung, Ho Tim and Lee were ninety-one, eighty-four and seventy-six respectively. They probably thought it was time to return to their roots and make a parting contribution to China's development. The foundation would give prizes each year to Chinese scientists with outstanding achievements in ten science and technology fields, including: physics, chemistry, astronomy, meteorology, geology, biology, physiology and medicine. Dr. Yang Chen Ning, the China-born American physicist and 1957 Nobel Prize winner, would be on the selection committee for the awards. On 13 May 1994, the day before the inauguration of the foundation, Vice Premier Zhu Rongji received the four patriarchs and their families at the Great Hall of the People in Beijing; it was the crowning moment for four highly successful business careers.

Leung Kau Kui died in November that year. Ho Sing Hang died on 4 December 1997 at the age of ninety-seven, a few weeks before he was due to retire completely. As I had stopped in Hong Kong on a visit to the Mainland at that time, I was able to attend his funeral. The service was attended by many Hong Kong and mainland dignitaries, and Chinese Premier Li Peng, Vice Premier Zhu Rongji and Hong Kong SAR Chief Executive Tung Chee Hwa all sent wreaths. Q.W. Lee, Chairman Ho's protégé, delivered the eulogy. I met many former colleagues from Hang Seng Bank who had also come to pay their respects; their hair had turned as grey as mine, and we were all saddened by the loss of our great teacher. Chairman Ho had been a constant source of inspiration for me throughout my career at the bank.

The two remaining patriarchs, Ho Tim and Q.W. Lee, stayed involved with Hang Seng Bank for a few more years, but in less active roles. Ho Tim remained a non-executive director until 2004 and died at the end of the year. Q.W. Lee retired from the post of chief executive and became non-executive chairman in 1996. Two years later, David Eldon of Hongkong Bank replaced Lee as chairman, and Vincent Cheng, also from Hongkong Bank, became vice-chairman and chief executive. When Q.W. Lee retired completely from the board in April 2004, the transition at the top was complete and the era of the patriarchs had come to an end.

Under the leadership of Chairman Ho and the patriarchs over a period of more than sixty years, Hang Seng Bank had grown from a small *yinhao* on Wing Lok Street to an international financial institution of world standing. On 31 December 2006 it boasted consolidated assets of HK$669 billion and net profits of HK$12 billion for the year, ranking it among the top banks in Hong Kong.

6
Home and Country

A Question of Nationality

I had considered the possibility of emigration during various periods in my life: first during the 1950s when political campaigns ravaged the Mainland, and later in 1967 when demonstrations turned violent in Hong Kong. On both occasions I had chosen to remain in Hong Kong, and I was able to advance my career as the economy rebounded and prospered.

When Sino-British negotiations started in 1983, I again thought about emigrating. Although I wanted to stay in Hong Kong to witness its return to Chinese sovereignty in 1997 — which had been the dream of my youth — I felt uneasy about the political situation in China. My concerns were echoed in a mainland Chinese movie, *Ku Lian* (Unrequited Love), which was shown in Hong Kong in the early 1980s. Based on a screenplay by mainland poet and writer Bai Hua, the film told the story of an artist who had returned to China out of patriotism after the war, but who later suffered political persecution and eventually died from cold and hunger during the Cultural Revolution. Towards the end of the film his daughter decided to leave China, and when her relatives begged her to stay she asked them a question they could not answer: "You love your country, but does your country love you?"

The movie was quickly banned on the Mainland and Bai Hua was forced to undergo severe "criticism and self-criticism", particularly regarding the daughter's question. When the film was shown in Hong Kong, the story resonated widely within the audience, especially among patriotic intellectuals. I asked myself the same question as I deliberated my future. I thought of my brothers who had gone to the Mainland out of patriotism, and of their wasted youth and betrayed loyalty. Did their country love them?

As I looked back on political developments in China during the past century, I became quite pessimistic about the prospects for individual rights and democracy in the country. China had been under authoritarian rule for over two thousand years; the only exceptions were the few hundred years during the Spring and Autumn and the Warring States Periods (770–221 BC) when the Middle Kingdom was split into many rival feudal states and "a hundred flowers blossomed and a hundred schools of thought contended". After the Qing dynasty was overthrown in 1911, there was hope of establishing a democratic government in China, but this was disrupted by the Japanese invasion. In 1949, the Chinese Communist Party took power and proclaimed that the Chinese people had finally stood on their feet, but the record of the CCP showed that authoritarian rule had returned and the party leadership had become the traditional despot which demanded the loyalty of its people. Although my family values were *chung* and *hao* — loyalty and filial piety — I was not prepared to give my loyalty to an authoritarian regime. Moreover, I had little faith that within my lifetime, and perhaps even my children's lifetime, China could become a modern democratic nation respecting the rights and freedom of its citizens. After much deliberation, I finally made up my mind to emigrate with my family.

This was a move that I would not have contemplated during my youth. I grew up in a family which was steeped in Chinese culture and tradition, and we had always considered ourselves Chinese rather than British even though we had lived in Hong Kong for three generations. Many of my friends and relatives considered the cession of Hong Kong to Britain after the Opium War a humiliation, and looked forward to the realization of Dr. Sun Yat-sen's "Three Principles of the People" — nationalism, democracy and people's livelihood — when China could be strong and prosperous again.

Most Chinese in Hong Kong shared such patriotic sentiments towards China both before and during the war, although everyone born in the colony was entitled to a Hong Kong birth certificate and British passport. During World War I, many local Chinese did not even register the births of their children with the colonial government, out of fear that their children might be drafted into the British armed forces when they grew up. Until the late 1940s, those who had to travel abroad usually applied for a Republic of China passport and, in general, only two types of people took up British nationality: those who wanted to go to Britain for their professional education and training, for example in medicine, law and engineering; and those who benefited from working for or with the British, such as the comprador class.

After the Chinese Communist Party took power in 1949, however, British nationality suddenly became much in demand by Hong Kong Chinese who did not want to live under communist rule and looked for a safety hatch in case China took back the colony. Those who had not registered their births with the Hong Kong government rushed to obtain birth certificates (under oath) in order to secure British passports, while those who were not born in Hong Kong sought naturalization by asking dignitaries and Justices of the Peace to be their guarantors. However, the British amended their Nationality Act in 1962 and denied all their colonial subjects the automatic right of abode in Britain. Hong Kong residents were upset by this act (which we considered discrimination), but many, myself included, still applied for British passports in the belief that being "second class citizens" of Britain might be preferable to being "first class citizens" of the People's Republic, especially in view of the growing hardships and turmoil on the Mainland.

The political concerns of the Hong Kong people escalated in 1967 as the violence of the Cultural Revolution spread to the colony. Many became alarmed and wanted to emigrate, in which case having a British passport without the right of abode was no longer sufficient. Those who could afford it sold their assets and emigrated to countries such as the US, Canada and Australia; I myself had considered emigrating to Canada at that time but eventually decided against it.

Many of those who emigrated in 1967 returned to Hong Kong later when the economy recovered and prospered during the 1970s, but this period of calm and confidence did not last long. The start of the Sino-British negotiations over the future of Hong Kong in 1983 triggered yet another wave of emigration. Many families who possessed the means or the appropriate professional qualifications packed up and emigrated, again principally for the US, Canada and Australia. Anticipating this new wave of emigration, the British government amended its Nationality Act once again in 1981, specifying that people who were born or naturalized in Hong Kong were now British Dependent Territory Citizens (BDTC) and had no right of abode in Britain. Later, as the Sino-British talks progressed, the British government made a conciliatory gesture and decreed that Hong Kong residents born in the colony before 1 July 1997 would be allowed to use a new type of British passport known as the British National (Overseas) (BNO) passport; but this right would not be transmissible to children born after 1 July 1997. In point of fact, BDTC and BNO passports were travel documents only, with no implication of British citizenship. Hong Kong people thus had no real choice but either to become a Chinese citizen after the handover or to emigrate, so I then decided to do the latter.

Leaving Hang Seng

My decision to emigrate was made easier by my retirement from Hang Seng Bank at the end of 1983. I suffered a heart attack in November 1983 and decided to retire at the age of fifty-nine, one year before the bank's official retirement age.

I was alerted to the risk of overwork in early 1983 when my elder brother Man Kwong, who was then the managing director of Dah Chong Hong in Japan, suffered a heart attack and went to Vancouver, Canada for bypass surgery. A dedicated and successful executive, Man Kwong worked long hours and frequently entertained both Japanese clients and mainland Chinese officials who were keen to start business relations with Japan. His guests included Chinese Minister of Foreign Economic Relations and Trade Madame Chen Muhua, who later reciprocated by inviting Man Kwong and Amy to attend the 1 October National Day parade in Tiananmen Square (in another United Front effort). The heavy work pressure and frequent business entertainment undoubtedly took their toll on Man Kwong's health.

Alarmed by Man Kwong's condition, I became more conscientious in taking early morning walks near my apartment on Arbuthnot Road before going to work. After finishing my walk one clear November morning, I felt a sharp pain in my chest and was reminded of Man Kwong's condition. I rushed to the hospital with Wing Kin's help and was treated immediately by a cardiologist and put on medication. Fortunately, I did not require surgery. As I lay on my hospital bed, I began to wonder whether it was worthwhile continuing to work under the daily pressures I faced at the bank. Man Kwok Lau was quite right when he said that the more demands Q.W. Lee made on me, the better my career prospects would be. My career did advance steadily, but it now became clear that the heavy workload had taken its toll on my health.

Many of my close friends and relatives came to visit me at the hospital and they agreed that I should slow down and take care of my health. Man Kwok Lau was especially sympathetic, since he too had been working under heavy pressure and his health had suffered as a consequence. Shortly after he visited me at the hospital, Man announced that he would retire and emigrate to Canada. The news caught everyone by surprise since Man's career at Hang Seng had been highly successful; he was then deputy general manager under Q.W. Lee and a member of the board. Moreover, he had been appointed a Justice of the Peace by the Hong Kong government and was only the third person within the bank (after Q.W. Lee and Ho Tim) to enjoy that honour. Although Man had already reached the official retirement age of sixty, he could easily have continued to work in Hang Seng as a director or advisor, but I suspected that he must have become weary of the work pressures within the bank.

Although Hang Seng tried to operate as a big family, as in other large corporations there was still heavy pressure to perform and I certainly felt the strains of my workload and the effects of the demands made by senior management. In my experience, in order to advance within the bank one needed to have not only professional knowledge, the ability to work hard, solid business connections and good relations with senior management, but also a willingness to sacrifice family time and, at times, even one's personal dignity. Realizing now that all this work pressure had put my health at risk, I decided to follow Man's example and retire.

When I handed in my resignation at the end of 1983, Hang Seng's patriarchs were both surprised and reluctant to see me leave. Chairman Ho, Ho Tim, Leung Kau Kui and the other old-time Hang Seng bankers who had known *Gung Gung* Tang Chi Ngong, Uncle Wai Chow and Father back in the days of the *yinhao* saw me more as a "nephew" than as a *foki* (an ordinary staff). Nevertheless, they respected my decision and wished me a happy retirement. Having resigned from Hang Seng, it then became quite easy for me to emigrate and leave Hong Kong.

Farewell to Hong Kong

When I considered possible destinations for emigration, Canada was a natural choice since my daughters Yvonne and Elaine had already left Hong Kong to attend their last two years of secondary school in Ottawa and Toronto respectively, and they would enjoy lower university tuition fees in Canada if we became residents. Canada also held many other attractions for me, including the wide open spaces, natural resources, a good social security and national health system, and a record of welcoming immigrants. Moreover, as members of the British Commonwealth, Canada and Hong Kong share a common heritage in British-based systems and institutions and the use of English as an official language, which would make our adjustment easier. Finally, from a political perspective, Canada embodied the values for which I had been searching and had incorporated the Charter of Rights and Freedoms in its constitution in 1982, thereby guaranteeing its citizens a wide range of constitutional rights and personal freedoms.

Having made up my mind, I submitted an application for myself and my family and, within a few months, we were asked to attend an interview at the Canadian Commission in Hong Kong. Yvonne and Elaine flew back to Hong Kong for the interview, which went smoothly, and we obtained our immigrant visas in June 1984.

When I told my friends and relatives about my plan to emigrate, their reactions were mixed; some were happy for us, but others worried that we would find it hard to adjust to a foreign country. Many of my older relatives believed in the traditional Chinese saying: "Once a person leaves his village, he will be looked down upon". Those who identified with New China, such as Chu Hark Keung and Tam Ting Kwong, my former classmates at King's College, and Kung Yulong, who accompanied me to visit the Mainland in 1977, were disappointed that I would forsake my motherland. They had hoped that I would play an active role after 1997 and tried to convince me to stay and serve China with my experience and qualifications. I thanked them for their good intentions, but tried to make them understand my thinking. "It is not that I love Hong Kong and China less, but I value personal freedom and democracy more," I told them. Unable to convince me to stay, they wished me luck in my adopted country. Unlike some of the more extreme patriots, they did not consider me a "coward" or a "deserter"; their sympathy and good wishes touched my heart.

The hardest part of leaving Hong Kong was saying goodbye to Mother. Since returning to Hong Kong from Singapore in 1958, Mother had lived with my family and I for more than twenty years: eight at Ying Fai Terrace and fifteen at Arbuthnot Road. During this time, Mother's relationship with Wing Kin had become increasingly stressed, which was not uncommon between mothers and their daughters-in-law in many traditional Chinese families. Mother had grown up in a large, traditional family where daughters-in-law had to be respectful towards their elders and perform many household tasks; she herself had been an obedient daughter-in-law in the Kwan family, working diligently in the house and serving Grandmother's every need. In turn, Mother expected the same from her own daughters-in-law, not realizing that times had changed.

In order to minimize the conflicts between Mother and Wing Kin, Man Kwong helped me to persuade Mother to move to an apartment that he had bought on Dragon Terrace in Causeway Bay. Mother finally agreed to move there in 1982 after Aunt Rose and other relatives promised to visit her frequently to keep her company. Aunt Rose, who had closed down her businesses after Uncle Leung passed away in the early 1950s, had moved to Sha Tin in the New Territories to live with her adopted granddaughter.

When we left Hong Kong in September 1984, Mother had turned eighty-four and looked very frail. When Wing Kin and I took Yvonne and Elaine to say goodbye to her, she embraced them tightly and the three of them started to cry. Wing Kin and I felt so guilty that we could hardly utter a word to comfort her; we ourselves were in tears when we gave her one last goodbye hug. That was the last time we all saw Mother.

Starting a New Life

We boarded a Canadian Pacific flight for Toronto on 6 September 1984, three months after we received our immigrant visas. Looking through the cabin window as our plane circled over Toronto's Pearson Airport, I was struck by the sharp contrast between the city and Hong Kong. While Hong Kong Island was packed with high-rise office and residential buildings, Toronto was completely flat except for a small cluster of skyscrapers and the landmark CN Tower near the waterfront on Lake Ontario. We found Toronto refreshingly spacious and relaxing after the noise and congestion in Hong Kong.

We were greeted at the airport by John Ho, who had been my comrade as a wartime interpreter, a colleague at Dodwell Motors and best man at my wedding.

Having moved to Toronto ten years earlier with his wife and three children, John was exactly the person we needed to help us settle down. Although he and his family lived in Etobicoke (at the western end of Toronto) in order to be close to his office, John suggested that we settle in Scarborough (at the eastern end of town) where there were more Hong Kong immigrants. With a population of nearly five hundred thousand and growing, Scarborough was thriving with the arrival of new immigrants and had become a "Little Hong Kong" where residents could speak Cantonese in most supermarkets, shopping malls, banks and restaurants, and even in the clinics of doctors and dentists.

The convenience of living in Scarborough appealed to Wing Kin, but Yvonne and Elaine objected strongly to the idea. "Since we have decided to live in Canada, we should participate fully in the lifestyle here," they said. "We should try to speak English, eat Western food and appreciate Canadian culture. Of course, you are retired, and you are happy as long as you have enough savings to pay for daily expenses, take the occasional tour, and go back once in a while to Hong Kong to see friends and relatives. We are different; we are in Canada to pursue our education and careers. We'll have no future here if we alienate ourselves from mainstream Canadian society. Living here in Hong Kong style simply will not work for us."

I understood my daughters' views very well; I would have felt the same if I were their age. However, I needed to take care of Wing Kin's wishes in order to make her feel comfortable in the new environment. In the end, we decided to settle in Scarborough and moved into an apartment near a large shopping mall. Soon after we had settled in, John moved his family into the neighbourhood as well.

My daughters' wishes were granted several years later. Yvonne got married in 1990 and moved to a house in Mississauga to the west of Toronto. Elaine moved first to an apartment in North York in uptown Toronto and later, after she got married, to a house in Vaughan in the northern part of the city. They have both developed their own careers and circles of friends, and their lifestyles have become increasingly Canadian. Wing Kin and I, on the other hand, continue to live in an apartment in Scarborough and our lifestyle has remained largely as it had been in Hong Kong.

We still associate primarily with friends who were originally from Hong Kong. New immigrants generally prefer to stay together as a group, and we are no exception. During the late 1800s and early 1900s, Chinese immigrants to Canada usually formed networks around hometown or clan associations, mixing with people from the same county or village who spoke the same dialect and shared the same customs and values. New immigrants from Hong Kong who settled in Scarborough in the 1980s had a similar tendency to stay together, but they used different networks such as professional societies, chambers of commerce, school and company alumni associations and, often, church groups.

Former Hang Seng staff who had immigrated to Toronto had formed a Hang Seng Friendship Association (HSFA) to keep in touch with each other and with current employees of the bank. The founding members were Man Kwok Lau, Wong Cho Sum and Ho Biu, who held the positions of deputy general manager, assistant general manager and senior manager respectively at the time of their retirement. I was invited to join the association's board of directors, but I decided to become just an ordinary member since I had already attended too many meetings while working for Hang Seng. With the support of the bank, the HSFA sponsored many social activities for its members and their families, including picnics, Christmas parties, Chinese New Year banquets and out-of-town excursions. The association also continued to maintain a close relationship with the bank; its members, myself included, regularly received the *Hang Seng Economic Monthly* and *Hang Seng Perspective*, a newsletter on the bank's current activities.

Of the three co-founders of HSFA, Man Kwok Lau was the only one who stayed on in Toronto. Wong Cho Sum could not tolerate the winter cold and returned to Hong Kong in the late 1980s; he passed away not long afterward. Ho Biu, who was relatively young, found life in Canada too quiet and returned to Hong Kong as soon as he obtained his Canadian passport. Man chose to remain in Canada; a devoted Christian, he often said: "God would guide me where I should go." He continued to chair the association and many younger Hang Seng alumni looked up to him as a leader. Man had never been keen to involve the HSFA in any political activity or community service, perhaps because he was tired of the political issues surrounding Hong Kong and the Mainland and wanted to stay away from politics in Canada. Although I respected Man, I disagreed with him on this matter and felt that we should be more involved in mainstream Canadian society.

Aside from the HSFA, I also interacted with two other groups of Hong Kong immigrants: my former King's College schoolmates and my wartime interpreter comrades. Compared to the HSFA, these two groups were more loosely organized and met only occasionally, but our gatherings were always warm and lively. We usually met in a tea house, restaurant or someone's home, where we would play *mahjong*, discuss current events (especially news from Hong Kong and China), or talk about our school days or wartime adventures. Sometimes we joked that we were "White Chinese", akin to the thousands of "White Russians" who had left their homeland and fled to northeastern China and Shanghai at the turn of the twentieth century to escape communism.

I had a wonderful time participating in the activities of HSFA and getting together with my former schoolmates and interpreter comrades. As time went by, however, participation at these gatherings started to drop as some of my friends went back to Hong Kong when the political uncertainly surrounding the handover dissipated, and others even went to live on the Mainland as living conditions there improved. Still others entered nursing homes in Toronto or died. It makes me sad and uneasy that I am seeing my friends less and less often.

Becoming Canadian

Many of my retired friends prefer to lead a quiet life and keep to themselves, subscribing to the traditional Chinese saying: "Shovel the snow in front of your own doorstep, and disregard the frost on the roof of your neighbours' house." Out of habit, some immigrants from Hong Kong even refer to the Caucasian people around them as "foreigners"; I find this highly ironic, even xenophobic, since the reality is the other way around.

Unlike many of my friends, I am always looking for ways to participate more fully in Canadian life rather than confining myself to such stereotypical immigrant activities as playing *mahjong* and visiting Chinese supermarkets. During long weekends or holidays, Wing Kin and I will often visit other provinces or cross the border to the United States, or even accompany our daughters to ski resorts although we do not ski. If I were younger and stronger, I would want to participate in such outdoor activities as skiing, skating, camping and fishing, in order to fully enjoy the Canadian way of life.

We finally acquired our Canadian citizenship in 1987, three years after we landed. My family and I attended an official ceremony, together with nearly a hundred other new citizens, to pledge our allegiance before a citizenship judge and sing the Canadian national anthem. I noted with a deep sense of irony that we were pledging allegiance to Queen Elizabeth II, who is Canada's queen and head of state in addition to being queen of the United Kingdom and head of the Commonwealth. When we all sang the national anthem, "O Canada", at the end of the ceremony, I joined in with a heavy heart and thought about the other anthems that I had sung in the past: "The Three Principles of the People" (national anthem of the Republic of China) in primary school; "God save the King" (national anthem of the United Kingdom) at King's College; and "March of the Volunteers" (national anthem of the People's Republic of China) after 1 October 1949 when many people in Hong Kong had such high hopes for New China.

I found a whole new dimension to my life in Canada after becoming a citizen. For the first time, I could elect officials to all levels of government — from the city council of Scarborough to the parliament in Ottawa — and participate actively in the country's political process. I felt a twinge of excitement when I mailed in my first ballot, which was for our neighbourhood representative on the Scarborough city council; it reminded me clearly why I wanted to immigrate.

I realized, however, that I should not take my right to vote for granted, and that the Chinese could enjoy immigration and citizenship rights in Canada only after decades of discrimination and political struggles. Canada's early immigration laws were highly racist and exclusionary, and listed the different peoples and races who could be admitted into the country in descending order of priority, and subject to economic needs. At the top of the list were the British and white Americans, followed by northern Europeans, central Europeans, southern and eastern Europeans, Jews and, finally, Chinese and blacks.

Early Chinese immigrants to North America were mainly poor peasants and workers from the Sze Yup region (comprising the four counties of Toishan, Sunwui, Hoiping and Yanping) in Guangdong Province, who had to leave their villages when the rural economy collapsed in the last decades of the Qing dynasty. Many of them departed for North America from Hong Kong, where the last glimpse of China they would see from their steamer was Victoria Harbour. The Sze Yup labourers were prepared to go wherever there was work, even under conditions of racial discrimination and extreme hardship. One of their earliest destinations was the Sacramento River in California where gold was first discovered in 1848; thereafter, the United States was known as *gumshan*, or Gold Mountain. In 1858, gold was discovered in the Fraser River Valley in what is now British Columbia, which drew the first wave of Chinese labourers to Canada. They later found work in other areas as well, such as lumber and fishing.

The second wave of Chinese immigration into Canada occurred during 1881–85 when more than fifteen thousand Chinese workers were hired for the construction of the transcontinental Canadian Pacific Railroad. Here again, Chinese labourers were sought after for their agility, endurance and willingness to accept low wages, which were often half the wages of other workers. Many Chinese workers were assigned to the dangerous task of dynamiting the path of the track through the mountains, and it was said that one Chinese worker died for every mile of railroad laid. When construction of the Canadian Pacific Railroad officially ended, on 7 November 1885, and Chinese workers were no longer needed, the Canadian government immediately imposed a $50 "head tax" on future Chinese immigrants in order to discourage them from coming to Canada. This amount was increased to $100 in 1900 and $500 in 1903; the Chinese were the only immigrants in Canada who had to pay a head tax.

When the Chinese continued to come to Canada despite the head tax, the Canadian Parliament passed the Chinese Exclusion Act of 1923, excluding all Chinese except for merchants and diplomats from entering Canada, and thus shattering many dreams of family reunion. The act also denied the Chinese any rights to Canadian citizenship and barred them from joining the army. It was only at the British government's request that ethnic Chinese were enlisted in the Canadian army in 1944 and sent to the Asian war front. Impressed by the loyalty of Chinese immigrants during the war, the Canadian government finally repealed the infamous Chinese Exclusion Act in 1947 and restored immigration and citizenship rights to the Chinese.

Taking Part in a Democracy

After the war, Hong Kong replaced Sze Yup as the main source of Chinese immigrants in Canada, but although the new immigrants from Hong Kong were generally better off than previous generations of Chinese immigrants, they too had to deal with racial discrimination and defend their democratic rights.

The arrival of Hong Kong immigrants peaked in the mid-1980s when it became clear that the British would hand Hong Kong over to China in 1997 (the Sino-British Joint Declaration was signed in 1984). The marked increase in the Chinese population in Scarborough led to racially sparked tensions. In 1984, some Scarborough residents started to blame Chinese immigrants for parking and traffic problems in the area and distributed hate literature targeting the Chinese community. The resulting racial tension prompted the mayor to appoint a task force to investigate and mediate race relations within the community.

In conjunction with this government effort, a group of dedicated Chinese Canadians organized the Federation of Chinese Canadians in Scarborough (FCCS), a non-profit organization, to promote equality and harmony within the city and to encourage the Chinese to participate in the social, economic and political life of the community. I was impressed by the mission of the FCCS and volunteered to work there as a director and secretary in 1989. Most of my colleagues were much younger than me, but I admired their energy and dedication and they respected my background and experience. It was the first time I had become involved with a major community organization, and gave me a first-hand education on civic duty and political participation. At that time, very few Hong Kong immigrants of my age had any interest in working for non-profit organizations such as the FCCS.

I had another experience in political participation that year, but under tragic circumstances. In the spring of 1989, politically active Chinese Canadians had formed the "Toronto Committee of Chinese Canadians Supporting the Movement for Democracy in China" (later re-named "Toronto Association for Democracy in China" (TADC)) to show their sympathy for students demonstrating in Beijing's Tiananmen Square and to support human rights and democracy in China. After the Chinese government declared martial law on 26

May, the committee planned to stage a demonstration in front of the Chinese Consulate General in Toronto to support the students. Since the FCCS was one of the organizations in the committee and I was its secretary, I quickly telephoned all our members and urged them to take part in the demonstration, which my family and I also joined. The group protesting outside the consulate that day reached over thirty thousand. I was sixty-four years old then, and this was the first and (so far) the only time in my life that I have taken to the streets for a political cause. Then, on 4 June, tanks rolled down the streets of Beijing into Tiananmen Square and brutally suppressed the nascent pro-democracy movement, thus crushing yet another dream of China embracing democracy and abandoning authoritarian rule.

A series of mass demonstrations also took place in Hong Kong during May and early June that year, and one of the demonstrations had over one million participants. I too would have joined the demonstrations had I remained in Hong Kong. Mass participation on this scale and with such unity of purpose was unprecedented in Hong Kong, and I wondered whether it signified the beginning of the people's involvement in the political process. I like to think that this had sown the seeds for greater political participation and activism in Hong Kong in later years, such as the demonstration on 1 July 2003 protesting the enactment of a national security bill under Article 23 of the Basic Law (which involved up to half a million people), and other demonstrations in subsequent years calling for universal suffrage.

This series of events affected me deeply. Through my participation in both the FCCS and the 26 May demonstration, I came to realize that democracy requires us to watch out for our rights constantly, and make our voices heard. Although we are able to vote for our representatives in government as Canadian citizens, in reality our rights and freedom can easily be eroded if we were not politically engaged and vigilant.

I have seen this clearly through the activism of my nephew Cheuk and his friends in the Chinese Canadian community over the past thirty years. After immigrating to Canada in 1976, Cheuk joined a group of friends in publishing *The Asianadian*, a magazine promoting Asian Canadian identity, arts, politics and community activism. Cheuk later became involved in the "Anti W-5" movement to protest against a nationally televised show called "Campus Giveaway" which claimed that "foreigners" were taking away places from Canadians in the universities, when in fact the "foreigners" were Chinese Canadians. The protest resulted in a public apology by the television network and the establishment of the Chinese Canadians National Council (CCNC) in 1980 to promote the rights of Chinese Canadians and to encourage their full participation in Canadian society. Both Cheuk and his friend Dr. Joseph Wong, who served as the CCNC's founding president, were active members of this organization.

Over the years, the CCNC has taken up a number of issues, including: the National Emergency Service for Chinese Students in Canada in the aftermath of June 4; the Chinese Exclusion Act and Head Tax Redress Campaign, which resulted in an official apology by the Canadian Government in 2006; and other movements promoting race relations and multiculturalism. The FCCS, where I volunteered, is itself a chapter of the CCNC.

A Long Farewell

My family and I have made our home in Canada since we immigrated in 1984 and have not thought about returning to live in Hong Kong. Wing Kin and I prefer the spacious living in Toronto to the cramped streets of Hong Kong. Both Yvonne and Elaine have pursued stable careers as medical technologists after graduating from the University of Toronto (although Yvonne later switched to teaching, which she enjoys more), and they have married and started their own families. Over the years, Wing Kin and I have taken several trips back to Hong Kong and mainland China, but we are always glad to return to our home in Canada.

Some of my initial trips back to Hong Kong were to say a last farewell to those who had been dear to me. My first return visit was in March 1985, only six months after I landed in Canada. On the morning of 28 March, my elder brother Man Kwong called me in Toronto to tell me that Mother had passed away. I rushed back to Hong Kong the next day, but Wing Kin could not accompany me since she had to stay and take care of our daughters. Unfortunately, our two younger brothers, Tse Kwong and Yuan Kwong, could not come to Hong Kong to attend the funeral since they were unable to obtain government approval in time. We followed Buddhist rituals for the funeral service, in accordance with our family tradition, and Mother's ashes are stored in Chi Lin Nunnery in Diamond Hill, Kowloon, in a niche that she had bought many years ago close to the niche where Father's ashes were stored and right next to the one that Aunt Rose had reserved for herself. Whenever I visit Hong Kong, I would go to Chi Lin to pay my respects to my parents.

My second trip back to Hong Kong to say farewell was in December 1988 when Man Kwong passed away. Although Man Kwong had reached the retirement age of sixty in 1981, Dah Chong Hong's board persuaded him to stay on in their Tokyo branch, first as managing director and later as an advisor. In the meantime, his wife, Amy, was diagnosed with Parkinson's disease and moved back to Hong Kong in 1986 for better medical care and support, and Man Kwong commuted between Hong Kong and Tokyo until he fully retired at the end of 1987. Just as he was finally ready to enjoy his retirement, however, he was diagnosed with cancer. Although he was immediately admitted to the hospital for treatment, it was too late as the cancer was at an advanced state; he passed away on 21 December 1988, the day of the winter solstice. I was shocked when I heard the sad news from Cheuk and rushed back to Hong Kong with Wing Kin. Man Kwong's funeral had a large attendance, including senior management and staff from both Dah Chong Hong and Hang Seng Bank, his former schoolmates from Pui Ching Middle School, and relatives from our extended families. Recalling Man Kwong's devotion to his work and family, I thought of the words of Zhuge Liang from the period of the Three Kingdoms: "Bending oneself to the task and exerting oneself to the utmost, until one's dying day."

Tse Kwong, who could not come for Mother's funeral, was there to attend Man Kwong's funeral since he had moved to Hong Kong after his retirement. Yuan Kwong's visit to Hong Kong was approved but he missed the funeral by a few days, again because of delays in processing his application. Since that brief period immediately after the war when we lived together in Hong Kong, the four brothers in our family had never had the chance to be together again. Tse Kwong and Yuan Kwong both left for the Mainland in 1949, and Man Kwong lived abroad for most of his career. I found it sad that, with Man Kwong's passing, we would never be together again; in fact, we do not even have a picture of the four of us together. Perhaps this was our fate.

Wing Kin and I visited Hong Kong a third time in April 1991 when Amy passed away, slightly more than two years after Man Kwong's death. We flew back in time to give our condolences and support to Man Kwong's children Cheuk and Nicole. I missed Amy; she was not only my sister-in-law but also my classmate at Western District Primary School, and I had fond memories of her. Tse Kwong, Yuan Kwong and I were able to get together at Amy's funeral, but I would not see them again until the handover of Hong Kong in 1997.

1997 — Hong Kong Returning to the Motherland

When the British finally handed sovereignty over Hong Kong back to China in 1997 — an event that I had dreamed about throughout my youth — I had already been living in Canada for thirteen years.

On 30 June 1997 I tuned in to the live television broadcast of the handover ceremonies in Hong Kong, and watched from the edge of my sofa as the rain turned heavy and Chris Patten, the last governor, stood to attention in front of Government House as the Union Jack was lowered for the last time. Drenched by the rain, he bowed his head as he took the neatly folded flag in his hands, as if feeling the weight of history. At midnight Patten attended the formal handing-over ceremony, and later that night he and his family boarded the royal yacht *Britannia* together with Prince Charles to leave the now-former colony.

After the broadcast, I immediately telephoned Tse Kwong and Yuan Kwong and shared with them my mixed feelings of joy and anxiety. On the one hand, it was an event that we had longed for ever since we were young — the end to colonial rule; on the other, I wondered what would happen to Hong Kong under Chinese rule. I had not seen my brothers for a long time but, through our correspondence, I knew that both of them had been enthusiastic about the economic reforms that Deng had introduced in 1979. They now urged me to visit China to see for myself.

Wing Kin and I followed their suggestion and visited Beijing, Shanghai and Shenzhen in November and December that year, stopping by Hong Kong on our way back to visit our friends and relatives. Even though I had read about economic developments in China as a result of Deng's Reform and Opening policy, I was amazed by the changes I saw. The streets of Beijing that were once cluttered with bicycles were now congested with cars and buses. Old buildings and *siheyuan* had been demolished and replaced by modern, multi-storey office buildings, hotels and blocks of apartments. Colourful and stylish clothing had replaced the once ubiquitous grey and blue Mao suits. A great variety of consumer goods crowded the shelves of stores and supermarkets, and many small retail shops and restaurants had opened up on the formerly grey, deserted streets. One of the most widely talked about topics in Beijing at that time was *xiagang* — stepping down from one's position. Millions of workers had been laid off as a result of the restructuring or closing down of state-owned enterprises. Remembering the industrial complexes that I had visited in the Northeast in 1977, I wondered about the fate of the workers who were once so proud of their factories. We asked our taxi driver, a man in his forties who had worked previously as a truck driver in a factory, how he felt about the changes. "I will try to pursue a better life," he said, "but I will have to work even harder. The state will no longer provide for us like in the days of Chairman Mao."

Construction sites had sprung up everywhere, in all the cities we visited, as if making up for lost time. I no longer recognized in Shenzhen the small dusty town that I had visited in the early 1980s. Tse Kwong and Yim Sheung had decided to make Shenzhen their retirement home. Yim Sheung had left Guangzhou for Hong Kong in 1983, and was later joined by Tse Kwong after he retired in 1986. Finding Hong Kong too expensive, they later settled in Shenzhen where their eldest son Niandong was working, and bought a two-bedroom apartment on the 27th floor of a high-rise condominium. The finishing on the outside walls was coarse and uneven compared to apartments in Hong Kong, but the building was equipped with all the facilities that they previously lacked in Guangzhou. Tse Kwong's apartment building was situated at the edge of a residential complex and had a clear view over the East Lake Reservoir, but elsewhere high-rise office and apartment buildings had sprung up all over the city. Cars, buses and trucks flooded the city streets and filled the highways connecting Hong Kong to Guangzhou. Watching all this from Tse Kwong's apartment, I could feel the strong pulse of China's economic reforms.

Both Tse Kwong and Yim Sheung were living on a government pension, which was (fortunately) indexed to inflation. At the time of his retirement, Tse Kwong's salary was just over 100 yuan, which was a very modest sum in view of the higher cost of living in Shenzhen. Fortunately, Yim Sheung had purchased a small apartment when she lived in Hong Kong and had sold it at a profit, thus generating sufficient savings for their retirement in Shenzhen. To be able to lead a relatively comfortable life in retirement seemed to be the least they deserved after a life of hardship and service to their country.

Tse Kwong was happy to see the opening-up of the economy and was quite relieved that he no longer had to deal with politics, but he was still concerned about the direction of the country's development. "We now have too much 'hardware' and too little 'software'," he said. "We are importing large quantities of machinery and equipment, but we don't have enough trained engineers and technicians to use them. I'm even more worried that China's legal system is not yet fully developed, which leaves many loopholes for mismanagement and corruption."

All his concerns were justified, but China seemed to be in a hurry to make up for all the years that had been lost in political turmoil. Large billboards with Deng Xiaoping's famous saying, "To get rich is glorious", had been put up everywhere in the city. Restaurants, shops, department stores and fast-food outlets (both the ubiquitous McDonald's and its many imitators) had sprung up everywhere. On the streets, the fashions and accessories of Shenzhen residents were no longer distinguishable from those of the people in Hong Kong. Tse Kwong confessed to me, however, that he felt nostalgic for the emphasis on equality and belief in self-sacrifice that had characterized the early days of the revolution.

Knowing my intellectual curiosity, Tse Kwong took me to visit Book City, the city's largest bookstore, which occupied an entire multi-storey building in a busy commercial district. Visiting the store with Tse Kwong reminded me of the days when he would take me to the pro-PRC bookstores in Hong Kong stocked full of the works of Marx, Lenin, Stalin and Mao Zedong. Now, half a century later, books on political ideology occupied only a quiet, almost deserted corner of Book City; instead, books on science, technology, management, philosophy and Western literature flooded the shelves. Many young people stood by the book shelves and read quietly, just as we did many years ago. What a long and winding road China had had to travel! But I was happy to see that, at long last, there was now some freedom in the people's quest for knowledge; I looked at Tse Kwong and felt quite sure that he shared my thoughts.

Since childhood I have always dreamed of a rich and independent China. In the late nineteenth century, intellectuals and officials of the Qing dynasty hoped to build a stronger China under the "Self-strengthening Movement", which advocated adopting Western technology while retaining traditional values. Their slogan was: "Chinese learning as the fundamental structure; Western learning for practical use." However, this did not stop Western and Japanese imperial forces from invading China and weakening the Qing dynasty, until it was eventually overthrown. More than a century and a half later, after trying to implement socialism for three decades, China had started to open up the country and introduce a market economy. Now the official policy was to build "socialism with Chinese characteristics" — which essentially meant introducing a capitalist market economy while retaining the existing Leninist party structure. Tse Kwong and I both wondered how it would work out this time. We promised each other to continue exchanging our views and observations on developments in China, as we had done when young.

"We have ended up living in two different worlds," Tse Kwong said before I left Shenzhen. "I only wish we could see each other more often. I have so much to share with you."

"China is my motherland," I said. "It will always have a place in my heart, but I do not regret emigrating. In Canada, I can still enjoy Chinese culture while the government upholds the rights and freedoms of its citizens. Can China offer me the same?"

"It will take a long time," Tse Kwong shook his head. "If I had been you I would have done the same."

Tse Kwong had become far more analytical and critical since we last met in Guangzhou in 1973. However, as far as I knew, Yuan Kwong remained staunchly and unquestioningly supportive of the Communist Party. I was not able to meet him on my trip, but he would often send me excerpts from Deng Xiaoping's writings, details of important party policies and news from China.

Yuan Kwong had resumed work at the Cultural Bureau of the Nanning City government after the Cultural Revolution ended in 1976. High-level city officials who shared the same "cow shed" with him during the Cultural Revolution had also been re-instated, which gave Yuan Kwong something of a network within the government and party bureaucracy. He later married Chen Cuihong, who worked in a factory in Nanning, and they had a daughter, Vicky. Yuan Kwong retired in 1991 but continued to follow the news of the country's political and economic developments actively.

Fortunately for both Yuan Kwong and Tse Kwong, the mainland government had a policy that those who joined the revolution before 1 October 1949 would be entitled to full medical benefits after their retirement. Yuan Kwong had made the cut-off just in time when he crossed the border from Hong Kong to the

Mainland on 30 September 1949. I felt somewhat comforted that he could at least enjoy this one benefit from the country that he had served so unswervingly for over forty years.

There is also some consolation in that even though our generation suffered war, revolution, separation and, in the case of Tse Kwong and Yuan Kwong, political and economic hardships, the next generation seems to have been able to enjoy peace and prosperity at last. Both of Tse Kwong's sons did well, although their schooling had been interrupted frequently during the Cultural Revolution. Niandong, who had a knack for business, first worked in a restaurant and later became a salesman for a factory in Shenzhen which produced porcelain ware for export. He was subsequently promoted to factory manager and actively ran the business between Shenzhen and Hong Kong. Sadly, Niandong died in 2007 at the young age of forty-seven. Nianfeng, Tse Kwong's younger son, left China with the help of Man Kwong to study in Tokyo and at the University of Western Ontario in Canada. He later settled in Japan, worked for Dah Chong Hong and several foreign multinational companies, and married a Japanese. Yuan Kwong's daughter, Vicky, pursued postgraduate studies in Australia with the help of Man Kwong's children, and later returned to China to work for a multinational company in Shenzhen. She emigrated to Canada in 2007.

After visiting the Mainland in 1997, I stopped in Hong Kong and visited Aunt Rose, who had brought me and my family so much joy and economic support when we were in need. Aged ninety-two, she was the only one of my parents' siblings still alive. Although her back was hunched and her movements had slowed, Aunt Rose was still extremely enthusiastic and charming, and her memory continued to serve her well; every year she would remember to send me a birthday card in Toronto. The first question she asked when we met was: "Have you received the birthday cards I sent you in the past years?" She had some hearing difficulties but her voice still boomed as we chatted eagerly about my childhood and our happy days together. Aunt Rose was the last link to my parents' generation; she passed away two years after our meeting, and I shall always miss her.

Fallen Seeds Taking Root

I find that the more experience I have of freedom and democracy in Canada, the more mixed are my feelings towards China — the land of my ancestors.

Thanks to Deng Xiaoping's Reform and Opening policy, China's economy has progressed by leaps and bounds, with GDP growing at a relentless rate of 8–10 percent per year. Deng Xiaoping's strategy of "letting a small group of people get rich first" has been successful, and China's status and influence in the international arena has never been so high. Some predict that the twenty-first century will be China's century, just as the twentieth century was America's. As far as its economic achievements are concerned, China is close to meeting the ideals of my youth, but in the areas of democracy, human rights and individual freedom, China is still far from meeting international standards. A large percentage of the population is still very poor, with a great disparity in wealth between ordinary people and those with means and political power. There is also rampant corruption, and Chinese citizens are still denied many of the basic democratic rights provided by the constitution.

The feelings of overseas Chinese towards their motherland are often mixed. Although many of us disagree with China's politics, we rejoice when its athletes win Olympic medals, or when its astronauts successfully complete a journey into space. We also contribute to charitable funds for disaster relief, and raise money for AIDS orphans on the Mainland. On the other hand, we are dismayed when we hear about peasants protesting at the seizure of their land by property developers in cahoots with corrupt cadres, or about dissidents being placed under arrest without due process of law.

According to an old Chinese saying, "Fallen leaves return to their roots", those who have gone overseas usually want to return to their native land. Many Chinese Canadians have returned to Hong Kong and the Mainland to take advantage of opportunities provided by China's vibrant economy. I am fortunate in that I have long since retired and no longer have to work for a living. In my circumstance, so long as the people's rights to freedom and democracy are not realized, my chances of "returning to my roots" are slim. I prefer instead to follow another traditional saying, "Fallen seeds take root where they land" — moving to a foreign country and establishing roots there.

Having said my long farewell to Hong Kong, I increasingly feel that Canada is my home. My last trip was in November 1999 when Wing Kin and I visited the Mainland, hoping to see my younger brothers one more time. We met Tse Kwong in Shenzhen and the three of us booked flights from Shenzhen to Nanning to meet with Yuan Kwong. Unfortunately, we were unable to make the trip because Wing Kin fell and broke one of her fingers. We returned to Hong Kong immediately and flew back to Toronto, heaving a sigh of relief when we reached home. This was my last visit to Hong Kong and mainland China.

Aside from becoming my home, Canada is also where I have finally found my spiritual belonging. Since retiring in 1984, I have had more time to ponder about my ideals and the meaning of life. Our daughters both converted to Christianity soon after arriving in Canada and, curious about their faith and their circle of friends, Wing Kin and I started to join them at Sunday worship, church events and meetings. We were baptized and became Christians in 1989.

My conversion was not an easy path for me, as I was inquisitive by profession and often took a rational and scientific approach to questions of religion and faith. However, I looked at the examples of Albert Einstein and Dr. Sun Yat-sen, the idol of my youth, who were both Christians. Einstein, especially, gave me much inspiration. He believed in a God "who reveals Himself in the harmony of all that exists". Searching for God's design was "the source of all true art and science", he said. He also said that we are but a speck in an unfathomably large universe; the more insights we gain into its mysterious forces, whether cosmic or atomic, the more reasons we have to be humble.

After much soul searching and reflection, I came to the conclusion that in order to pursue an ideal life, we need not just knowledge but also religion: knowledge to understand and tackle the issues we face in life, and religion for our peace of mind and a positive attitude in pursuing our paths.

I was fortunate to have found faith, since it has given me much-needed strength and solace as I have come to a sad and difficult period of my life. In 1999, when Wing Kin and I were both over seventy and should have been happily enjoying the golden years of our lives, she was diagnosed with Alzheimer's disease. I became her caregiver and have had to face many challenges in my new role. My perseverance, confidence, and patience have been constantly put to test. When she makes a blunder, I pick up the pieces. When she is upset, I have to comfort her. When she becomes unreasonable, I try to treat her like a child. Fortunately, my mental and physical health are still sound, even though I have developed hypertension. To comfort me, Yvonne gave me a copy of the Serenity Prayer:

> God grant me the serenity to accept things I cannot change; courage to change the things I can; and wisdom to know the difference.

We were also fortunate to be able to enjoy the social and medical benefits provided by the Canadian government, and to benefit from the efforts of Chinese Canadians to take care of their elders. In June 2005 we moved to Yee Hong Garden Terrace at the advice of Cheuk and Dr. Joseph Wong, who founded the Yee Hong Centre for Geriatric Care. Our new home is nestled in a senior-friendly, Chinese-speaking apartment complex which offers community programmes, a medical emergency system, and medical facilities in an adjacent building, all of which allow us to live independently and with dignity.

I therefore have much to be thankful for. Even though it has been difficult at times, my care-giving experience has helped me understand the meaning of love, and thus the spirit of Christianity:

> Love never gives up; and its faith, hope, and patience never fail.
> (Corinthians 13)

Appendix I

The Chinese Gold and Silver Exchange Society

Established in 1910, the Hong Kong Chinese Gold and Silver Exchange Society specialized in the buying and selling of gold bullions. However, gold and silver coins and paper currencies of the United States, Japan, Indo-China, the Philippines and Mexico were also traded in the pre-war days and during the early post-war years.

Gold traded in the society is of 99 percent fineness, weighed in *taels* and quoted in Hong Kong dollars, whereas gold traded in the European and American markets is of 99.5% fineness, weighed in troy ounces and quoted in US dollars. *Tael*, also known as *"liang"* (兩), is a Chinese weight measuring unit. One *tael* is equivalent to 38.5 grams and 1 troy ounce is equivalent to 31.1 grams; therefore 1 *tael* is equivalent to 1.24 troy ounces.

The minimum unit of transaction in the society is 100 *taels*. Members of the society are allowed to hold an open position of up to 3,000 *taels* in the buying and selling of gold. If this limit is exceeded a margin deposit of HK$75,000 per 100 *taels* will have to be paid. This limit and the amount of margin deposit are subject to change, depending on the fluctuation of gold prices.

The amount of margin deposit paid by clients to members varies with the amount of margin required from members by the society. In certain cases, however, clients are allowed smaller margin deposits.

In principle, settlement of all transactions in the trading hall has to be effected within one business day. However, settlement can be rolled over until the next business day or indefinitely subject to the constraints of the "carried over charges system" whereby interest is to be paid either by the seller or the buyer, depending on which party defers either delivery or taking delivery. There is also a "daily storage fee" of HK$6 per 100 *taels* outstanding at the close of business.

The so-called "carried over charges system" works as follows. On each business day, at 11.00 a.m. (10.30 a.m. on Saturday) the society takes stock of the amount of physical gold for spot delivery. If there is an excess demand for spot delivery, sellers deferring delivery of the gold will be charged interest in favor of the buyers. Interest so paid is known as "positive interest". In a situation of excess supply, buyers deferring taking delivery will be charged interest in favor of the sellers. Interest so paid is known as "negative interest". No interest will be paid either by the seller or the buyer if the demand for and supply of physical gold delivery is in equilibrium. If this is the case a situation of "even interest" arises.

This "carried over charges system" stipulates that payment of interest is divided into five classes. If a disequilibrium situation in demand and supply persists, interest will be adjusted upward — one class for every three consecutive days (from first class to second class and so on until the fifth highest class). If the disequilibrium subsides interest will be back to an "even interest" level after which it will scale up again should either a "negative interest" or "positive interest" situation develop. The amount of interest is expressed as $x per 10 *taels* and is calculated on the previous day's afternoon price fixing. In order to avoid complications, in the gold trading contracts the term "interest" is referred to as the "handling charge".

The existence of such a system enables the society, which is basically a physical spot market, to evolve into something akin to an undated future market. (Market participants have the option of deferring delivery with no fixed date of delivery).

To facilitate the settlement of members' accounts the society fixes prices twice daily (i.e. the morning fixing and the afternoon fixing.) These fixings are clearance prices for members to compare the contract prices of various deals with the fixed prices and transfer the proceeds of net profit or loss to the society. In this way the society assumes the duty of a clearing house.

Source: Excerpts from the article "Hong Kong — An International Gold Trading Centre" published in *Hang Seng Economic Quarterly*, January 1983.

Appendix II
The Hang Seng Index

When was the Index started?

The Hang Seng Index was first published in November 1969. It started out at 100 on 31 July 1964, which is the original base date of the Index. Since its inception, it has been the most widely quoted indicator of the general price movements in the Hong Kong stock market.

What does the Index reflect?

The Hang Seng Index is composed of a representative sample of stocks. It serves two main purposes. First, it traces the day-to-day general price movement of the market. Second, it reflects the performance of the market as a whole, i.e., the combined experience of all investors in stocks. The Index literally sets a standard, against which investors and portfolio managers could measure their own performance over a period of time.

Above all, the Hang Seng Index reproduces the performance of a hypothetical or model portfolio. The interest in each constituent stock is always proportionate to its market value. This characteristic is not affected by any capital changes of the constituent stocks or changes in the list of constituent stocks.

In case of a rights issue, for instance, the model portfolio would "take up" the rights and increase its interest in that particular constituent stock, thereby reducing its relative holdings in all others. Hence, the resulting interest in each constituent stock is still proportionate to its "new" market value.

Similarly, if any constituent stock is replaced, the model portfolio would dispose of all its interest in the old constituent and take up an interest in the new constituent, thus reducing its relative holdings in the remaining stocks. Therefore, replacement of constituent stocks from time to time will not create any havoc or inconsistency. It is but a feature of portfolio management.

Computation Methodology

Basic Concept

In statistical terms, the Hang Seng Index is a Laspeyre's type price index, weighted by the number of outstanding issued shares of the constituent stocks on the base day.

The basic formula is simple: divide the aggregate current market value of constituent stocks (i.e. the sum of the products of the current market prices of stocks and their respective numbers of issued shares) by the aggregate base market value of these stocks. That is:

$$\text{H.S.I.} = \frac{\text{Aggregate Market Value at Current Market Prices}}{\text{Aggregate Market Value at Base Market Prices}} \times 100$$

Allowances are made for capital changes in the constituent stocks or changes in the list of constituent stocks, and the Index in effect consists of a number of "chain-linked" series, each link occurring at the point of time of such changes.

Computation Formula

For convenience in computation, the daily chaining approach is used. The computation formula is as follows:

$$\begin{matrix} \text{Today's} \\ \text{Current} \\ \text{Index} \end{matrix} = \frac{\text{Today's Current AMV}}{\text{Yesterday's Closing AMV\#}} \times \begin{matrix} \text{Yesterday's} \\ \text{Closing} \\ \text{Index} \end{matrix}$$

\# Yesterday's closing AMV (aggregate market value) is adjusted for any capital changes in the list of constituent stocks.

Treatment of Suspended Stocks

When a constituent stock is suspended from trading, it is temporarily excluded from the computation of the sub-index concerned. If suspension occurs during trading hours, the necessary adjustments will be made at the end of the current trading session. Until then, the suspended stock will be included in the real time index calculation at the last market price before suspension.

Source: Excerpts from *A Guide to Hang Seng Index* published by HSI Services Ltd. in 1988.

Appendix III
The Teachings of Chairman Ho

An excerpt from *Yue Si Qian Tan* 閱世淺談 (A Talk about My Life Experience)

Your success or failure in life depends upon the strength of your will. A strong will allows you to overcome difficulties and succeed in your undertakings. However, knowledge and experience are also important, and a lack of either would be a major weakness. You will become susceptible to outside influence or material temptations, and will waver and become indecisive. This is the major cause of failure in one's career.

Young people lack experience and are therefore more impulsive and easily offended. When they encounter setbacks, which are inevitable in life, they become angry and will often resort to verbal abuse or even physical violence. This not only upsets the people around them but also harms their relationships with other people. In human relationships, therefore, one must start by cultivating oneself; the keys to success are patience and forgiveness.

人生過程的成功或失敗，與意志是否堅定有關。立志堅定，才可克服困難，任重致遠，以底於成。但認識與經驗，也是很重要的。認識不夠與經驗缺乏，都是人生兩大弱點。每當受到外間物質的引誘，或旁人的唆擺，便把心不定，見異思遷，進退失據，這就是形成事業失敗的主因。

青年人入世未深，缺乏人生經驗，故此較為沖動及易怒。其實人生中總有一些無可避免的挫折，但是他們只要稍遇逆境，怒氣便形於言表，進而惡言相稽，甚至以武力傷人，以洩一時之憤。這不但令所有人不安，亦破壞了彼此的交情。因此處世之道，在於內心的修養，能夠堅守"忍，恕"的原則，才是達到成功的不二之門。

Source: The booklet *Yue Si Qian Tan* (A Talk about My Life Experience) by Ho Sin Hang, (何善衡著：閱世淺談), Hong Kong, 1969. (English translation by the authors.)

Hang Seng Bank Service Motto 恆生銀行服務箴言

Greet your customers with an amiable smile,	笑容生和氣
And salute them by calling their names out loud.	高聲道姓名
Perform your duties expeditiously,	工作須迅速
And be sincere when rendering your services.	服務要忠誠
Always be humble towards your customers,	態度常謙敬
And be brief and concise when answering their questions.	問答簡而精
Be considerate of the needs of your customers,	對客皆周到
And bow and thank them for their patronage.	鞠躬謝盛情

Source: Service motto written by Ho Sin Hang in the 1960s for the Hang Seng Bank staff. (English translation by the authors.)

Quotations, Sayings and Slogans in Chinese

1. Roots

The Tang Family to the Rescue

Many fortunes, long life, and many male descendents.
多福，多壽，多男子

School Days and the Seeds of Patriotism

Only by bearing the hardest hardship can one rise to the top.
吃得苦中苦，方為人上人

2. Baptism by Fire

The Battle of Hong Kong

We will pay taxes to whoever is the emperor.
誰做皇帝向誰納糧
Those who understand the trend of the times are heroes.
識時務者為俊傑

Free China

A young man should have the ambition to go to the four corners of the world.
男兒志在四方
The blue sky, the white sun and the red earth underneath.
青天白日滿地紅
One drop of gasoline, one drop of blood.
一滴汽油，一滴血
The entire nation in arms.
全國武裝

Every citizen a soldier.
全民皆兵
A good son should never join the army.
好男不當兵

Wartime Interpreter

In heaven and on earth, there is no more dreadful din than that of a Cantonese speaking Mandarin.
天不怕地不怕，最怕廣東人講官話

The Burma Campaign

Join the war of resistance and build up our nation. To build our nation, we must first build our army. The building of our army starts here.
Vanquish our enemies and achieve our goals. To achieve our goals, it is important to follow a virtuous path. With virtues on our side we will be invincible.
抗戰建國，建國必先建軍，建軍即自此始。
殺賊立功，立功尤貴立德，立德所向無前。
(Source: the couplet on the gate pillars at the entrance to the Qujing Motor School)

4. Hang Seng Bank

New Career

A grasp of worldly affairs is genuine knowledge; the understanding of human relations is true learning.
世事洞明皆學問，人情練達即文章。
(Source: *A Dream of Red Mansions*, Chapter 5)

Humble Beginnings

At thirty, we stand on our own feet.
三十而立

The Teachings of Chairman Ho

He who wishes to be established assists others to be established;
He who wishes to be successful assists others to be successful.
己欲立而立人
己欲達而達人
(Source: *The Analects* of Confucius)

If you can one day renovate yourself, do so from day to day. Yea, let there be daily renovation.

苟日新，日日新，又日新。

(Source: *The Great Learning*, one of the *Four Books*)

Is it not pleasant to learn with a constant perseverance and application?

學而時習之不亦悦乎

(Source: *The Analects* of Confucius)

Years of Turmoil

Oppose the British and resist violence.

反英抗暴

5. New China

The Price of Patriotism

The Revolution has not yet been successfully concluded.
Let all our comrades continue to make every effort to carry it out.

革命尚未成功

同志仍須努力

(Source: Dr. Sun Yat-sen's *Last Will and Testament*)

If you have not been to the Great Wall, you cannot be a brave man.

不到長城非好漢

Self-reliance

Return to the motherland to witness her reconstruction.

回國參觀建設

Use, criticize, alter, create

用，批，改，創

Deeply dig caves and extensively store grains.

深挖洞，廣積糧

6. Home and Country

A Question of Nationality

A hundred flowers blossomed and a hundred schools of thoughts contended.

百花齊放，百家爭鳴

Farewell to Hong Kong

Once a person leaves his village, he will be looked down upon.
人離鄉賤

Becoming Canadian

Shovel the snow in front of your own doorsteps, and disregard the frost on the roof of your neighbours' house.
個人自掃門前雪，不管他人瓦上霜

A Long Farewell

Bending oneself to the task and exerting oneself to the utmost, until one's dying day.
鞠躬盡瘁，死而後已

1997 — Hong Kong Returning to the Motherland

Chinese learning as the fundamental structure; Western learning for practical use.
中學為體，西學為用

Fallen Seeds Taking Root

Fallen leaves return to their roots.
落葉歸根
Fallen seeds take root where they land.
落地生根

Glossary

All-Hong Kong Students' National Salvation & War Relief Association 全港學生救國賑災會

Anti-Rightist Campaign 反右運動

Apollo Book Store 智源書店

Ba Jin 巴金

Babu 八步

Bai Hua 白樺

Baojia 保甲

Bei Jiang 北江

Big Character Poster 大字報

Bing Di 昺帝

Bo Ai Tang 博愛堂

Boh loh 菠蘿

Cai Yuanpei 蔡元培

Cangshan 蒼山

Canton Merchants' Volunteer Corps 廣州商團

Canton Trust and Commercial Bank 廣東信託商業銀行

Central College 中央書院

Chan Chark Tong 陳澤棠

Chan Kwan Po 陳君葆

Chan Lim Pak 陳廉伯

Chan Yee Yeung Tong 陳義讓堂

Cheng Bao 正報

Cheng Hoi Chuen, Vincent 鄭海泉

Cheongsam 長衫

Cheung Wing Min 張榮冕

Chi Lin Nunnery 志蓮淨苑

China Emporium 中華百貨公司

China Mutual Trading Company 廣大華行

Chinese Gold and Silver Exchange Society 金銀業貿易場

Chinese Representative Council 華民委員會

Ching Lin Terrace 青蓮臺

Chu Hark Keung 朱克強

Chung Hwa Book Store 中華書局

Chung Sze-yuen 鍾士元

Chung Wah Distillery 中華酒廠

Chung Wah Music Academy 中華音樂學院

Commercial Press 商務印書館

Convention of Chuanbi 穿鼻草約

Cow shed 牛棚

Dah Chong Hong 大昌行

Dao Heng Bank 道亨銀行

Dazhalan 大柵欄

Defend Our Country China 保衛中華

Dong Jiang 東江

Dongcheng district 東城區

Dream of Red Mansions, A 紅樓夢

Du Zong 度宗

Duan Zong 端宗

Dunn, Lydia 鄧蓮如

Dushan 獨山

Eight Thousand Miles of Cloud and Moon 八千里路 雲和月

Entertainment Building 娛樂行

Erhai Lake 洱海

Lee Quo Wei/Q.W. Lee 利國偉
Leung Chik Wai 梁植偉
Leung Fung Ki 梁鳳岐
Leung Kau Kui 梁銶琚
Leung Ki Chai 梁杞儕
Leung Nai Hei 梁乃熙
Leung Nai Ying 梁乃英
Liang Shuming 梁漱溟
Liao Chengzhi 廖承志
Liao Yao-hsiang 廖耀湘
Liao Zhongkai 廖仲凱
Lingnan University 嶺南大學
Liu Chong Hing Bank 廖創興銀行
Liu Yan Tak 廖恩德
Liuzhou 柳州
Lo Hung Kwan 老洪鈞
Longling 龍陵
Lu Ban 魯班
Lu Shui 蘆水
Lu Xun 魯迅
Lung Tai Hong 隆泰行

Ma Kam 馬鑑
Ma Lin 馬臨
Ma Liu Shui 馬料水
Ma Shizeng 馬師曾
Ma Sicong 馬思聰
Man Kam To 文錦渡
Man Kwok Lau 文國鎏
Man Sing 文承
Mao Dun 茅盾
Marco Polo Bridge 盧溝橋
Mausoleum of Revolutionary Martyrs
    黃花崗七十二革命烈士陵園
May 7 Cadre School 五七干校
Ming On Edible Oil Shop 明安油莊
Mu Guiying 穆桂英

Nam Pak Hong 南北行
Nan Fang College 南方學院
Nanfang Daily 南方日報
Nanhai 南海
Nankai University 南開大學
Nanxiong 南雄
National Southwest Associated University
    國立西南聯合大學
National Times, The 國民日報
New Evening Post 新晚報
Nu Jiang 怒江

Ode to the Eight Hundred Heroes
    歌八百壯士
On New Democracy 新民主主義論
On the Songhua River 松花江上

Panyu 番禺
Ping Tsai 平妻
Plan for National Reconstruction
    建國方略
Po Leung Kuk 保良局
Poh Poh 婆婆
Poon Yee Kit 潘以傑
Pui Ching Middle School 培正中學

Qianzhuang 錢莊
Qiao Guanhua 喬冠華
qipao 旗袍
Queen's College 皇仁書院
Qujiang 曲江
Qujing 曲靖

Rainbow Chorus 虹虹歌詠團
Return to Native Village Certificate
    回鄉證
Returned Overseas Chinese Certificate
    歸僑證
River of Spring Water flowing to the East, A
    一江春水向東流
Romance of the Three Kingdoms
    三國演義
Rushang 儒商

Sai Nam Middle School 西南中學
Sam Chi Yan 沈智仁
San gui jiu kou 三跪九叩
Self-strengthening Movement 自強運動
Seng Yuan Company 生源號
Shang Chen 商震
Shanhaiguan 山海關
Shaoguan 韶關
Shea, William 佘汝麟
Shek Tong Tsui 石塘咀
Sheng Tsun Lin 盛春霖
Shiu Yuan Yinhao 肇源銀號
Shixilu 世系錄
Shoe Money 鞋金
Shrine of Successive Generations of Kwan
    Family Ancestors 關門堂上歷代祖先

Young Pioneers 少先隊
Yulin 玉林
Yuntai 雲臺

Zhang Hanzhi 章晗之
Zhang Shizhao 章士釗
Zhanjiang 湛江
Zhaoqing 肇慶
Zhijiang 芷江
Zhongshan 中山
Zhuge Liang 諸葛亮

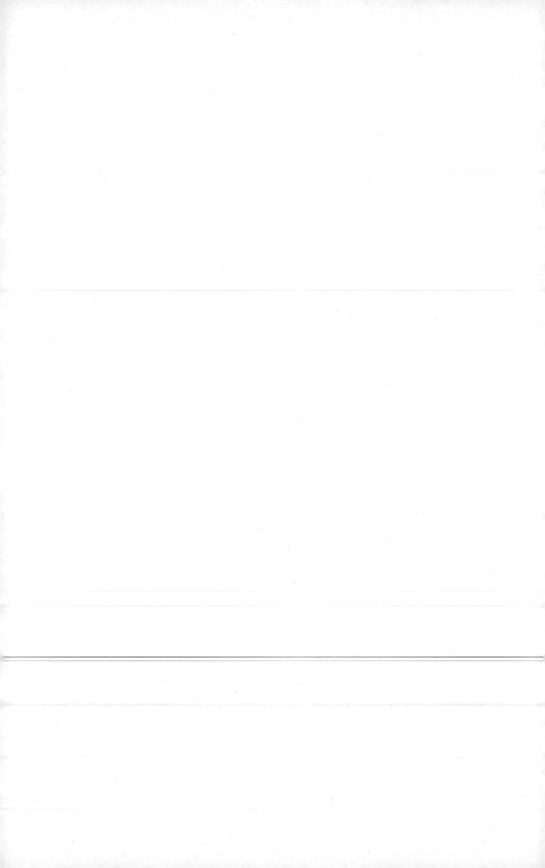

Sources

The contents of this book are primarily derived from my own memories, observations and reflections, which were later supplemented by my research and personal interviews over fifteen years, and more recently with the help of Nicole. We used the following sources for background information on the history of Hong Kong and China. Our sources on specific topics are listed by chapter below.

Stanley Kwan

(1) *A Borrowed Place — The History of Hong Kong*, Frank Welsh, Kodansha America Inc., New York, 1993.
(2) *China: A New History*, John King Fairbank and Merle Goldman, The Belknap Press of Harvard University Press, Cambridge, Massachusetts, 1998.
(3) *Jindai Zhongguo Shigang* (An Outline of Modern Chinese History), Guo Tingyi (郭廷以著：近代中國史綱), The Chinese University Press, Hong Kong, 1974.
(4) *Precarious Balance: Hong Kong between China and Britain, 1842–1992*, Ming K. Chan editor, Hong Kong University Press, Hong Kong, 1994.
(5) *Xianggang Shi Lue* (A Brief History of Hong Kong), Yuan Bangjian (元邦建著：香港史略), Zhongliu Press, Hong Kong, 1988.

1. Roots
The history of my ancestors:
> The *Shixilu* (世系錄) — a genealogical record of the Kwan family written in ink brushes by my father, Kwan Tsai Tung.

The *yinhao* and the banking industry in Hong Kong:
(1) *The Banking System of Hong Kong*, T.K. Ghose, Butterworths Asia, Hong Kong, 1995.
(2) *Xianggang Jinrong Ye Bainian* (A Century of Hong Kong Financial Development), Fung Bong Yin (馮邦彥著：香港金融業百年), Joint Publishing (H.K.) Ltd., 2002.

On the history of the Kwan and Tang families, I am truly grateful to the following persons for providing me with invaluable information:
(1) My parents
(2) Cousin Kwan Lin Chee
(3) Cousin Kwan Sai Kwong
(4) Aunt Rose Tang

(5) Cousin Tang Wai Han (daughter of my maternal uncle Shiu Woon), in particular her taped interview with Aunt Rose in May 1991 which was a wealth of information

The history of the patriotic activities of students of King's College:

Yinghuang Shisheng Aiguo Aigang Qing (The Patriotic Feelings for China and Hong Kong Among Teachers and Students of King's College), Leung Chik Wing (梁植穎著：英皇師生愛國愛港情), Ming Pao Press Ltd., Hong Kong, 2007.

Dr. Sun Yat-sen's writings and comments:

(1) *Last Will and Testament* as translated in *All Change Hong Kong*, Robert Adley, Blandford Press, Poole, Dorset, U.K., 1984

(2) Remarks during his visit to the University of Hong Kong in 1923: *Old Hong Kong*, Volume Two 1901–1945, Trea Wiltshire, Form Asia Books Limited, Hong Kong, 1995.

2. Baptism by Fire

The Battle of Hong Kong:

(1) Wiltshire, *Old Hong Kong*, Volume Two

(2) Yuan, *Xianggang Shi Lue* (A Brief History of Hong Kong)

On the Canadian soldiers:

The Search of Global Citizenship: The Violation of Human Right in Asia, 1935–1945, the Canadian Association for Learning & Preserving the History of WWII, Toronto Chapter, 2005

The Japanese occupation:

The Fall of Hong Kong: Britain, China and the Japanese Occupation, Philip Snow, Yale University Press, New Haven and London, 2003

On Chan Lim Pak:

(1) Guo, *Jin Dai Zhongguo Shigang* (An Outline of Modern Chinese History)

(2) *The Soong Dynasty*, Sterling Seagrave, Sidgwick & Jackson Ltd., Great Britain, 1986.

The American Volunteer Group (AVG):

Seagrave, *The Soong Dynasty*

While Claire Chennault was the commander of the AVG, Soong May-ling (Madame Chiang Kai-shek) and her brother T.V. Soong, who had held the posts of Acting Premier, Finance Minister and Foreign Minister, were responsible for the formation of the AVG behind the scene.

On wartime interpreters:

An article written by my former army interpreter comrade, Mei Zuyan (梅祖彥), titled *Junshi fanyiyuan jingli zuiyi* (A Recollection of the Experiences of Military Interpreters)軍事翻譯員經歷追憶 provided a wealth of information on the training of wartime interpreters and Chinese soldiers and airmen by US instructors and liaison officers. Mei was then a fourth-year student at the National Southwest Associated University in Kunming; his father Mei Yiqi (梅貽琦) was a chancellor of the university and a well-known educator. The Meis did not leave China following the Communist takeover of the Mainland, and Zuyan eventually became a member of the Chinese People's Political Consultative Conference (CPPCC) in Beijing. The ten-page article was part of a collection of articles written by CPPCC members in March 1995, in commemoration of the 50th anniversary of China's victory in the War of Resistance against Japan.

On the China-Burma-India Theatre of War, General Stilwell, the Burma Campaign and later the China Theatre of War, I am heavily indebted to the following two sources:

(1) *Stilwell and the American Experience in China 1911–45*, Barbara W. Tuchman, Macmillan Company, New York, 1971

(2) *Huanghe zai paoxiao — Zhongguo de kangzhan* (The Roaring Yellow River — China's Anti-Japanese War), Yang Yi Min (楊一民著：黃河在咆哮——中國的抗戰), Feng Yun Shi Dai Publishing Company, Taipei, 1994

3. Hong Kong after the War

The surrender of Japanese forces in Hong Kong:

Wiltshire, *Old Hong Kong*, Volume Two

The organization and operation of the US Defense Department and Foreign Service:

Encyclopedia Americana, 1997 Edition, Volume 8, pp. 628–629, and Volume 11, pp. 577–581.

I used information that I had gathered from my relatives over the years. I am especially grateful to the following persons:

(1) My brothers, Tse Kwong and Yuan Kwong, for recounting their experiences in post-war Hong Kong and New China

(2) My cousin Leung Nai Hei for sharing his experiences in his letter dated 3 April 1990 from England

(3) My cousin Kwan Sai Kwong for sharing his experiences

(4) Wong Man Fai for information regarding the Wong family

4. Hang Seng Bank

For the history of the bank and general information on Hong Kong's banking industry, I have used as my main reference: *Hang Seng — The Evergrowing Bank*, which was published in 1991 by Hang Seng Bank Ltd. to commemorate the inauguration of the bank's new headquarters building.

In addition, I have used the following sources for more specific topics.

The Chinese Gold and Silver Exchange Society:

"Hong Kong — An International Gold Trading Centre", *Hang Seng Economic Quarterly*, January 1983. (See Appendix A)

The Teachings of Chairman Ho:

The booklet *Yue Si Qian Tan* (A Talk about My Life Experience) (閱世淺談), and the *Hang Seng Bank Service Motto* (恆生銀行服務箴言) written by Ho Sin Hang, which were to be read and observed by all bank staff.

Bank runs during the 1960s:

Banking and Currency in Hong Kong, Y.C. Yao, The Macmillan Press Ltd., London, 1974.

Hong Kong during the 1960s:

I am grateful to my cousin Kwan Hung Kwong and Sam Chi Yan, my former classmates at King's College, for sharing their experiences with me.

Other sources:

(1) Wiltshire, *Old Hong Kong, Volume Two*

(2) An article entitled "Na Yi Ye — Xianggang Jingcha Ba Wo Dai Zou" (That night, the Hong Kong Police took me away) by Choi Wai Hang (蔡渭衡：那一夜——香港警察把我帶走), former Secretary of Hong Kong Chinese Reform Association, *Ming Pao Daily News*, Toronto, 22 March 2007

Compilation of the Hang Seng Index:

> An article titled "Hang Seng Index" in the October 1979 issue of the *Hang Seng Economic Quarterly*, and the pamphlet *A Guide to Hang Seng Index* published by H.S.I. Services Limited in 1988. (See Appendix B)

5. New China

I relied heavily on information that I had gathered from my relatives over the years, especially from my brothers Tse Kwong and Yuan Kwong, and Wing Kin's sister Shook Ling.

In addition, I have consulted the following sources:

My tour of Beijing 1973:

> *Beijing — China's Ancient and Modern Capital*, Liu Junwen, Foreign Language Press, Beijing, 1982.

On the Cultural Revolution:

> *Zhongguo Wenge Shinian Shi* (Ten Years of Cultural Revolution in China), Yan Jiaqi and Gao Gao (嚴家其、高皋編著"中國文革十年史"), Ta Kung Pao, Hong Kong, 1986

My tour of northeast China and Beijing in 1976:

> I used information from a log book that our tour group kept on our visits and from my own notes.

On Lee Ming Chak (R.C. Lee):

> *Profit, Victory & Sharpness: The Lees of Hong Kong*, Vivienne Poy, Canada and Hong Kong Project, York Centre for Asian Research, York University, Toronto, 2006

Q.W. Lee's meeting with Deng Xiaoping on 23 June 1984:

> (1) *The End of Hong Kong*, Robert Cottrell, John Murray (Publishers) Ltd., London, 1993
>
> (2) *South China Morning Post*, Hong Kong, 24 June 1984

Sir Edward Youde and the *Amethyst* Incident:

> (1) *Xianggang Huiyilu* (Hong Kong Memoirs), Xu Jiatun (former Director of Xinhua News Agency, Hong Kong) (許家屯著：香港回憶錄), published by United Newspaper Press, Taipei, 1993
>
> (2) "Wushi Nianqian De 'Zhishuijing Shijian' Yu Xianggang" (The *Amethyst* Incident Fifty Years Ago and Hong Kong) by cousin Leung Nai Hei (梁乃熙著：五十年前的"紫水晶"事件與香港), *Brushstroke* magazine, Liverpool, England, June 1999

The Ho Leung Ho Lee Foundation (何梁何利基金):

> *Hang Yuan* (Hang Seng Garden) *Bi-monthly* (恆生銀行出版'恆園'雙月刊), Hang Seng Bank Ltd., Hong Kong, No. 281, June–July, 1994

6. Home and Country

Bai Hua and the movie *Ku Lian* (苦戀):

> I am grateful to Lisa Shi for her research.

On the question of British citizenship and Hong Kong:

> *The Government and Politics of Hong Kong*, Norman Miners, Oxford University Press, Hong Kong, 1986

The history of early Chinese immigrants to Canada:

> *Gold Mountain — The Chinese in the New World*, Anthony B. Chan, New Star Book Ltd., Vancouver, B.C., 1983

The activities of Chinese Canadians:

> I relied on documents and publications from the Federation of Chinese Canadians in Scarborough (FCCS), the Toronto Association for Democracy in China (TADC), and the Chinese Canadians National Council (CCNC).

On my conversion to Christianity:

> I received much inspiration from the 31 December 1999 issue of *Time* Magazine nominating Albert Einstein as "The Person of the Century".

I am also grateful to Hang Seng Bank for continuing to send their publications to me in Toronto, which has helped me keep in touch with the bank's activities and Hong Kong's economic developments over the years.

Index